Writing in the Elementary Classroom

A Reconsideration

Edited by
Janet Evans

HEINEMANN
Portsmouth, NH

Heinemann
A subsidiary of Reed Elsevier Inc.
361 Hanover Street
Portsmouth, NH 03801–3912
www.heinemann.com

Offices and agents throughout the world

The authors and publisher would like to thank those who have given their permission to include material in this book:
"Using Graphic Organizers to Write Information Texts" by Steve Moline, copyright © 2000 by Cockatoo Publishing Pty Ltd. Reproduced with the permission of the author.

Library of Congress Cataloging-in-Publication Data

Writing in the elementary classroom : a reconsideration / edited by Janet Evans.
        p. cm.
     Includes bibliographical references.
     ISBN 0-325-00351-3 (pbk.)
     1. English language—Composition and exercises—Study and teaching (Elementary)
  2. Language arts (Elementary) I. Evans, Janet, 1952–

  LB1576 .W743 2001
  372.62'3—dc21   00-054120

Editor: Danny Miller
Production service: Denise Botelho, Colophon
Production coordinator: Lynne Reed
Cover design: Joni Doherty
Manufacturing: Louise Richardson

Printed in the United States of America on acid-free paper
05 04 03 02 01 DA 1 2 3 4 5

To Les my husband...writing a book can even try the patience of a saint...nevertheless he remained one throughout.

Contents

Foreword

In the last several decades, research on the writing process has expanded rapidly. Researchers have documented such aspects as children beginning to learn literacy at birth and continuing that learning throughout their lives (Doake 1988; Hall 1987; Teale and Sulzby 1986); actively constructing knowledge about literacy through their inventions of written language (Ferreiro and Teberosky 1982; Goodman 1984); growing and developing as writers through writing for a variety of meaningful and authentic purposes in an environment that encourages their experimentation (Clay 1987); discovering and learning the purpose of conventions in written language as they grow as writers (Calkins 1994; Graves 1983); being influenced by experiences in their social worlds when they write (Dyson 1993); and learning to read and write simultaneously (Baghban 1984; Bissex 1980). Now we have *Writing in the Elementary Classroom: A Reconsideration.* Don't be fooled, however; this is *not* merely "another book" on writing. It is a collection of work by educators and researchers who are not satisfied with what they know about children and writing and have pushed the boundaries of their (and, fortunately, our) knowledge into new territory. Each chapter is theoretically grounded and invites its readers into classrooms and/or the presence of children to learn more about the writing process, children's perceptions of writing and themselves as writers, the role of writing in learning, and the critical importance of writing in all areas of the curriculum.

As a literacy researcher, I have documented children's writing development (Martens 1996, 1999; Martens, Adamson, and Wood 2000). Reading this book and considering aspects of writing through the eyes and minds of the authors was exciting. I learned so much in areas such as poetry, nonfiction, information technology, bilingual writers, notemaking, young children's writing . . . the list goes on. Each chapter addresses writing development from a different direction, creating a rich collage focused on children and how to support their growth as competent writers.

From chapter to chapter, the key factor that continually leapt out at me was the critical role of knowledgeable teachers in children's growth as writers. It is knowledgeable teachers who understand literacy learning as a lifelong process; focus their students first and foremost on constructing meaning as they write; see and support the relationship between reading and writing; encourage their students to experiment and invent how to represent their meanings; understand how to facilitate children's learning of writing conventions as they read and write; "kidwatch" (Goodman 1985) to learn what their students know and need to know as readers and writers; find large blocks of time for their students to read and write; provide a variety of rich authentic literacy experiences so their students read and write for a range of meaningful purposes; and help their students perceive themselves as competent readers and writers. And, it is knowledgeable teachers who realize they don't know it all and have so much yet to learn about children and literacy development.

This volume is one that will make readers more knowledgeable. The international authors are innovative, reflective risk takers who invite readers to think and work side by side with them as they use children as their "informants" (Harste, Woodward, and Burke 1984) to explore writers and writing. Readers will come away with a deeper understanding of children as thinkers and writers and how to create environments that support their students.

As I write this Foreword, education in the United States is under close scrutiny and attack. Public schools are blamed for the state of education. Teachers are pressured to raise their students' test scores. Students are denied promotion, and even high school diplomas, based solely on how they score on standardized tests. Parents are accused of not doing enough at home to support their children, the teachers, and the schools. And, political candidates are promising more standardized testing to hold teachers, students, and schools accountable.

In the midst of this storm emerges *Writing in the Elementary Classroom: A Reconsideration.* Janet Evans and her collaborators remind us of the brilliance of children as readers and writers, the ingenuity of teachers, and the critical necessity of rich and varied writing experiences to students' learning. And, through their work, the authors push us into new and deeper understandings in the twenty-first century.

Prisca Martens
Indiana University, Indianapolis
November 2000

References

Baghban, M. (1984) *Our Daughter Learns to Read and Write: A Case Study from Birth to Three.* Newark, DE: International Reading Association.

Bissex, G. (1980) *Gnys at Wrk: A Child Learns to Write and Read.* Cambridge, MA: Harvard University Press.

Calkins, L. (1994) *The Art of Teaching Writing.* Portsmouth, NH: Heinemann.

Clay, M. (1987) *Writing Begins at Home.* Portsmouth, NH: Heinemann.

Doake, D. (1988) *Reading Begins at Birth.* New York: Scholastic.

Dyson, A. (1993) *Social Words of Children Learning to Write in an Urban Primary School.* New York: Teachers College Press.

Ferreiro, E. and Teberosky, A. (1982) *Literacy Before Schooling.* Portsmouth, NH: Heinemann.

Goodman, Y. (1985) "Kidwatching: Observing Children in the Classroom," in Jaggar, A. and Smith-Burke, M. T. (eds.), *Observing the Language Learner* (pp. 9–18). Newark, DE and Urbana, IL: International Reading Association and the National Council of Teachers of English.

Goodman, Y. (1984) "The Development of Initial Literacy," in Goelman, H., Oberg, A., and Smith, F. (eds.), *Awakening to Literacy* (pp. 102–109). Portsmouth, NH: Heinemann.

Graves, D. (1983) *Writing: Teachers and Children at Work.* Portsmouth, NH: Heinemann.

Hall, N. (1987) *The Emergence of Literacy.* Portsmouth, NH: Heinemann.

Harste, J., Woodward, V., and Burke, C. (1984) *Language Stories and Literacy Lessons.* Portsmouth, NH: Heinemann.

Martens, P. (1996) *I Already Know How to Read: A Child's View of Literacy.* Portsmouth, NH: Heinemann.

Martens, P. (1999) "'Mommy, how do you write "Sarah"?' The Role of Name Writing in One Child's Literacy," *Journal of Research in Childhood Education* **14**(1), 5–15.

Martens, P., Adamson, S., and Wood, J. (2000) "Making Meaning Visible: Children Invent the Orthographic System" (submitted and under review).

Teale, W. and Sulzby, E. (1986) *Emergent Literacy: Writing and Reading.* Norwood, NJ: Ablex.

Acknowledgments

I wish to thank each one of the very hard working writers who have contributed to this edited volume. They have given so splendidly of their time and expertise, and it is very much appreciated.

Many people have given support during the writing of this book and to all of them I am indebted. However, I would particularly like to thank Nigel Hall for his advice whenever I have needed it, Robin Campbell for reading and making suggestions on certain aspects of my work, and Mary Hewson who is always willing to give an outside opinion whenever it is needed.

Special thanks go to the staff and children of St Gregory's RC Primary School in Liverpool. They freely gave of their time whenever I asked them for writing, drawings, and ideas in general.

Children's Views of Writing

Children's views of writing from three to eleven years—a journey through their ages

Children from three to eleven years old were asked to consider and jot down their thoughts in relation to the statement, "What I think about writing and myself as a writer."

3-year-olds
Courtney 3.11 years

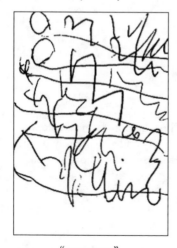

"my mum"
"my dad"
"Georgia and me . . ."
". . . and that says you"

4-year-olds
David 4.6 years

"I like writing but not that much."

5-year-olds
Jordan 5.5 years

"I like writing because it gets your brain working."

6-year-olds
Lewis 6.3 years

"I like writing because it is good to
   learn and it makes me behave."

7-year-olds
Sean 7.4 years

What I think about writing and myself as a writer.

I Just like story's and finding out about whats going on. I'de like to be a writer becaus e I'de like people hearing my story's because I like writing about adventures and things like dinosaur. and James bond.

8-year-olds

Paul 8.5 years
"I'm not a good story writer, I can only do about twenty two lines."

Joanne 8.3 years
"I like writing because it is fun and when you are having fun time flies."

9-year-olds

Hanna 9.5 years
"Every time I write a story in school or at home I feel that I am going to be laughed at because people might think it is stupid."

Jenny 9.2 years
"I think I am a pretty good writer but I just don't want to be one."

10-year-olds

Graeme 10.6 years
"I think writing is interesting because you sometimes get to use your imagination. For example when you write a story you have to plan it because if you go straight into a story and straightaway publish it you could have made a mistake and people would say, 'This writer doesn't know how to spell.'"

Michael 10.1 years
"I don't like writing because it makes your hand hurt after a while."

11-year-olds

Warren 11.1 years
"I don't like writing because after a while my hand goes dead and I'm slow at writing and sometimes you only get a few minutes to write something and it is boring to do plus I don't like dictation and copying off writing sheets."

Steven 11.2 years
"I think writing is important even though I don't like it that much."

Introduction: Learning and Teaching the Complexities of Writing

Janet Evans

> I like writing because it learns you things and when you write stories you imagine your own world. Writing is educational. When you write it learns you how to spell and if you get it wrong you remember not to spell it like that again and then it makes you spell better. When you write you learn new things.

Ten-year-old Ellie tells us a great deal about the process and complexity of writing. Writing stimulates the imagination, helps learning, and develops spelling. It is no wonder, therefore, that in the last two decades international research into writing has focused on the ways in which it is learned and taught. More recently, the drive to improve standards of literacy in general and writing in particular has been given top priority in many countries. This has resulted in a tremendous upsurge in the interest in writing as a process and has brought the debate about how best to teach writing onto center stage.

Writing as a Process

Donald Graves was one of the first researchers to take a closer look at the way writing was being taught in primary schools. He was very dissatisfied with the lack of progress that some American children made when exposed to traditional approaches to the teaching of writing, and he despaired of the way in which educators often ignored the knowledge about writing that children already possessed when they started school. His basic premise included the need to encourage children to write with an audience in mind, for a particular purpose, and in a style appropriate to the purpose (Graves 1983). To do this, children must have ownership of the writing process in terms of deciding what they should write. They should also have opportunities to write every day, talk about their

1

writing with other people, produce drafts, revise their work as a result of the discussions, and present their work for others to read. This *process approach* to writing, a term which is now almost synonymous with Graves' work, also demands the presence of knowledgeable teachers who know how children learn to write and are able to support them in appropriate ways as they work on their writing.

Other researchers, such as Frank Smith (1982) and Lucy McCormack Calkins (1986), were in agreement with Graves. They stated that in order to write effectively we must have something to write about, we need to plan the writing prior to starting, and we need to talk with someone about the writing. Graves (1983) used the term *conference* to describe this discussion process.

Learning How to Write

The current drive to raise standards of literacy has led to a renewed interest in the way in which children learn. The previously published work of researchers such as Vygotsky and Bruner has been reconsidered, and in Vygotsky's case re-translated from the Russian, in an attempt to shed more light on how children learn. In looking at the interaction between learning and development, Vygotsky (1978) felt that there are implications for learning in that initially children will be able to learn much more in collaboration with others than they will be able to achieve alone, and that this learning will then feed back into future learning situations. This gap between what children can achieve collaboratively with others and what they can achieve individually has been called the "zone of proximal development" (ZPD) by Vygotsky. Children are supported in the ZPD primarily through dialogue, and for this reason it can be seen that talk is central to the learning process. Vygotsky compares children's "actual development level" with their "mental development level" and suggested that what children can achieve with help is more indicative of their mental developmental level, as it is an indication of their potential, that is, what they are actually capable of. He states that, "The state of a child's mental development can be determined only by clarifying its two levels: the actual development level and the zone of proximal development" (p. 54).

Bruner's more accessible work on scaffolding, derived directly from Vygotsky's work, has meant that many more educators now know how important it is to work alongside children, modeling writing processes and guiding them towards processes which they will be able to do alone at a later stage (Bruner 1985).

These ideas were reflected in the work of Brian Cambourne, an Australian teacher–researcher. Based on twenty years of classroom observation, he proposed a model of how children could learn to write effectively. Importantly, he suggested that the right conditions needed to be in place before effective learning would occur. In his writing he demonstrates how, with those conditions in place, effective learning is evident (Cambourne 1988).

The Complexities of Writing

Writing is clearly a complex, multifaceted process requiring the ability to manipulate many subskills stimultaneously. Some of the thought-provoking research from the early 1980s highlights the differences between merely being a writer and being someone who learns through their writing. Frank

Smith (1982) posed a question in relation to this point when he asked, "How does a writer create a text, and in what manner is the writer changed in the process?" (p. 103). Smith visualized writing not as a simple "think, write, think, write, think, write" continuum but as a more complex, deep-seated process involving ongoing thought processes which every so often manifest themselves in bouts of writing, which he calls "writing episodes." These thought processes and the corresponding episodes of writing interact with each other, and there is an almost symbiotic relationship between the two as they influence, nurture, and support each other, weaving their way towards the writer's finished piece of writing. Smith was intrigued to know what was going on in a writer's mind when writing was being produced, and Aldous Huxley's description of the composing process helps us to appreciate how even accomplished writers struggle with the inherent complexities of the writing task:

> Generally, I write everything many times over. All my thoughts are second thoughts. And I correct each page a great deal, or rewrite it several times as I go along . . . Things come to me in driblets, and when the driblets come I have to work hard to make them into something coherent! (*Writers at Work* 1963, p. 197)

Other researchers had been looking at the psychological processes involved in writing. Hayes and Flower's (1980) research looked at how mature writers operate. They concluded with outcomes which were not dissimilar to those of Smith. They stated that the stages involved in writing—planning, writing, and revising—are not linear stages but are recursive; they are intertwined and link with one another as the writer works towards a finished product. They form a kind of spiral which can be moved along in both directions as the writer draws upon information to inform and help develop the ongoing process of composing (Flower and Hayes 1981).

Bereiter and Scardamalia (1987), in their research into the relationship between easy and difficult cognitive functions, focused on writing because of its traditionally accepted complexity as a skill to acquire. They proposed two different models of writing. One model, "knowledge telling," shows writing to be a reasonably natural task that makes maximum use of already existing cognitive structures, while the other model, "knowledge transforming," makes writing a task that keeps growing in complexity to match the expanding competence of the writer. The difference between the two lies in the contrast between what someone is able to do using naturally acquired abilities and what can be done when a person works on a piece of writing to achieve intended effects and to reorganize one's knowledge in the process.

In knowledge telling, writers draw on everything they know about a topic and write it down. The quality of the finished product is reliant on their ability to recall their own knowledge and experiences, and the ability to utilize the vocabulary and syntax of the writing system they are using. With knowledge transforming, however, the finished product has usually been subjected to reviews and revisions through close scrutiny of vocabulary and refinements of meaning through manipulation of syntax used. The resulting text often bears no resemblance to the original piece of writing. It is this ability to work on and thereby transform a piece of writing that allows the writer to learn: Words and associated grammar are reworked until different meanings emerge. These different meanings not only make the writing a better piece to read, but also often change the author's understanding of what was being considered.

It is this ability to work on texts that many educators want to promote in young writers. However, young writers often consider doing rough drafts a painfully boring waste of time—in many cases they are not shown how to revise effectively—they are taught to focus on secretarial skills as opposed to compositional skills and this focus means that their attempts at revising become mere error correction with nothing at all to do with the meaning and composition of the piece of work. How can these attitudes be changed? Will an all-pervading change in approaches used to teach writing help?

Teaching Writing

The need to change children's attitudes to writing and the need to make the approaches to teaching more effective in order to raise standards have led to a closer examination of the relevant research. Margaret Mooney's "to," "with," and "by" continuum (see Figure I.1) gives an indication

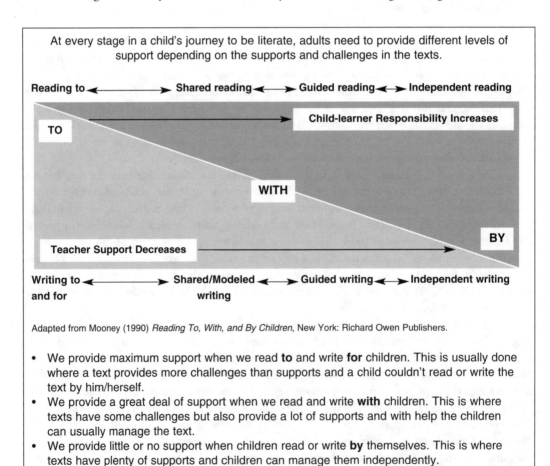

At every stage in a child's journey to be literate, adults need to provide different levels of support depending on the supports and challenges in the texts.

Reading to ← → Shared reading ← → Guided reading ← → Independent reading

TO

Child-learner Responsibility Increases

WITH

BY

Teacher Support Decreases

Writing to and for ← → Shared/Modeled writing ← → Guided writing ← → Independent writing

Adapted from Mooney (1990) *Reading To, With, and By Children*, New York: Richard Owen Publishers.

- We provide maximum support when we read **to** and write **for** children. This is usually done where a text provides more challenges than supports and a child couldn't read or write the text by him/herself.
- We provide a great deal of support when we read and write **with** children. This is where texts have some challenges but also provide a lot of supports and with help the children can usually manage the text.
- We provide little or no support when children read or write **by** themselves. This is where texts have plenty of supports and children can manage them independently.

Figure I.1 The "To," "With" and "By" Continuum in Relation to Reading and Writing

of how much support and guidance teachers need to give at various stages when young children are learning how to write. Her work has influenced the teaching of reading and writing at an international level, and teachers are now familiar with an approach which includes modeled and shared writing, guided writing, and independent writing. In talking of each of these parts of the whole approach, Hornsby (2000) says,

> In modeled writing, you provide maximum support by composing the text, putting it on paper, and talking about it. The children are free to witness the act of writing—to see what it is to be a writer. At the other end of the writing continuum, you expect children to write "by" themselves, or independently. (p. 23)

The "with" part of the continuum, where child and expert writer are working together, is a crucial stage of the teaching process and represents the time where children are beginning to write for themselves but still need help and guidance. Children can be best helped with their writing at the point of composition, and this working with the children in a guided-writing situation is the equivalent of Vygotsky's ZPD and Bruner's scaffolding approach.

Hornsby (2000) expertly describes the components in this approach to the teaching of writing and very clearly identifies the levels of support needed for each of the components (see Figure I.2).

Independent Writing

To gift children with the capacity to work on their writing, and thereby transform their thinking processes and knowledge, must surely be the ultimate aim of writing teachers. Michael Rosen (1996) sums up this way of working:

> When we draw on the whole body of language every time we write, we change that resource. We search around in our memories for words, phrases and combinations that will help us say what we want to say. Literacy theorists have described us as living in an "intertextual space." That's to say, all words, phrases and forms of language arrive in a sense, *already used*. We talk and write within inherited traditions and modes of discourse: everything we say and write comes to us in shapes and patterns that are part of shared knowledge. Writing is a way of working with available repertoires and patterns of language to make *new* combinations. (p. 15)

Each of the authors in this book considers various approaches to teaching and learning which support children as they move towards competence as writers. It has been organized into four sections.

The first section consists of four chapters which focus on support for the young writer. In the second section the authors explore how the writing of narrative and poetry is influenced by a variety of issues and approaches. The third section, which looks at nonfiction, considers ways into effective nonfiction writing. The final section provides us with food for thought in relation to preparing writing to be read by an audience—the mechanics of the writing process.

All of the authors recognize, as Ellie did, that writing "learns you things." Children learn about writing as they write. They also develop knowledge and understanding as they write. As Ellie clearly stated, "writing is educational."

Component	Description	Supports & challenges
Modeled writing	The teacher composes and writes down the text. The children observe, respond, and question. As the teacher composes and writes the text, he or she "thinks aloud" to help the children understand the process.	Maximum support from the teacher
Shared and interactive writing	In shared writing the children work together (whole class or groups) to compose a text. The teacher, as a member of the group, may contribute to the text and help to guide the way in which the text is constructed. The teacher writes for the children so that they can focus on composing the text. Interactive writing is a form of shared writing. However, the teacher sometimes hands the pen over to a child and asks that child to write the next word, or the first letter of the next word, or whatever is appropriate; i.e., a "shared pen" technique is used.	Shared and interactive writing
Guided writing	Guided writing can be managed in two different ways. Each approach has a different main purpose. (1) One or two sessions may be planned for small groups of children who need assistance with specific writing skills. (2) Many sessions, building upon shared reading and writing of a particular genre, are planned. Firstly, the children are immersed in the genre during reading. Secondly, they compose a text in that genre during shared/interactive writing. Finally, they are guided to write their own text in that genre.	Children take responsibility for writing, but with teacher support
Independent writing	Independent writing must be a daily component of the writing program. Children need opportunities to choose to write for a variety of purposes and a range of audiences. They need opportunities to enjoy writing about their own topics and for their own purposes. Opportunities for independent writing help children to "catch the writing habit." The children will have access to a wide variety of writing materials.	Children challenged to attend to all aspects of writing
Language experience	The class shares an experience and the children are given opportunities to express their understandings of that experience, or to respond to it, through talk, drama, art/craft, music. The experience and the children's responses are used (with groups) to generate an oral text that is dictated to the teacher and written down as a "wall story." The text is reproduced in individual booklets for each of the children in the group. The text is used for study of conventions (such as punctuation, spelling, vocabulary).	Support from shared experience, oral language base, and teacher

Figure I.2 Components of a Comprehensive Literacy Program (Hornsby 2000)

References

Bereiter, C. and Scardamalia, M. (1987) *The Psychology of Written Composition.* Hillsdale, NJ: Lawrence Erlbaum Associates.

Bruner, J. (1985) "Vygotsky: A cultural and historical perspective," in Wertsch, J. (ed.) *Culture, Communication and Cognition: Vygotskian perspectives.* Cambridge: Cambridge University Press.

Calkins, L. (1986) *The Art of Teaching Writing.* Portsmouth, NH: Heinemann.

Cambourne, B. (1988) *The Whole Story: Natural Learning and the Acquisition of Literacy in the Classroom.* Sydney: Ashton Scholastic.

Flower, L. and Hayes, J. (1981) "A cognitive process theory of writing," *College Composition and Communication* **32**, pp. 365–86.

Graves, D. (1983) *Writing: Teachers and Children at Work.* Portsmouth, NH: Heinemann.

Hayes, J. and Flower, L. (1980) "Identifying the organization of writing process," in Gregg, L. and Steinberg, E. (1980) *Cognitive Processes in Writing.* Hillsdale, NJ: Lawrence Erlbaum Associates.

Hornsby, D. (2000) *A Closer Look at Guided Reading.* Melbourne: Eleanor Curtain Publishers.

Mooney, M. (1990) *Reading To, With and By Children.* New York: Richard Owen Publishers.

Rosen, M. (1996) "Into the red brick factory," in Powling, C. and Styles, M. (eds.) (1996) *A Guide to Poetry 0–13.* Reading: Books for Keeps and The Reading and Language Centre.

Smith, F. (1982) *Writing and the Writer.* Portsmouth, NH: Heinemann.

Vygotsky, L. (1978) *Mind in Society: The Development of Higher Psychological Processes.* Cambridge: Harvard University Press.

Writers at Work: The Paris Review Interviews (2nd Series) (1963) New York: Viking Press (160).

Part I

Supporting the Young Writer

Chapter 1

"That's How I Used to Write My Name When I Was Little": Under-fives Exploring Writing

Robin Campbell

When Alice was four years ten months old she produced a drawing and a piece of writing which included a few words written conventionally, a string of five letter-like shapes and her own name. When asked about the unrecognizable writing of letter-like shapes, she indicated: "That's how I used to write my name when I was little" (Campbell 1999, p. 147).

Figure 1.1 "That's How I Used to Write My Name When I Was Little"

That piece of writing was completed at home. It indicated that Alice was able to write a small list of words. It was not unlike the genre of writing a shopping list of words that she produced on other occasions—although that would be written in a vertical line rather than on the horizontal. Alice was also able to indicate the marks that she might have used previously as she attempted to create her own name. Inevitably her name had been written in a number of invented formats before the conventional was achieved. Finally, in this writing, her name was written at the bottom of the sheet, denoting both ownership and achievement.

That simple vignette suggests a number of points about young children's exploration of writing in their first five years. Those include the opportunities for writing at home and in preschool settings which encourage children to become writers; the early marks made by children; the child's own name as a bridge to literacy (Davies 1988); invented spellings in children's writing; and, as an extension of those matters, young children writing in different genres.

Opportunities for Writing at Home

Children need to be provided with many opportunities for writing at home and in preschool settings. It is during those explorations with writing that children learn about print. To paraphrase Smith (1978, p. 5): To learn to write, children need to write. The issue is as simple and as difficult as that. Of course, Smith was debating learning to read. But children also need to write in order to learn about writing and to learn to write. That was exemplified by Casbergue (1998), who noted that it was through exploring and experimenting with print that Emily was able to use written language confidently by the time she was six years old.

At home it is helpful if there is an availability of writing materials. With a variety of papers to draw and write on, plus pencils and crayons, the child is well placed to explore mark-making. However, it is also the opportunities provided by, and the encouragement from, significant adults to use those materials, which is important. Sitting alongside the child, talking with them about their marks and taking an interest in what they are attempting, supports their understanding of literacy (Clark 1976).

The parent who makes a note while on the telephone or who creates a shopping list is providing a model for the child about writing for a real purpose. If, in addition, the parent can find time to wait while the child makes a note or a list, then that helps the child to differentiate between drawing and writing and to see a purpose for writing. Of course, at other times the child will determine what needs to be recorded. So the excitement of seeing a swan, a truck, a plane, etc., sometimes needs to be followed by a drawing and/or writing by the child, in whatever form that they are able to achieve at that time.

As children begin to note and understand the use of writing, they will occasionally want to include some form of writing in their play activities. After a trip to the dentist or doctor they might want to write a prescription or fill out a note pad just like the medic. Of course, that free use of writing materials during play does lead to the occasional mishap. Children gradually acquire an understanding of where to use writing equipment. Initially, many surfaces might be seen to have the potential for mark-making!

Reading and writing are linked, so the child learns about writing also during engagements with reading. In particular, noticing environmental print and participating in story readings support children's writing. In various studies we learn of children as young as two years old who recognize the logo and therefore the first letter of McDonald's, e.g., Baghban (1984) and Laminack (1991). Furthermore, when stories are read aloud regularly and frequently with young children, they begin to perceive that the squiggles on the page have meaning and importance. That is especially so in the one-to-one adult/child story readings where the child is next to the adult and close to the book. The pictures of such interactions in Taylor and Strickland's (1986) text on family storybook reading demonstrate the variety of contexts where that occurs. When children can see the print, in that way, they begin to wonder why the adult from time-to-time follows the print with a finger as the story is read. That leads children towards making their own marks, and they have the model of writing from the environmental print and the story print to help in their endeavors.

Opportunities for Writing in Preschool Settings

The opportunities for writing at home are reflected, although typically developed further, in preschool settings. So writing during sociodramatic play, creating classroom print, modeling writing, encouraging the writing of own name, and a writing center will all be evident (Campbell 1996).

Many children will have written during sociodramatic play at home. In the preschool, that is extended as the adults create and arrange the home corner in a variety of ways to facilitate the children's play. Morrow and Rand (1991) and Hall and Abbott (1991) describe the organization of the home corner or play area into various settings. A post office, veterinarian's office, travel agency, or airport are merely a few of the possibilities. Within those settings there will be numerous opportunities to provide for mark-making and writing. The message pad by the telephone, appointment cards, a variety of forms, note pads as well as key boards, typewriters, and perhaps computers are indicative of the possibilities. In one observation of a preschool, the adults had organized the post office in one corner of their large hall. In that setting the children filled out forms, made a mark to indicate the cost of stamps, and used a telephone pad to make a record of their telephone conversations. One child was content to sit at a typewriter and type the alphabet. In doing so, she scanned the keyboard for the required letter, typed each letter, checked her typing to make sure it was the right letter, recalled the sequence of the alphabet, and sang an alphabet song to herself. She was enjoying her play, but developing her literacy knowledge at the same time

Children learn about writing from the environmental print. As Whitehead (1999) indicated, we need to bring that print to the children's attention, make collections of it, and read it with them. She also suggests that children should be encouraged "to play with the print, taking it apart and reassembling it, or making copies of it for their play areas" (p. 131). However, it can be useful if the children move beyond that to creating their own classroom print with support from the adults. In one preschool the teacher worked with the children to create a notice reminding the parents to close the latch on the gate into the playground (Lally 1991). The teacher talked with the children about the notice, and modeled the writing of it with them. Over the next few days, many of the children produced further notices for other purposes in the classroom during their play.

We have just noted how effective the modeling of writing can be for young children. Adults can use that to link to other activities. So when a nursery rhyme has been enjoyed by the children, a shared writing of that rhyme can be helpful. In one preschool the teacher and children worked together to produce a nursery rhyme on a big sheet of paper:

Teacher:	So if I write
	Humpty Dumpty
	Now what comes next?
Children:	*sat on a wall*
Teacher:	I'll write *sat on a . . .*
Children:	*wall*
Teacher:	*wall* (Campbell 1996, pp. 34–5)

As that process continued, the children were able to see their contributions being written onto the sheet. They watched as each word was written and saw the letters being formed. They were learning further about writing. Later they had a piece of classroom print, which they returned to from time to time as they recited that nursery rhyme.

One feature of writing in the preschool classroom will be the children's writing of their own name. Adults will encourage the children to recognize and also to write their name. Indeed, a wide range of activities are likely to be provided (Campbell 2001). Finding name cards each day, posting them, looking at an alphabet book of class names, writing of names on paintings and drawings, and creating their own name in various media are all possibilities. In some classrooms the children, as young as three years of age, are encouraged to sign in each day (Harste, Woodward, and Burke 1984). Of course, that demands that the adults are ready to accept what the children are able to achieve and to support them as they move towards conventional writing. However, this is such an important aspect of writing for the child that we shall consider it in more detail below.

A writing center is often simply a table with a variety of paper of different sizes and colors and pencils, crayons, chalk, and felt-tip pens. Some preschool teachers suggest it is best to vary the writing implements on a regular basis to create an interest for the children. It is important, too, that the adults visit the center to model writing "I think I'd better make my shopping list," or "We need a notice to keep the pet box tidy." In addition, the adult can act as an audience for the marks and writing made by the children. Given that environment for writing and the acceptance of what the child is able to achieve, a variety of products will be evident.

In one preschool classroom, the children produced scribbles, linear scribbles, pseudo-letters, actual letters, own name, invented spellings, and conventional words (Campbell 1996) at the writing center. They learned from the modeling of writing by, and support from, the adults. However, they also learned from each other as they talked about what they were producing. And their learning was facilitated because the opportunities to explore writing were regular and frequent.

Making a Mark

We have just noted how, at one writing center, a group of children produced a variety of marks, letters, and words. That gradual development from apparently unintelligible scribbles to conventional writing is common (Temple *et al.* 1992). A key role for the adult is to accept what the child is able to offer and to provide appropriate support and guidance to encourage the learning.

A major step for children, in their development, is when they begin to differentiate between drawings and writing. For instance, Martens (1996) noted that her daughter Sarah began to distinguish between drawing, with various circular forms, and writing, with a number of horizontal parallel lines, when she was two and a half years old. Similarly, Alice began to differentiate between drawing and writing at that age. Her picture of "Grandad smiling" (Figure 1.2) could be recognized (Campbell 1999, p. 52). And her marks alongside that picture indicated very clearly that she had an understanding of writing.

Although for Alice the writing indicated "d, d, b, i, d," they appeared as relatively similar marks on the paper. Nevertheless, the importance of those marks was substantial. Alice was writing. The conventional presentation of letters and words was merely some months and years in the future. Mark-making will be an important part of the writing process for most young children. It needs to be recognized and celebrated, with the frequent opportunities for mark-making helping the children on their path towards recognizable conventional writing.

Writing Own Name

We have noted that preschool classrooms will provide opportunities for children to recognize and write their own name. Why is that regarded as being important? Initially, because young children are intrigued by their own name. That should not surprise us. After all, in their first year children learn how significant their name is. Their given names are used by those around them for many purposes.

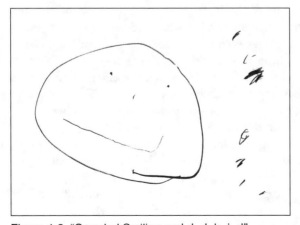

Figure 1.2 "Grandad Smiling and d, d, b, i, d"

Subsequently, many young children draw themselves as well as depicting those important adults around them. Then, as they become aware of the use of print, it is the given name that often provides the first word to be explored.

In a number of studies we noted how, for young children, it was the given name which served as an entry into writing. As Adam began to produce letters at two years nine months, it was the "A" which was most frequently evident—leading to the writing of his name by three years (Schickedanz 1990). Similarly, with other children between two and three years of age, it was the first, and capital, letter of their given name which dominated their mark-making and writing. For Giti it was the use of the "G" (Baghban 1984) and for Cecilia a "C" (Payton 1984) which was evident in the samples of writing which were published. The children were naturally inclined to explore their own names.

Children acquire a considerable amount of knowledge about letters, words, and writing as they explore their names. They learn that particular marks have to be made, knowledge of some letter shapes is acquired, and they are able to recall those letters. The letters of their name can be written and the children become aware of the importance of the sequence of those letters. They also begin to note that their name has to be separate from other words, and subsequently they note that is the case for other words as well. When all of that learning is considered, we can see why Davies (1988) regarded the child's name as a bridge to literacy.

Alice showed how that link might be made as she looked at some words. She noted, "That's like Alice but it's an apple." She appeared to be using her knowledge of her own name and the all-important first letter as she considered and recognized the word *apple*. As Bloodgood (1999) indicated, children's name writing provides support for learning about many aspects of literacy.

Using Invented Spellings

When Bissex (1980) chronicled her son's development as a writer and reader, she noted particularly his use of invented spellings. In that analysis, she was following the earlier work of Read (1971), who had recorded how children develop towards conventional spelling. A number of writers have described children's attempts to write freely and the appearance of spellings, which approximate to the conventional and are recognizable but which are not accurate.

A number of terms have been used to describe those spellings. Graves (1983) referred to invented spellings and subsequently inventive spellings (1994). Strickland (1998) noted both of those descriptors but also recognized the use of temporary spelling, constructive spelling, developmental spelling, or phonics-based spelling. Casbergue (1998) wrote about phonemic spelling. Behind all of those descriptors is the recognition of young children actively using their knowledge of letters and sounds to construct the words that they wish to write.

The invented spellings are, therefore, a very positive indicator of what children are able to achieve. For instance, by the time Alice was five years old, she produced a piece of writing entitled "How to Make a Shepherd's Pie" (Figure 1.3).

In that writing we can see that she was able to write "to, a, of, and," with each spelled conventionally. Furthermore, her invented spellings of hao (how), mack (make), sepas (shepherd's), piy (pie), uyn (onion), ptatos (potatoes), biass (beans), cess (cheese), as well as various interpretations of "grams," all demonstrated her active, constructive role as a writer.

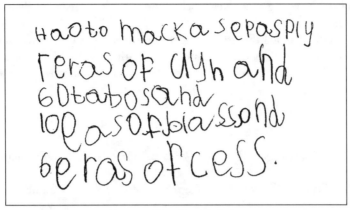

Figure 1.3 "How to Make a Shepherd's Pie"

The writing also demonstrates why some have referred to such unconventional writing of words as being phonic-based spellings or phonemic spellings. With each of the words it is possible to follow the likely means by which Alice arrived at her spelling. She was indeed using her knowledge of letters and sounds to represent each word. That was a strategy that, when linked to other strategies and knowledge, would serve her well in the future.

Writing in a Variety of Genres

Young children are helped to understand the process of writing as they write in a variety of genres. For instance, it was after Alice had helped her grandmother to do some cooking that she decided that she, too, needed a recipe book. However, Alice wanted to construct her own book. So "How to Make a Shepherd's Pie" became one page of that book. Her writing was for a real purpose, and she enjoyed producing a book just like adults used.

There are other genres that intrigue young children. Many adults produce a list before going out on a shopping expedition, and young children enjoy making their own shopping list. It might be that the typical vertical list of words is one that attracts them. Then, making birthday cards requires a particular layout and children enjoy creating cards for others. Labeling the objects in their own drawings leads to children writing stories when they are older, or recreating stories they have heard and enjoyed.

All of that might appear like a simple use of the notion of genre. Yet, the children do have to adjust their writing according to which writing they are producing. That is part of the process that will support the reading and writing of various genres as the child develops as a literacy user.

The Role of the Adult

Throughout this chapter the emphasis has been upon children. However, it will have been evident that the adult has a prominent support role as children develop as writers. It is not the direct teaching of writing that will help the young child. Nevertheless, the adult does need to facilitate, guide, and support children in their literacy learning.

Weinberger (1996) noted that the parents of three-year-olds were "providing resources and opportunities, acting as literacy models, and interacting with their children on literacy practices and events" (p. 43). We have noted each of those three important attributes as we considered aspects of young children's writing.

References

Baghban, M. (1984) *Our Daughter Learns to Read and Write*. Newark, DE: International Reading Association.

Bissex, G. (1980) *GNYS AT WRK: A child learns to read and write*. Cambridge, MA: Harvard University Press.

Bloodgood, J. (1999) "What's in a name? Children's name writing and literacy acquisition," *Reading Research Quarterly* **34** (3), pp. 342–67.

Campbell, R. (1996) *Literacy in Nursery Education*. Stoke-on-Trent: Trentham Books.

Campbell, R. (1999) *Literacy from Home to School: Reading with Alice*. Stoke-on-Trent: Trentham Books.

Campbell, R. (2001) "'I can write my name I can': Looking at the importance of the writing of own name," *Education 3–13*. Spring 2001 (in press).

Casbergue, R. (1998) "How do we foster young children's writing development?" in Neuman, S. and Roskos, K. (eds.) (1998) *Children Achieving: Best practices in early literacy*. Newark, DE: International Reading Association.

Clark, M. M. (1976) *Young Fluent Readers*. London: Heinemann.

Davies, A. (1988) "Children's names: Bridges to literacy?" *Research in Education* **40**, pp. 19–31.

Graves, D. (1983) *Writing: Teachers and Children at Work*. Portsmouth, NH: Heinemann.

Graves, D. (1994) *A Fresh Look at Writing*. Portsmouth, NH: Heinemann.

Hall, N. and Abbott, L. (eds.) (1991) *Play in the Primary Curriculum*. London: Hodder & Stoughton.

Harste, J. C., Woodward, V. A. and Burke, C. L. (1984) *Language Stories and Literacy Lessons*. Portsmouth, NH: Heinemann.

Lally, M. (1991) *The Nursery Teacher in Action*. London: Paul Chapman Publishing.

Laminack, L. (1991) *Learning with Zachary*. Richmond Hill, ON: Scholastic.

Martens, P. (1996) *I Already Know How to Read: A child's view of literacy*. Portsmouth, NH: Heinemann.

Morrow, L. M. and Rand, M. K. (1991) "Promoting literacy during play by designing early childhood classroom environments," *The Reading Teacher* **44** (6), pp. 396–402.

Payton, S. (1984) *Developing Awareness of Print: A young child's first steps towards literacy*. Birmingham: Educational Review, University of Birmingham.

Read, C. (1971) "Pre-school children's knowledge of English phonology," *Harvard Educational Review* **41** (4), pp. 1–34.

Schickedanz, J. A. (1990) *Adam's Righting Revolutions*. Portsmouth, NH: Heinemann.

Smith, F. (1978) *Reading*. Cambridge: Cambridge University Press.

Strickland, D. S. (1998) *Teaching Phonics Today: A primer for educators*. Newark, DE: International Reading Association.

Taylor, D. and Strickland, D. (1986) *Family Storybook Reading*. New York: Scholastic.

Temple, C., Nathan, R., Temple, F. and Burris, N. A. (1992) *The Beginnings of Writing*, 3rd ed. London: Allyn and Bacon.

Weinberger, J. (1996) *Literacy Goes to School*. London: Paul Chapman Publishing.

Whitehead, M. (1999) *Supporting Language and Literacy Development in the Early Years*. Buckingham: Open University Press.

Chapter 2

Using Nursery Rhymes, Jingles, Songs, and Poems as a Way into Writing

Janet Evans

Nursery Rhymes as a Popular Genre

Nursery rhymes have always been popular with children . . . but why? Very often they don't relate to our contemporary life, and frequently they seem to make no sense at all. Yet the rhythm and rhyme of the sentences, the simple story lines, humorous innuendoes, and play on words make them good fun not only to recount, but also to sing along with other people. Books of nursery rhymes, poems, and jingles have often been given as presents on the birth of a child or on a baby's christening day. Now more than ever there is a tremendous choice on the market, and rhyming poetry, verse, and books of songs to sing are all available for parents to purchase. Many adults have pleasurable memories of sharing books when they were young children and are able to go straight to a bookshelf and pick up an old, battered copy of their much-loved childhood nursery rhyme book.

Some of the original nursery rhymes were never written down but were passed from generation to generation by word of mouth. Indeed, many are extremely old, some dating as far back as 500 BC, e.g. *Rain, rain, go away come again another day*. The apparent nonsense and innocence of some of these verses can sometimes belie more somber origins, as the words of *Ring-a-ring o' Roses* show:

> Ring-a-ring o' roses
> A pocket full of posies
> A-tishoo! A-tishoo!
> We all fall down.

This popular rhyme—ostensibly quite innocuous—describes the sudden deaths of people succumbing to the Great Plague. The tell-tale red circle on the skin, or "*ring of roses,*" and the sneezing, "*A-tishoo! A-tishoo!*" signified that the disease had been caught. Carrying special herbs, "*A pocket full of posies,"* was thought to keep the plague at bay, but it worked infrequently. The effects of the plague were so rapid and severe that people often dropped dead in the street as they walked—hence the final line, *"we all fall down"* (Trussell-Cullen 1989).

We are often led to believe that in Victorian times fortunate youngsters went to sleep while nursery rhymes and songs were being read and sung to them in bed. Indeed, some of the first books of nursery rhymes, rhyming verse, traditional stories, and poetry, often illustrated by such acclaimed illustrators as Kate Greenaway, Norman Caldecott, and Leslie Brookes, were the ones which popularized the idea of sharing such books with young children.

Iona and Peter Opie (1987), in their comprehensive documentation of children and their playground rhymes and jingles, also did a great deal to promote the importance of exposing young children to nursery rhymes, jingles, and songs. Originally, much of this exposure was for the pure pleasure of listening to stories and rhymes being told and sung out loud; however, the simple, ubiquitous nursery rhyme has more recently been attracting attention in education circles for other, quite different reasons.

Linking Nursery Rhymes with Writing

My personal interest in using nursery rhymes and jingles to teach reading to young children, coupled with an awareness of the ongoing research into how educators can effectively teach the process of writing, led me to link these two areas in some work I was doing with six- and seven-year-old children. My aim was to share a big book with the whole class of children, followed by some written work to be done with a mixed-ability group of ten girls and boys. I wanted to examine their knowledge of traditional nursery rhymes and jingles; would they know a lot of them and be able to chant them, or would they think that nursery rhymes were too babyish for children of their age? I also wanted them to choose one of their favorite rhymes, and, taking the main character(s) in the original rhyme, write a sequel, maybe in the form of the further adventures of Jack and Jill, or Mary and her little lamb, or whichever rhyme character they chose. My third intention was to observe the children organizing their narrative writing, offering structured help where applicable to enable the children to become more effective writers.

To be able to write an adventure sequel, the children needed to respond to the narrative element of the rhymes and to explore their structure. I wondered if the rhymes would be seen as short stories, some with very clear structures in terms of characters, setting, plot, events, and resolution, or if they would just be listened to, chanted, and regarded as simple verses for babies. I knew that I would need to talk with the children about their favorite rhymes and the personalities of the characters in the rhymes. I also knew that I would need to model each stage of the writing process for the children as we progressed from our initial ideas to a finished book which the other children could read.

Nursery Rhymes as a Stimulus

The book which became the stimulus for many of their ideas was called *Times and Rhymes* (Davidson 1997). Written in rhyming verse, it is really good to read to young literacy learners because of the way it guides them into using all of the cueing systems: syntactic, semantic, and graphophonic. It specifically encourages the use of picture cues, predicting, guessing, reading on, reading back, initial and final letter sounds, patterns of letters in words, and the use of onset, rime, and analogy in rhyming words. It is also wonderful in the way it alludes to the nursery rhymes to come, giving clues of all kinds before eventually, as one turns each page, exposing the full version of the nursery rhyme to the reader. Ten familiar and not so familiar nursery rhymes are referred to throughout the story.

This book was shared with the class of six- and seven-year-old children, along with some other books about nursery rhymes and traditional stories, such as *The Nursery Rhyme Picnic* (Wignell 1990), *Goodnight, Goodnight* (Parkes 1989), *The Enormous Watermelon* (Parkes and Smith 1986), *Each Peach Pear Plum* (Ahlberg 1996), *Mr Wolf's Pancakes* (Fearnley 1999), and *Little Bo Peep's Library Book* (Cowell 1999). The children started to consider what kind of personalities the rhyme characters had when they were not "in role" in their story. The idea of writing about the further adventures of some of these characters came later, after listening to the story of *Struwwelpeter* (Hoffman 1845), the boy who had his fingernails cut off. The children questioned how Struwwelpeter could carry on in life without fingernails. This led them to relate back to the nursery rhyme characters and to consider what would happen to some of them after their adventures—some of which were quite traumatic, such as Humpty Dumpty, who was shattered, and Rock-a-Bye Baby, who fell from a tree in a cradle when one of the branches broke. We re-read the original book and started to discuss each of the main characters in even more detail. As well as Humpty Dumpty and Rock-a-Bye Baby, what further adventures would Jack and Jill get up to? What about Jack, who was nimble and quick and who jumped over the candlestick . . . what would he do? Contrary Mary: what other things could she do as well as having silver bells, cockle-shells, and pretty maids all in a row in her garden? Polly with her kettle, the old woman who lived in a shoe, and the baby who fell from the tree top complete with cradle, were all subjects for discussion.

> John, a very insightful child, commented, *"With no fingernails, Struwwelpeter wouldn't be able to hold his knife and fork, or draw and colour in . . . he wouldn't be able to pick his nose either would he?"*
>
> Sean, who went on to write about Humpty Dumpty, said, *"Perhaps every broken bit of Humpty's shell will grow other body bits and become complete eggs like worms when they get chopped in half."*
>
> Chris, who didn't always find it easy to contribute to class discussions, said in relation to Hickory Dickory Dock, *"That mouse will be well shattered running up and down the clock everytime it rings."*

The children talked eagerly and thoughtfully about their ideas, and each child chose the rhyme and character they wanted to work with. Having worked with them before, I knew they were certainly not afraid of putting their ideas down on paper and they were used to doing shared writing followed by guided writing. However, at this point I was mindful of the recent Office for Standards in Education (OFSTED) interim report on the National Literacy Strategy (1999), which states that greater emphasis needs to be given to the teaching of writing. With both girls and boys, writing expertise seems to be lagging behind reading. The whole process of writing needs teaching more explicitly right across the five to eleven age range. I started to question myself. Was I doing enough to help these children organize their narrative writing?

Research—Past and Present

What impact has research on writing from the last two decades had on classroom practice? I think back to the 1980s when a great deal of international research (Calkins 1986; Calkins and Harwayne 1991; Clay 1991; Graves 1983, 1989; Hall 1987, 1989; Parry and Hornsby 1985; Temple *et al.* 1993) was conducted in relation to children, learning and writing. In England, action-based research resulted in newsletters which reported on the work of teachers during the period of the National Writing Project (1985–1989). This project was set up to look at how writing was being taught, to identify good practice in the teaching of young writers, and to create competent and confident writers who could write for a range of purposes. Many teachers found that their personal and professional knowledge about how children learn to write was augmented and broadened through the child-centered research which they conducted in their own classrooms. The research undertaken was wide ranging in its content and fascinating in its findings; some teachers in the south of England encountered disturbing and yet salutary viewpoints when they asked children a series of questions about writing, including what makes a piece of writing good? The majority of children said a good piece of writing must be long, have all words spelled correctly, have correct punctuation (including capital letters and periods), and it must be neat! The children were not considering the content, audience, purpose, or appropriateness of style when writing, indicating that much work needed to be done in relation to changing children's attitudes to writing.

It is evident that, to develop as effective writers, children need:

- the opportunity to try things out and to relate their previous knowledge of print to their own personal situation;
- to feel able to take risks without being frightened of making mistakes;
- to be exposed to an adult role model who will share writing and the whole writing experience with them;
- to have something to write about and reasons to write.

And incontrovertibly, children must have:

- exposure to top-quality literature and books, as children write what they read.

Much of the very relevant and creative international research of the 1980s has informed our current practice and is still influencing new research into the teaching of writing. One such piece of teacher research, small scale in its range but still so refreshingly relevant that it could almost have been written yesterday, was by Chris Rayers (1987). The article about *shared, guided,* and *independent* writing outlines a methodology for modeling the process of writing with five- to eleven-year-old children. It is evident, however, that Rayers' main aim was for teachers to teach children how to write through acting as role models and encouraging the children to "have a go" in a relaxed, child-friendly atmosphere where they were expected to succeed when they were scaffolded by the teacher. Rayers alluded to some of the problem areas that children faced when trying to become writers, from tired hands for the very youngest children, through to a lack of knowledge of the conventions of print and the inability to spell new words, with older children. He stated that instead of learning writing in a piecemeal, bit by bit manner, where the skills are focused on to the exclusion of the meaning of the whole text, the young child:

> needs to experience the whole writing process as soon as possible, and shared writing with an adult is an ideal method of providing such early writing success. The shared writing technique immediately involves the children in talking about writing and in redrafting at a very early age. (p. 118)

With Rayers' ideas in mind, it is interesting to read what the training details from the National Literacy Strategy (DfEE 1998) have to say about shared writing:

> In Shared Writing sessions, you will be using known texts to create new ones, demonstrating different aspects of the writing process and helping pupils to understand purpose, organization and conventions of different genres. In their group activities, pupils will be encouraged to write collaboratively and be taught how to respond helpfully to others' work. They will be asked to write parts of whole texts—an opening, or a paragraph of dialogue, or an outline plan—which is not necessarily developed into a full blown novel. These activities develop out of reading and should involve pupils in returning to the text rather than departing further and further away from it. They will use the original as a model, but change one or more ingredients—perhaps the setting, or author's viewpoint, characters, or outcome. Further revision of pupils' own writing will be going on in guided group work at Text, Sentence or Word level. At these times they will be concerned with further crafting and refining, rather than correcting spelling mistakes. (DfEE 1998)

It is evident that the issues have not changed despite the passage of time. Children and their educators need to know that writing is not simply a process of thinking about an idea, jotting it down and then tidying it up. As the Ministry of Education for New Zealand consider in their book, *Dancing with the Pen* (1996), writing is recursive in that the writer can move from one stage to another, depending on what has already been written and what is yet to be written. The audience and purpose will affect whether drafting and proof reading are needed, while the desired outcome will determine how the piece of writing is eventually presented, if at all.

The Process of Writing

The small group of children with whom I was working, although eager, enthusiastic writers, were not always aware of all the stages in relation to the process of writing, so as they worked their way towards their completed book, I carefully guided them through each stage (see Figure 2.1).

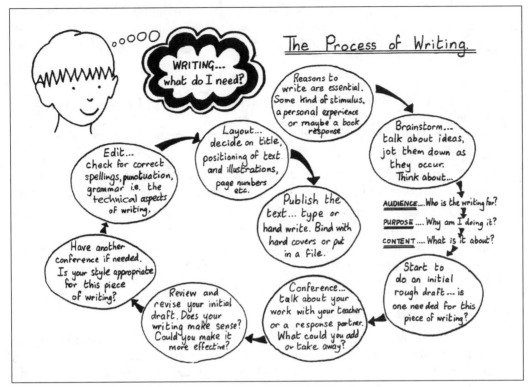

Figure 2.1 The Process of Writing

1. Initially we related to our personal **experiences** of reading and responding to the big book, *Times and Rhymes*. All writers must have reasons to write and something to write about; an experience, preferably first hand but more usually a second-hand experience relating to a book which has been shared with the children. Nigel Hall (1989) wrote extensively about the need for children to write in purposeful ways, while Casbergue (1998) talks about young children writing about authentic purposes in real situations.

2. We talked about our responses to the book and started to jot down our ideas in a random fashion for a shared write relating to one of the characters; this was the **brainstorming** part of our writing. At this stage we asked ourselves:

- Who is this writing for? (AUDIENCE)
- Why am I doing this writing? (PURPOSE)
- What is this writing about? (CONTENT)
- Is it necessary to do a brainstorm?

If so:

- What STYLE of writing will be APPROPRIATE in relation to the above questions?

3. We wrote our **initial rough draft**. At this point we were not in the least bit worried about correctness in terms of grammar, punctuation, neatness, spelling, and layout; we were interested in placing some of the ideas from our brainstorming in a simple written form. At this stage we asked ourselves:

   - Is a rough draft always needed?
   - Do I need to do a rough draft to write a quick message to my best friend or to write a shopping list?
   - Do I need to do a rough draft to write an important letter or to write a story to be read by the other children in school?

4. We then stopped to read what we had written and to **talk about it**, that is, **conference**. Initially this was done with the teacher, then in small groups, then in "response partner" pairs before "going it alone." At this stage we asked ourselves:

   - *Where* does this adventure take place?
   - *Who* are the characters in this story?
   - *What* does that character look like; can you describe him/her?
   - *What* else do I need to know about what is happening?
   - *How* can I make this piece of writing better? Should I use more descriptive language or take some bits out as they are repetitive?

The concept of conferencing as initiated by Donald Graves (1983) really allows children to think about and reflect on their work in nonthreatening, helpful situations. Hodgson (1995) feels that conferencing is a time when child and teacher get together to discuss the child's writing, while Mandel Morrow and Gambrell (1998) report on some five- and six-year-old children who write, then conference with partners: "After writing, the partners read their stories to each other. Then they suggested ideas for change or additions to their partner's work. The partners made the suggested revisions and then read their stories to each other again." (p. 156)

5. We **reviewed** and **revised** our initial rough draft to include some of the ideas which had come from our conferencing—amendments were made where appropriate. At this stage we asked ourselves:

   - Does my writing make sense?
   - Does it need amending?
   - How can I improve my writing?
   - What else do I want to know?
   - Do I need to add bits or take bits away?
   - Should the writing be more descriptive?

6. We **conferenced** once again to reassure ourselves that the writing was appropriate for the audience, and any further additions and omissions were made to the content of the writing. At this stage we asked ourselves:

   - Have I carefully considered how my audience will relate to this?
   - Is the style appropriate for the purpose?

7. We started to **edit** the writing at this stage and began to give full attention to spelling, punctuation, grammar, i.e. the technical aspects of the writing. At this stage we asked ourselves:

   - Are the words spelled correctly?
   - Does the punctuation help with reading the text?
   - Are the capital letters and periods in the right place?
   - Are the adjectives, adverbs, and pronouns being used properly?

8. Finally we decided on the **layout**, as this writing was being written as a book for readers of all ages. At this stage we asked ourselves:

   - Is the layout appropriate for the content of this piece of writing?
   - Are the illustrations in the right place? Are there enough illustrations?
   - Is there a title page, a contents page, an index, page numbers, acknowledgments, ISBN, bar code, etc.?
   - Is the cover suitably designed? Do the authors and illustrators have their names in place?
   - Is the work neat?

9. How shall we **publish** our book? At this stage we asked ourselves:

   - Should the text be typed or handwritten?
   - Should it be bound between hard covers, spiral bound, or placed in a ring file?

Each stage of the writing process was carefully considered; however, it was the notion of rough drafts that created most discussion with the most asked question being, "Are rough drafts always necessary?" It was through being involved in a piece of writing which was going to be fully published for a particular audience (in this case, the other children in the class) that each child came to see that reviewing rough drafts was not simply a case of copying the writing out neatly with correct spellings. The conferencing aspect of the writing became important to this group of six- and seven-year-olds; each child thought about his or her own idea but collaborated with the teacher and then with a response partner when it came to conferencing. It was very evident that, by offering ideas, making suggestions for improvement, and responding to each other's work, the children's writing was much improved, as was their concept of themselves as writers. The knowledge that writing is recursive is an important concept for children, and the notion of a piece of work being important enough to think about, talk about, and return to . . . just as real authors do . . . was a real support to them. They realized that all stages in a writing process are important, from the initial stages where they are composing and getting their ideas down without worrying about what they looked like, through to the later stages where finer adjustments to make the writing better are made as part of the reviewing and editing process.

The Children's Alternative Adventures

Out of the ten contributors to the book, which they called *Mixed Up Nursery Rhymes*, four children in particular showed a real understanding of the purpose for doing the writing and a growing ability to write humorously for an intended audience. Their further adventures of the nursery rhyme characters kept the essence of the nursery rhyme genre, the lightheartedness of which often has a hidden message. However, one or two of their adventures had a rather forlorn, darker side to them.

Figure 2.2 "Jack Be Nimble" and "Jack and the Burning House"

It is very evident from this short narrative that John had fully understood the potential danger in Jack's athletic actions, and he was more than able to weave this into an interesting, humorous adventure.

Jack and the Burning House. Jack jumped back over the candlestick but oh no! He fell onto the candlestick, ow, he burned his botty he landed on the table cloth, he had started a fire, it spread, it burnt the whole house down. One day he was walking round the debris and he met some mice. The next day Jack and the mice went to London.

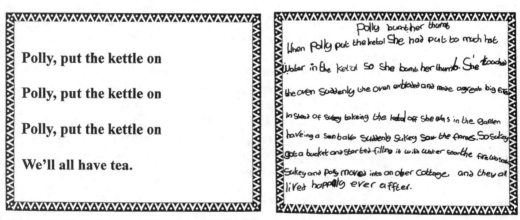

Figure 2.3 "Polly Put the Kettle On" and "Polly Burnt Her Thumb"

Caroline used the simple action of Polly putting the kettle on as a stimulus for a further adventure. In similar ways to John, she could evidently see the danger of getting burned in the original rhyme, and she used this theme in her narrative about Polly and Sukey.

Polly Burnt Her Thumb. When Polly put the kettle on she had put too much hot water in the kettle so she burnt her thumb. She touched the oven, suddenly the oven exploded and made a great big fire. Instead of Sukey taking the kettle off she was in the garden having a sunbathe suddenly Sukey saw the flames. So Sukey got a basket and started filling it with water, soon the fire was out. Sukey and Polly moved to another cottage and they all lived happily ever after.

<table>
<tr><td>

Humpty Dumpty sat on a wall.

Humpty Dumpty had a great fall.

All the king's horses and all the king's men

Couldn't put Humpty together again.

</td><td>

sellotepd Dumpy

Humpty Dumpoy saw on wall well
then he crack The King's men cunt
him togther so they sellocep him wo
to guver then he watched mandunwood
evry tamie thay scored ones wen
they scored he crased and all the
yonk cem out then he died.

</td></tr>
</table>

Figure 2.4 "Humpty Dumpty" and Sellotaped (Taped) Dumpty"

It was the idea of poor Humpty Dumpty shattering into a myriad of pieces that inspired Sean to write his very comical piece.

Taped Dumpty. Humpty Dumpty sat on a wall then he cracked. The King's men couldn't put him together so they taped him to together then he watched Man (Manchester) United, every time they scored. Once when they scored he crashed and all the yolk came out then he died.

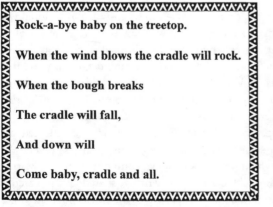

<table>
<tr><td>

Rock-a-bye baby on the treetop.

When the wind blows the cradle will rock.

When the bough breaks

The cradle will fall,

And down will

Come baby, cradle and all.

</td><td>

Rock a bye baby

Waa! Waa! mama! mama! the branch brock and I
fell down to the ground Waa! Waa! be quiet becoise
you wont have any dinner! ok. The baby was silent
for a minet then said: but then I wont have my
baby food will I? no you wont will you! Said mummy
(you now relise this story-has a lot of Shouting going
on) Grandma come shush! lisen to this rock a bye baby
on the tree top when the wind blows the cradle
will fall. That all I Know up to now Sorry Come
on lets go to Bolton. When they got there they
had lots of fun.

</td></tr>
</table>

Figure 2.5 "Rock-a-bye Baby"

In Laura's work we see another child who is able to relate the nursery rhyme incident to real life. She included dialogue and a real sense of the here and now, coupled with the whimsical nature of the nursery rhyme setting. Laura read her story out with such conviction, expression, and enthusiasm that it was impossible to have anything other than full respect for her work. She was already showing signs of becoming a very competent writer at the age of six.

> *Rock-a-bye Baby. Waa! Waa! Mama! Mama! the branch broke and I fell down onto the ground. Waa! Waa! be quiet because you won't **have any** dinner! OK. The baby was silent for a minute then said, "But I won't have my favorite baby food will I?"*
>
> *"No you won't will you?" said Mommy.*
>
> *(You now realize this story has a lot of shouting going on).*
>
> *Grandma came, "Shush! Listen to this rock a bye baby on the tree top, when the wind blows the cradle will fall."*
>
> *"That's all I know up to now, sorry. Come on let's go to Bolton."*
>
> *When they got there they had lots of fun.*

The children in the group immensely enjoyed their work; they were enthusiastic and motivated—noted by their requests to work through playtimes during the mornings I was able to spend with them! Their writing benefited, as could be seen by their increasing ability to plan, to jot their initial ideas down, to write their first draft, to structure interesting short story lines in terms of plot and events, and in their more sophisticated use of words. However, despite my encouragement to write more stimulating endings, they wrote rather mundane, uninspired, and stereotyped endings. It was evident that we needed to read and study the endings in many more stories, both traditional and contemporary, before considering the kinds of endings which would be suitable for our simple short stories. The children would also need exposure to more teacher modeling focusing on resolutions in narratives. Many teachers find this a problem area, as Maureen Lewis (1999) noted in relation to her work on narrative writing.

What Have We Learned?

Despite the fact that this collaborative piece of work done with six- and seven-year-old children was small scale in terms of time, numbers, and range of intentions, it was very positive in terms of its outcomes. It was very encouraging to find that nursery rhymes and traditional stories make excellent stimuli for narrative writing because of their predictability and their ability to make children feel at ease with their apparent simplicity. I was convinced that slightly older children would benefit from a more detailed examination of the nursery rhyme genre and was pleased to confirm that this was indeed the case; the nursery rhymes were humorous, witty, and thought-provoking.

The children's developing ability to organize and plan their written work confirmed my thoughts that they need a role model at each stage of their journey towards full competency as authors. Hornsby (2000) discusses five stages which he feels are crucial components in the writing part of a comprehensive literacy program: These include modeled writing, shared and interactive writing, guided writing, independent writing, and language experience, which can fuel the other aspects of the program. These stages move from maximum support from the adult to a variety of different levels of support, depending on the children's needs. Hornsby's extra stages augment the now-recognized shared, guided, and independent stages while also highlighting the fact that the teacher's role is crucial in the teaching of writing.

It was noteworthy that the children were now beginning to see their writing as a process, something which couldn't be done in one session but needed a much longer period of time. Their growing awareness of how each stage of the process fitted into the whole was evident from their responses to the work as it developed and came together as the finished book. With help from me, these children had also begun to see writing as recursive. They were more prepared to work on parts of it, rereading, revisiting, adding bits, taking bits away, chatting about it, and generally improving its fluency. Time, exposure to a knowledgeable role model and many more opportunities to practice, consolidate, and continually apply their existing knowledge to new and different writing situations will now be needed to allow these children to grow as writers.

The whole writing process can be very difficult. It is time-consuming, labor-intensive, and often frustrating. Even professional writers find it difficult and really have to work at it. If schools make the process of writing part of a whole-school policy, starting with four- and five-year-olds and leading up to ten- and eleven-year-olds in a cyclical, recursive fashion, then they are more likely to produce effective writers who find writing a rewarding experience.

References

Ahlberg, J. and A. (1996) *Each Peach Pear Plum*. London: Oliver & Boyd.

Calkins, L. (1986) *The Art of Teaching Writing*. Portsmouth, NH: Heinemann.

Calkins, L. and Harwayne, S. (1991) *Living Between the Lines*. Portsmouth, NH: Heinemann.

Casbergue, R. (1998) "How do we foster young children's writing development?" in Neuman, S. and Roskos, K. (1998) (eds.). *Children Achieving: Best practices in early literacy*. Newark DE: International Reading Association.

Clay, M. (1991) *Becoming Literate: The construction of inner control*. Portsmouth, NH: Heinemann.

Cowell, C. (1999) *Little Bo Peep's Library Book*. London: Hodder Headline.

Davidson, A. (1997) *Times and Rhymes*. London: Kingscourt.

DfEE (1998) *The National Literacy Strategy Framework for Teaching*. London: DfEE.

Fearnley, J. (1999) *Mr Wolf's Pancakes*. London: Methuen Children's Books.

Graves, D. (1983) *Writing: Teachers and Children at Work*. Portsmouth, NH: Heinemann.

Graves, D. (1989) *Experiment with Fiction*. Portsmouth, NH: Heinemann.

Hall, N. (1987) *The Emergence of Literacy*. London: Hodder & Stoughton.

Hall, N. (1989) *Writing with Reason: The emergence of authorship in young children*. Sevenoaks: Hodder & Stoughton.

Hodgson, M. (1995) *Show Them How to Write: The writing process for children from seven years on*. New Zealand: Lands End Publishing.

Hoffman, H. (1845) *Struwwelpeter*. London: Belitha Press.

Hornsby, D. (2000) *A Closer Look at Guided Reading*. Melbourne: Eleanor Curtain Publishing.

Lewis, M. (1999) "Developing children's narrative writing using story narratives," in Goodwin, P. (1999) (ed.). *The Literate Classroom*. London: David Fulton Publishers.

Mandel Morrow, L. and Gambrell, L. (1998) "How do we motivate children toward independent reading and writing?" in Neuman, S. and Roskos, K. (1998) (eds.). *Children Achieving: Best practices in early literacy*. Newark, DE: International Reading Association.

Ministry of Education (1996) *Dancing with the Pen: The learner as a writer.* New Zealand: Learning Media.

National Writing Project (1989) Walton-on-Thames: Nelson.

OFSTED (1999) *The National Literacy Strategy: An interim evaluation.* London: OFSTED.

Opie, I. and Opie, P. (1987) *The Lore and Language of Schoolchildren.* Oxford: Oxford University Press.

Parkes, B. (1989) *Goodnight, Goodnight.* London: Kingscourt.

Parkes, B. and Smith, J. (1986) *The Enormous Watermelon.* London: Kingscourt.

Parry, J. and Hornsby, D. (1985) *Write On: A conference approach to writing.* Portsmouth, NH: Heinemann.

Rayers, C. (1987) "Writing should be sharing," *Reading* **21**(2).

Temple, C., Nathan, R., Temple, F. and Burris, N. (1993) *The Beginnings of Writing.* Needham, MA: Allyn & Bacon.

Trussell-Cullen, A. (1989) *A Pocket Full of Posies: A history of nursery rhymes.* London: Kingscourt.

Wignell, E. (1990) *The Nursery Rhyme Picnic.* London: Kingscourt.

Chapter 3

Do You Hear What I Hear? Helping Children Read and Spell Using Letter-Onset/Rime Analogy

Margaret Moustafa and Rosalie Franzese

Children who have not yet learned to read have difficulty analyzing spoken words into their constituent phonemes (any of the units of sound that distinguish one word from another). That is, they have difficulty analyzing a spoken word such as *play* into /p/, /l/, and /ay/.

While the number of phonemes in words may appear obvious to adults, they are not obvious to children as they are learning to read and write. When adults are asked to analyze spoken words into phonemes, they, in fact, typically analyze words on the basis of their spelling (Scholes 1998). That is, they might say there are three phonemes in *box* and five phonemes in *school* when there are actually four phonemes in both words.[1]

If being able to analyze spoken words into phonemes is a consequence of becoming literate, then asking children to spell words by sounding them out is actually a cart-before-the-horse approach. If a child doesn't know how to spell a word, how can a child analyze it into its constituent phonemes?

We are saved from this seemingly impossible conundrum by the fact that children who have not yet learned to read and write can and do hear other units of sounds: syllables, onsets, and rimes (Treiman 1983, 1985; Goswami and Bryant 1990). Onsets are any consonants that occur before a vowel in a spoken syllable. In play, /pl/ is the onset. Rimes are the vowel and any consonants that occur after the vowel in a spoken syllable. In play, /ay/ is the rime. While all syllables have rimes, not all syllables have onsets. Playing has two syllables, so it has two rimes, /ay/ and /ing/, but only one onset, /pl/. Once children learn letter-syllable/onset/rime correspondences in known words, they are able to multiply this knowledge by making analogies between familiar and unfamiliar print words with like letters or groups of letters representing like onsets, rimes, or syllables to pronounce unfamiliar print words (Goswami 1986, 1988; Goswami and Bryant 1990; Goswami and Mead 1992; Moustafa 1995).

Elsewhere, Moustafa has written about how we can build on English-speaking children's ability to analyze spoken words into syllables, onsets, and rimes to teach them letter-syllable/onset/rime correspondences in the context of words they have learned via shared reading so that they can make analogies between familiar and unfamiliar print words to pronounce unfamiliar print words (Moustafa 1997; Moustafa and Maldonado-Colon 1999; Moustafa 2000). Franzese has extended the approach to teaching children to spell new words by analogy to print words they already know how to spell. Here we will review teaching letter-syllable/onset/rime correspondences in reading and then describe how these same principles used in teaching reading can be applied to teaching spelling.

Letter-Onset/Rime Analogy in Reading Instruction

Early readers read print words better in context than out of context (Goodman 1965; Nicholson 1991; Nicholson, Lillas, and Rzoska 1988). They also read text with familiar language better than text with unfamiliar language (Rhodes 1979; Ruddell 1965). Hence, instruction in letter-onset/rime analogy in reading begins with the teacher selecting several books, songs, and poems with natural, familiar language for his/her emergent readers.

Once the teacher has located appropriate reading materials, he/she then reads aloud one of the books (or songs or poems) to the children for overall understanding, and then, repeatedly over several days, as a shared reading. In shared reading the teacher points to the words in the story in full view of the children as he/she reads (Holdaway 1979). Once the children have memorized the language of the text, the teacher gives every two children a copy of the story and asks each child to read the story to his/her partner. With the first book or two, the teacher checks that each child can match spoken words to print words.

Once all the children can read the story with one-to-one spoken-word/print-word matching, the teacher begins whole-to-parts phonics instruction, using words the children have learned to recognize in the story. First, the teacher asks the children their favorite words in the story and writes each word on a separate piece of paper with a logo on it that represents that particular story. As each child nominates his/her favorite word, the teacher asks all the children in the group to find the word in the story.

After class the teacher plans which letter-syllable, letter-onset, or letter-rime correspondences he/she would like to teach in the words the children have selected. The next day, the teacher reviews each word the children have chosen with the children, asking them to find the words in the story, if necessary, in order to identify them. Once the children identify a word, the teacher highlights a letter or groups of letters in that word which represent(s) a syllable, an onset, or a rime, saying something like "Yes, this word is *play* and these letters (referring to the letters he/she is highlighting) say /ay/. Can you hear /ay/ in *play?*"

After the teacher has taught *one part* in each word, he/she then models grouping the words according to the letters that are highlighted, saying something like "Oh, look! There's a yellow square around the *ay* in *play* and a yellow square around the *ay* in *say*. I'm going to put these words together under the *A* in our word wall. Who can find another pattern?" (See Figure 3.1.)

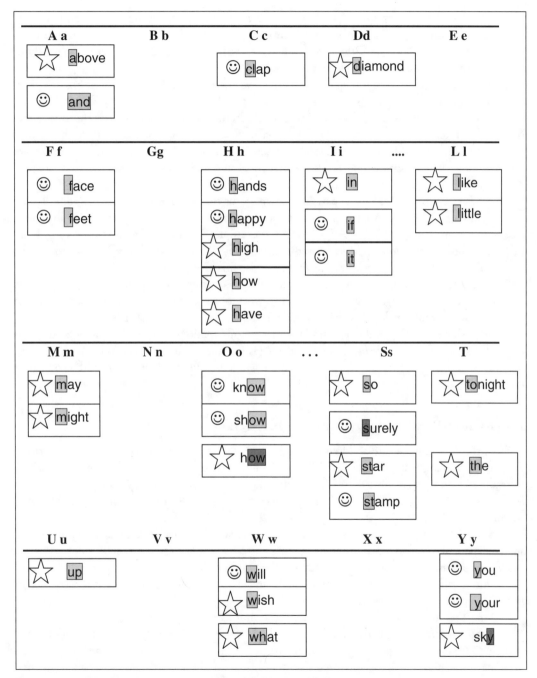

Figure 3.1 A Whole-to-Parts Phonics Word Wall in Progress
(In this example, the words came from the children's poems *If You're Happy and You Know It* and *Twinkle, Twinkle, Little Star.*)

The teacher then repeats the cycle of shared reading, partner reading, and whole-to-parts phonics instruction with other stories, songs, or poems with familiar language. As more and more words go up on the word wall, the logo beside each word helps the children return mentally or physically to the context where they saw the word.

As more and more words go up on the phonics word wall, alternative pronunciations of a given letter or group of letters (such as the *g* in *g*|o and *g*|iant or the *-ow* in n|ow| and sh|ow|) will come up within the context of the children's reading. As the alternative pronunciations of the same letter or group of letters come up *within the words on the wall*, the teacher then teaches to the alternative pronunciations. For example, the teacher might say "Oh, look! When we see the *-ow* in n|ow| we say /ow/, but when we see the *-ow* in sh|ow| we say /o/. I'm going to color all the *-ow*'s that are pronounced /o/ green."

As children learn to recognize parts of known words that represent onsets, rimes, or syllables, they can then use their knowledge of letter-sound correspondences to pronounce unfamiliar print words (Goswami 1986, 1988; Moustafa 1995). For example, if, through shared reading and whole-to-parts phonics instruction, children learn that *sm-* in |sm|all and |sm|ile is /sm/ and that *-art* in c|art| and p|art| is /art/, they can then work out that *smart* is /smart/.

As children learn multiple pronunciations of a given letter or group of letters, they are then able to use their knowledge of spoken English to work out which pronunciation of that letter or group of letters would make sense within the context of the story they are reading. For example, if, through shared reading and whole-to-parts phonics instruction, children have learned that *h* is /h/ and that *-ow* can be /ow/ (as in *now*) and /o/ (as in *know*), when they encounter *-ow* in *how*, they can try out both pronunciations of *-ow* to see which would make sense within the context of the story.

Letter-Onset/Rime Analogy in Spelling Instruction

Rich writing programs where children have a personal investment in and commitment to writing foster good spelling (Hughes and Searle 2000). Hence, as instruction in letter-onset/rime analogy in reading begins with reading whole text with familiar language via shared reading, instruction in letter-onset/rime analogy in spelling begins with composing whole, authentic messages via shared writing.

Shared writing (McKenzie 1985), like the Language Experience Approach, begins with a shared experience (a read-aloud, a movie, a science experiment, a class event, etc.) followed by the teacher acting as a scribe, writing the message the children dictate on chart paper in full view of the children. Additionally, shared writing solicits the children's active involvement in the conventions (i.e. spelling, punctuation, etc.) of writing.

First the message is established orally. For example, after the teacher has read the children a story about John Henry, he/she might ask, "What would you like to write about John Henry?" If the children decide to write, "John Henry was a big man," the teacher would show the children that the sentence consists of six words by counting aloud the words on his/her fingers. Then the teacher would write the message in full view of the children. Once the sentence is written, the teacher reads the sentence to and with the children, pointing to each word as he/she reads.

Then the teacher asks, "What else would you like to say about John Henry?" If the children decide to write, "He was a big baby," the teacher would again count aloud the words in the sentence and then write the sentence. However, this time the teacher would also ask the children to spell the words that are repeated in the second sentence (e.g. "How do you spell *was?*" "How do you spell *a?*" "How do you spell *big?*"). As the children spell the words orally, the teacher writes the words while spelling them. "Yes, *w-a-s.*" The teacher may also ask the children to spell words that are on the phonics word wall or in previous shared-writing stories posted around the room as the words come up in the current story. "Do you see *baby* in any of our other stories? That's right. There it is on the word wall. There it is in this story we wrote yesterday. Now tell me how to write it in this story."

During shared writing, in addition to writing what the children dictate and asking the children to spell words orally, the teacher can also encourage children to use their visual memory for print words by demonstrating the "have a go" strategy. This is done by placing another piece of paper next to the message page and using it as a practice page. When questions come up as to how to spell a particular word (e.g. *they* or *thay* for *they; like* or *lik* for *like*), the teacher can write the word in the different ways the children suggest on the practice page and ask the children, "Which way do we see it in books?"

Each shared writing session is followed by children writing independently on topics of their choice, applying what they have learned in the writing demonstrations. Before independent writing begins, the children can be shown how to divide their paper in half and use one side of the paper (e.g. the left-hand side) for practice and the other side for their drafts. Alternately, they can be provided with a journal or notebook and shown how to use the pages on one side as practice pages and the pages on the other side for their drafts. Then, as they are writing they can be encouraged to use the "have a go" strategy when they need it.

As children learn to read and spell more and more words through shared reading, shared writing, and independent writing, the teacher can introduce spelling by analogy. In teaching spelling by analogy, the teacher can use words children can spell to show them how to spell words that are analogous at the onset, rime, or syllable level. For example, if the children have dictated a sentence with the word *bike* in it and the word *like* is on the phonics word wall or in previous shared writings posted around the room, the teacher can say, "*Bike* sounds like *like*. We can use *like* to spell *bike*. Do you see *like* in our other stories? Yes, there it is." The teacher then writes *like* on the practice page, circles the *ike* in *like* and says, "These letters say /ik/. We can take the *i-k-e* in *like*, add a *b*, and get *bike*." As the teacher speaks, he/she writes *ike* beneath the *ike* in *like* on the practice page and puts a *b* in front of it. She then writes *bike* in the story.

Similarly, if the children dictate a sentence with the word *star* in it and the word *stop* is on the phonics word wall or in previous shared writings posted around the room, the teacher can say, "*Star* sounds like *stop*. We can use *stop* to spell *star*. Do you see *stop* in our other stories?" The teacher then writes *stop* on the practice page, circles the *st* in *stop* and says, "These letters say /st/. We can take the *s-t* in *stop* to write the beginning of *star*. *Car* sounds like *star*." The teacher then writes *car* on the practice page, circles the *a-r* in *car* and says, "These letters say /ar/. We can take the *a-r* from *car* and use it to write *star*." The teacher then writes *a-r* after *st* on the practice page to make *star* and writes *star* in the story.

After multiple demonstrations of spelling by analogy, the teacher encourages children to use the strategy on their practice pages during independent writing. Figures 3.2a and 3.2b show a story and the practice page of a six-year-old boy, Carl, in Rosalie Franzese's inner-city New York class. Figures 3.3a and 3.3b show a story and the practice page of a seven-year-old girl, Ruth, in Franzese's class. (We use pseudonyms with both children.)

In dealing with the multiple ways certain phonemes, onsets, and rimes can be represented in English script, readers have an advantage that writers do not have. When readers encounter a letter or group of letters that can be pronounced in multiple ways (as the *-ow* in *now* and *snow*), they can use their knowledge of spoken language to decide which pronunciation makes sense within the context of the story.

The converse is not true for spellers. When there are multiple ways to represent a given onset or rime in print (e.g. /k/ is represented in one way in *cat* and another in *kangaroo*, /ut/ is represented one way in *cut* and another way in *what*, /ay/ is represented one way in *say* and another in

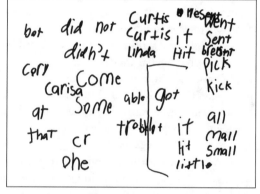

Figure 3.2a Carl's Story   Figure 3.2b Carl's Practice Page for His Story

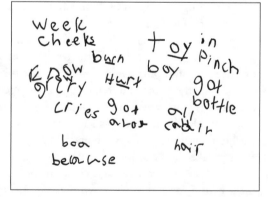

Figure 3.3a Ruth's Story   Figure 3.3b Ruth's Practice Page for Her Story

they), neither spellers' knowledge of spoken language nor their knowledge of letter-sound correspondences can help them decide which plausible spelling (e.g. *kat* or *cat*, *wut* or *what*, *thay* or *they*) to use. Their knowledge of letter-sound correspondences can get them to an approximate spelling of a given word, but it cannot, *in and of itself*, help them to decide which plausible spelling is correct.

Early writers' most accessible tool to get them from approximate spelling to conventional spelling is their visual memory for print. Hence, instruction in spelling by analogy needs to be checked with "have a go" strategies where spellers ask themselves which spelling "looks like book spelling." After introducing children to using analogies to spell words, teachers can teach a two-step process of using analogies and then checking to see if the analogy "looks right." For example, during shared writing a teacher might say, "*They* sounds like *say* (writing *say*). I'll take the *a-y* from *say* (writing *ay* below *say*) and add a *th*. There. *T-h-a-y*. That doesn't look like the way we see it in books, does it? Let's see if we can find *they* in a story we've read."

As the children have more and more experience with shared and independent writing, the teacher may move into interactive writing, a form of shared writing where the children, rather than the teacher, act as scribes, writing the group's message on the chart paper (Button, Johnson, and Furgerson 1996; Pinnell and McCarrier 1994). For example, if, after a trip to the mall, the class decides to write, "We went to the mall," the teacher might ask, "What is the first word?" Once the children agree the first word is *we*, the teacher would ask, "Who would like to come up and write *We?*" The teacher would call on a volunteer to come up and write *We* on the chart paper, orally guiding the child to use a capital letter to begin the first word in the sentence. As the child writes *We* on the chart paper, the other children write *We* on their own wipe-off boards. As each child takes a turn writing a word in the evolving story on the chart paper, the other children and the teacher help the child stretch the word and apply letter-sound correspondences the class has learned, using analogy and "have a go" strategies on the practice page as needed. When words which are beyond the children's developmental level come up, the teacher helps the children through these words. Interactive writing, like shared writing, is followed by independent writing, where children have an opportunity to write on topics of their choice, applying what they have learned in the writing demonstrations.

As the children have more and more experience with letter-onset/rime analogy and with reading and writing, they make analogies in their minds. For example, Carl misread "so he decided to play a trick" as "so he decided to play a truck." He then reasoned aloud, saying, "That doesn't make sense. It starts like *truck* but it has the *ick* chunk like *pick*. It's *trick*." For another example, Ruth misread "Such a grand house" as "Such a garden house." Then, realizing the sentence didn't make sense within the context of the story, she re-read the sentence saying, "Such a . . . there's the *and* chunk and it starts like *grapes*. It's *grand*. Such a grand house." For still another example, one of Margaret Moustafa's graduate students, a teacher in an inner-city school in Los Angeles, had a child who asked her, "Teacher, how do you spell *say?*" When the teacher responded, "Well, I know you know how to spell *day*," the child replied (spelling the word) "Oh, s-a-y!"

Figures 3.4a and 3.4b show Carl's September 1998 to May 1999 growth in writing. Figures 3.5a and 3.5b show Ruth's September 1998 to May 1999 growth in writing.

The advantage of letter-onset/rime analogy instruction in reading and spelling instruction is that it works with units of sounds early readers and writers can hear: onsets, rimes, and syllables.

WHn I WS LIttLe

I like to go To The

moves.
MON

MON

Sept 1998

Figure 3.4a Carl's Writing in September 1998

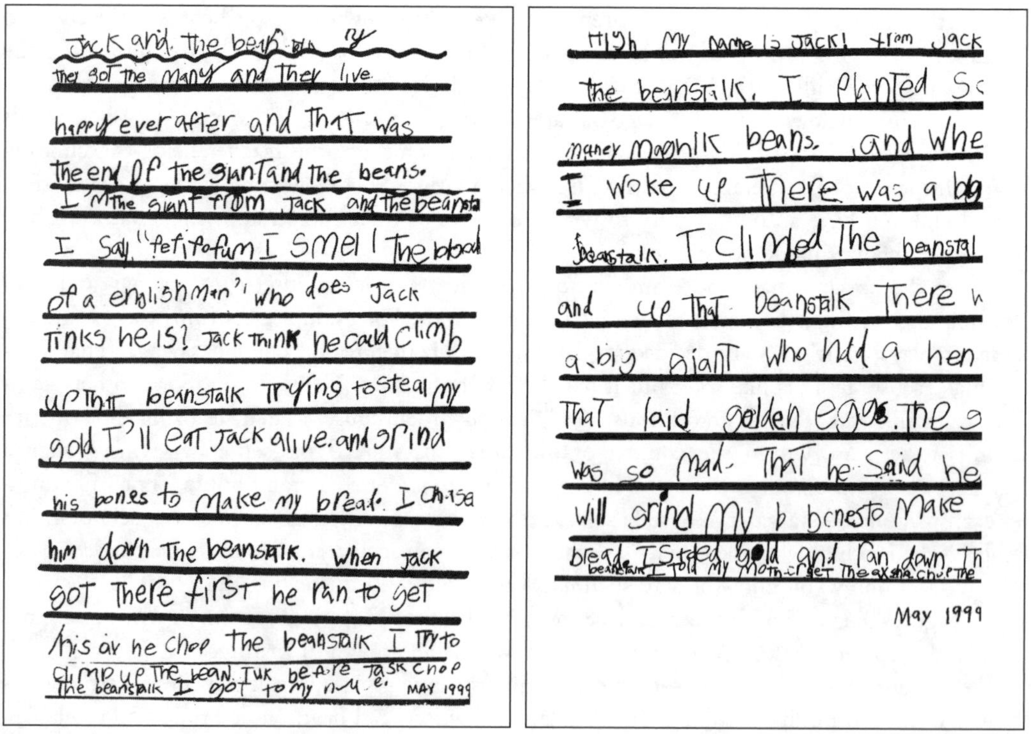

Jack and the beans...
they got the money and they live
happy ever after and that was
the end of the giant and the beans.
I'M the giant from Jack and the beanst
I say "fetifofum I smell the blood
of a englishman", who does Jack
tinks he is? Jack think he could climb
up that beanstalk trying to steal my
gold I'll eat Jack alive. and grind
his bones to make my bread. I chasa
him down the beanstalk. When Jack
got there first he ran to get
his ax he chop the beanstalk I try to
climb up the bean tuk befare Jask chop
the beanstalk I got to my nu e. MAY 1999

HIgh My name is Jack! from Jack
the beanstalk. I phnted so
maney maghllk beans. and whe
I woke up There was a big
beanstalk. I climped The beanstal
and up that beanstalk There w
a big giant who had a hen
that laid golden eggs. The g
was so mad. That he said he
will grind my b bonesto make
bread I stled gold and ran down. Th
beanstum I told My mother get the ax and chop the
May 1999

Figure 3.4b Carl's Writing in May 1999

She box I wet to The Prk!
ah blpp em

Sept. 1991

Figure 3.5a Ruth's Writing in September 1998

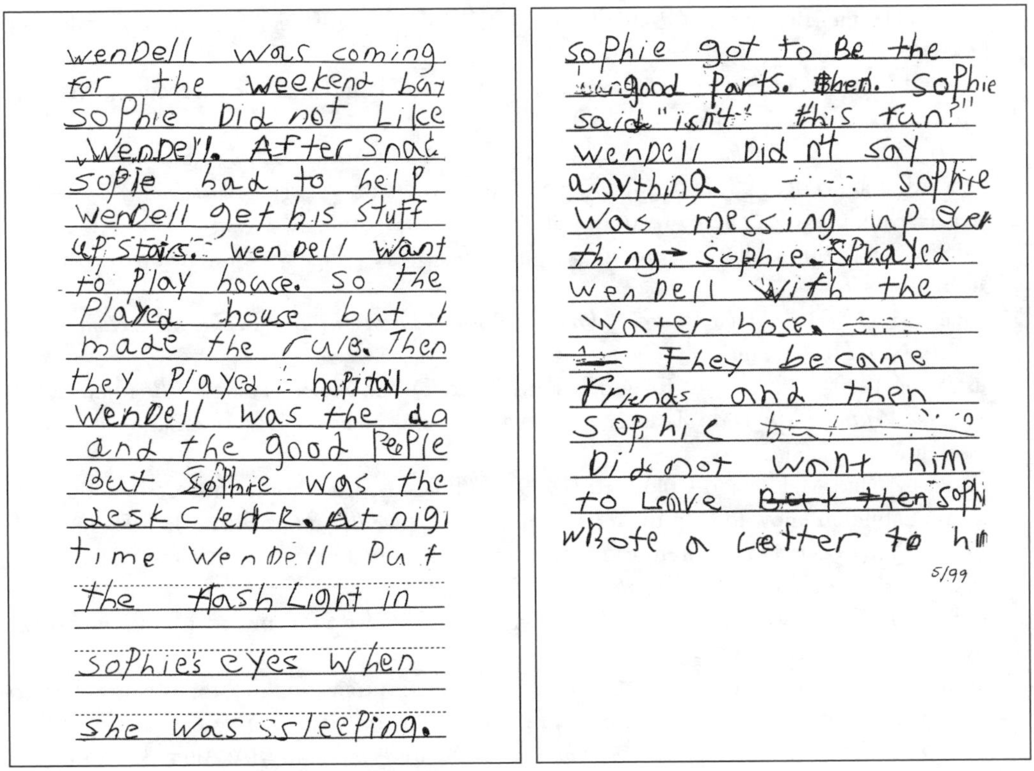

wenDell was coming
for the weekend but
soPhie Did not Like
Wendell. AfterSnac
soPie had to help
wenDell get his stuff
upstairs. wen Dell want
to Play house. So the
Played house but I
made the rule. Then
they Played hopital.
wenDell was the do
and the good PeoPle
But SoPhie was the
Desk clerk. At nigi
time WenDell Put
the flash Light in
soPhies eyes when
she was ssleeping.

soPhie got to Be the
good Parts. then. SoPhie
said "isn't this fun?"
wenDell Did nt say
anything. soPhie
Was messing uP eer
thing. sophie sprayed
wen Dell with the
Water hose.
They became
Friends and then
SoPhie
Did not want him
to Leave But then soPi
wRote a Letter to hi
5/99

Figure 3.5b Ruth's Writing in May 1999

When letter-onset/rime analogy spelling instruction is embedded in real, purposeful reasons for writing, coupled with instruction that encourages children to use their visual memory, it is a powerful tool in teachers' tool boxes for helping children learn to spell conventionally.

Note

1. *Box* is /boks/ and *school* is /skol/.

References

Button, K., Johnson, M. J., and Furgerson, P. (1996) "Interactive writing in a primary classroom," *The Reading Teacher* **49**(6), 446–54.

Goodman, K. (1965) "A linguistic study of cues and miscues in reading." *Elementary English* **42**, 639–43.

Goswami, U. (1986) "Children's use of analogy in learning to read: A developmental study," *Journal of Experimental Child Psychology* **42**, 73–83.

Goswami, U. (1988) "Orthographic analogies and reading development," *The Quarterly Journal of Experimental Psychology* **40A**(2), 239–68.

Goswami, U. and Bryant, P. (1990) *Phonological Skills in Learning to Read*. Hillsdale, NJ: Lawrence Erlbaum.

Goswami, U. and Mead, F. (1992) "Onset and rime awareness and analogies in reading," *Reading Research Quarterly* **27**(2), 150–62.

Holdaway, D. (1979) *The Foundations of Literacy*. New York: Ashton Scholastic.

Hughes, M. and Searle, D. (2000) "Spelling and 'the second R'," *Language Arts* **77**(3), 203–8.

McKenzie, M. G. (1985) "Shared writing: Apprenticeship in writing," *Language Matters,* 1–2, 1–5.

Moustafa, M. (1995) "Children's productive phonological recoding," *Reading Research Quarterly* **30**(3), 464–76.

Moustafa, M. (1997) *Beyond Traditional Phonics: Research discoveries and reading instruction*. Portsmouth, NH: Heinemann.

Moustafa, M. (2000) "Phonics instruction," in Strickland, D. and Morrow, L. (eds.) *Beginning Reading and Writing*. New York: Teachers' College Press and Newark, DE: International Reading Association.

Moustafa, M. and Maldonado-Colon, E. (1999) "Whole-to-parts phonics instruction: Building on what children know to help them know more," *The Reading Teacher* **52**(5), 448–58.

Nicholson, T. (1991) "Do children read words better in context or in lists? A classic study revisited," *Journal of Educational Psychology* **83**, 444–50.

Nicholson, T., Lillas, C., and Rzoska, M. A. (1988) "Have we been misled by miscues?" *The Reading Teacher* **42**, 6–10.

Pinnell, G. S. and McCarrier, A. (1994) "Interactive writing: A transition tool for assisting children in learning to read and write," in Hiebert, E. and Taylor, B. (eds.) *Getting Reading Right from the Start: Effective early literacy interventions* (pp. 149–70). Needham, MA: Allyn & Bacon.

Rhodes, L. K. (1979) "Comprehension and predictability: An analysis of beginning reading materials," in *New Perspectives on Comprehension* (monograph in Language and Reading Studies). Bloomington: Indiana University School of Education.

Ruddell, R. B. (1965) "The effect of oral and written patterns of language structure on reading comprehension," *The Reading Teacher* **18**, 270–5.

Scholes, Robert J. (1998) "The case against phonemic awareness," *Journal of Research in Reading* **21**(3), 177–89.

Treiman, R. (1983) "The structure of spoken syllables: Evidence from novel word games," *Cognition* **15**, 49–74.

Treiman, R. (1985) "Onsets and rimes as units of spoken syllables: Evidence from children," *Journal of Experimental Child Psychology* **39**, 161–81.

Chapter 4

A Place to Start From: Encouraging Bilingual Children's Writing

Charmian Kenner

Writing needs a source and it needs a motivation. Although curriculum tasks can be used for teaching and assessment, they do not necessarily provide a reason to write. Particularly for young children adapting to school life, connections need to be made with the purposeful everyday writing they observe in their homes and communities. For bilingual children, their source material comes from literacy events in other languages as well as English: They may see, for example, a parent writing an airletter in Thai, a grandparent filling in a crossword from the newspaper in Gujarati, or an older sibling doing homework from after-school Arabic classes. Young children also participate in these events: sitting alongside their parents and writing their own letters to family in other countries, asking questions about the symbols used in the crossword, or using their siblings' homework as a model to write from.

Teachers are often not aware of bilingual children's literacy experiences outside school. Whereas emergent literacy in English is relatively well documented, there has been little research concerning young children growing up in multilingual communities. In most schools in English-speaking countries—even those where pupils come from a wide variety of language backgrounds—learning and teaching is conducted entirely in English and texts in other languages are unavailable. So children have no opportunity to display their multilingual knowledge in the classroom. Whether inside or outside school, this knowledge remains invisible to educators.

It is, however, possible for teachers to find out about and tap into bilingual children's sources for writing. The project I shall describe here took place in a multilingual class in South London. When families brought home literacy materials into school and wrote together in the classroom, children's writing was stimulated in their first languages and also in English. In this chapter I focus on the responses of two children who had previously been "reluctant to write."

Everyday Literacy in the Classroom

Young children are keen to write as they see adults and older siblings do, in order to build relationships (for example, through letters and greetings cards), to obtain resources (writing menus to sell pizza in a role-play "café"), and to organize events (making a list of friends to invite to a party). The rich opportunities which arise for literacy learning as part of family life were first described in detail through research such as that of Taylor (1983) in the United States and Hall (1987) in Britain. Home and community experiences can provide a fruitful basis for school literacy work, as when the classroom "home corner" (role-play area) is turned into an office or clinic and children can write as part of play (Neuman and Roskos 1991; Hall and Robinson 1995). These contexts provide familiar purposes for writing and reading, giving children the chance to explore and build on their existing understandings.

The Importance of Bilingual Literacy Learning

The transfer of knowledge between home and school could also occur in other languages as well as English. Research on bilingualism suggests that there is a fertile interrelationship between children's learning in different languages: for example, concerning how written symbols represent sounds, how sentence grammar is structured, and how to guess meanings within a text (Cummins 1991; Baker 1995). Literacy instruction could draw on bilingual children's learning strategies (Gregory 1996) and knowledge of vocabulary and word meaning (McWilliam 1998). In fact, this is explicitly recognized in the National Literacy Strategy for England, where the following statement appears:

> *The place of languages other than English*
> EAL [English as an Additional Language] learners who already know the sound system of another language and the principles of phonology and spelling can bring that awareness to bear when learning to read and write in English . . . Managed carefully, talking about literacy in languages other than English can help EAL pupils to identify points of similarity and difference between languages at word, sentence and text level. (DfEE 1998, p. 107)

However, the National Literacy Strategy gives no specific guidance as to how this approach could be put into practice. The main body of the documentation, where schemes of work are spelled out in detail for each year group in primary school, refers only to English. Further steps need to be taken to fully integrate multilingualism into classroom literacy tasks, in ways such as those discussed below.

Bilingual Children's Literacies Outside School

In order to plan for bilingual learning, it is vital for teachers to have some knowledge of texts and practices in multilingual communities which provide the basis for early biliteracy. Connections between classroom learning and children's out-of-school literacy experiences can then be more successfully made.

Ethnographic studies have begun to give some insights into bilingual children's literacy lives. Martin-Jones and Bhatt (1998) found that in the Gujarati community in Leicester, England, children and young people aged nine to twenty participated in family letter-writing sessions, reading and writing for religious purposes, and cultural activities such as song writing. The ways in which six-year-olds learn both Arabic and Bengali in community language classes after school in London's East End are documented by Gregory, Rashid, and Williams (see Rashid and Gregory 1997). The world of an even younger child, a multilingual four-year-old growing up in Southall, West London, is described by Saxena (1994); this boy could already identify several different scripts because he had observed family members reading and writing for everyday purposes, from magazines to shopping lists.

Research in other countries includes work with Samoan-origin communities (Ochs and Duranti 1982) and Latino communities (Reese *et al.* 1995) in the United States, and with Torres Strait Islanders in Australia (Luke and Kale 1997). Such research studies provide a source of ideas for teachers who would like to know more about their bilingual pupils' literacy learning.

The South London Project: Making Home–School Literacy Connections

This project began as a year-long piece of action research in a nursery school class, and continued with further multilingual literacy activities over the next two years of the children's school lives. The nursery school class consisted of thirty-five children whose families spoke languages including Arabic, Spanish, Thai, Tigrinya, Gujarati, Filipino, Yoruba, and Cantonese. With an awareness that literacy events of the type described above might be taking place in children's homes, the teacher and I began a dialogue with bilingual parents at the start and end of nursery school sessions each day. These conversations about children's participation in reading and writing at home were supplemented by informal interviews with parents later in the term (for further details, see Kenner 1999, 2000).

We encouraged families to bring into school any materials which interested children, and invited parents to act as writers in the classroom. Children could write alongside their parents, and talk about home literacy materials and bilingual writing with their classmates and their teacher. The project was part of a wider initiative in which the home corner was filled with everyday literacy materials in English as well as other languages; children could write as part of sociodramatic play and display their texts on the home corner walls.

As the children moved on to kindergarten (at age 5) and first grade (at age 6), multilingual work continued with a weekly language workshop for families based around the making of newspapers in different languages.

Discoveries About Children's Home Literacy

Among the nursery school parents, several were teaching their children to write in other languages as well as in English. Ace's mother, for example, was writing numbers with her three-year-old daughter in Chinese, and working with a set of picture cards which showed the Chinese characters for concepts ranging from "sister" and "brother" to "moon" and "stars." Mohammed's mother was using an Arabic alphabet chart to prepare him for Qur'anic classes, which he would soon begin when he reached age five. Mohammed was also learning to write English alphabet letters from his parents and older siblings. Billy, at four, was being taught the alphabet in both Thai and English by his mother.

As well as this more formal instruction, children were gaining ideas about written language by participating in everyday family activities. Meera saw her mother doing word searches from Gujarati newspapers and magazines. She also watched Indian film videos in Hindi with her parents and sister. Billy's favorite video in Thai was of romantic karaoke songs, in which the words rippled across the screen in Thai script against the background of a fishing village by the river. Mohammed sat next to his mother when she wrote letters to relatives in Gujarati. He asked for paper in order to write, too, and commented that the script looked different.

In the following years, when parents and children brought newspapers to school for the Language Workshop, their teacher and I found further evidence of bilingual literacy knowledge. Recep, for example, knew about Turkish language and culture both from newspapers and from satellite TV.

Linking Home Literacy with the Curriculum

As parents told us about home literacy activities, the nursery school teacher and I began to devise ways of linking these with classroom work. Materials such as Mohammed's Arabic alphabet songs on tape, with an accompanying poster made by his mother, could be used to help the whole class sing the song together and compare the Arabic and English alphabets. This supported children's understanding of how spoken language was represented by written symbols, an important concept in early literacy learning. Watching a cartoon video in Chinese, and incorporating Chinese food packets into café role-plays, prompted children to look carefully at the details of written language and become more aware of the features which differentiated English symbols from those of other scripts.

Multilingual literacy could be linked with the themes on which the class focused each term. For example, when the topic was "travel," the home corner was turned into a "travel agency" where children could play at arranging visits to other countries, using maps and travel brochures. Parents and children made pages for a class "travel brochure" showing the countries their families came from (for example, Billy and his mother made pages about Thailand, combining their own writing in Thai and English with family photographs and a map cut out of a printed brochure). Knowing that letter writing was a significant home literacy activity for several bilingual children, the teacher and I planned to integrate this work into the travel topic. We asked parents if they could write airletters in the classroom to relatives in other countries, requesting pictures and information for our "travel agency." Children wrote alongside their parents and later continued to write letters to friends and family, both in English and in home languages.

Monolingual children joined in enthusiastically with the multilingual activities, intrigued by the variety of scripts now present in their environment. The use of home literacy materials in the nursery school, and the chance to see adults writing in different languages, offered extra writing opportunities and stimulation for the whole class.

Parents as Model Writers

Children showed great interest when their parents wrote in the classroom. After Meera's mother had helped her to make greetings cards for the class "postbox," Meera commented to the nursery staff, "My mum writing in the nursery." When adding to one of her mother's texts she stated, "I write Gujarati—I write like my mum." Adedamola's mother also participated in the card-making activity, and he responded by concentrating hard on producing the same symbols in Yoruba. When Marta's father wrote an airletter in Tigrinya to his family in Eritrea, Marta sat beside him and wrote on her own airletter form. Later she used both letters as a resource in order to do more writing, which she showed proudly to the nursery school workers.

In all these cases, children were inspired by the presence of their parents as writers. Home languages were now visible in the classroom, and given status as part of the school literacy agenda.

Billy and Recep: Becoming Writers in the Classroom

Some of the bilingual children were already enthusiastic writers in school. The multilingual literacy activities gave them opportunities to draw on their knowledge of other languages and expand their learning still further. For other children, who were initially less involved in writing in the classroom, the enriched literacy environment encouraged them to participate as writers in school for the first time. This was the case for both Billy and Recep, whose stories I will now tell.

Billy: The Inspiration of Letter-writing

Billy's language background included Thai, his mother's language, and English, spoken by his father. Billy had grown up in England, and had a baby sister, Elizabeth. As I mentioned earlier, his mother was making efforts to teach him the alphabet in Thai—using a booklet with brightly colored pictures—as well as English. But she was concerned that, at the age of four, he was not enthusiastic about writing at home. Billy did not often choose to write in nursery school either; occasionally, he produced one or two letters from his name.

However, Billy's mother told us that he became enthusiastic at home when she wrote letters to the family in Thai. He would sit next to her and ask her to include his name and his sister's as well as her own, saying, "Do you, Billy, Elizabeth." He would also write symbols on his own sheet of paper. The teacher and I had heard similar descriptions from the parents of Meera and Mohammed, for example, and we therefore decided to involve parents in letter writing in nursery school for the travel topic as described above.

So Billy's mother sat in nursery school one morning, writing several lines addressed to Billy's grandmother in Thai. Billy sat alongside her with his own airletter form, which he filled with symbols and lines in several colors. Mother and son talked together in Thai and English as they wrote, linking their literacy activity to its purpose of communicating with family far away. As with their home letter writing, Billy's mother was showing him how to write in Thai and giving him a reason for doing so. She also modeled writing in English, by putting his name on a separate piece of paper.

When Billy's mother went home, the texts she had written remained in the classroom. We had suggested that her airletter could be a resource for the children to use. Billy's mother was familiar with this arrangement because, like the other bilingual parents, she knew that such materials were regularly used as part of literacy learning in nursery school. Her actual letter to the family in Thailand could be written again later and sent from home.

Later that morning, Billy spent about fifteen minutes in the classroom's writing area, at the table where the airletter event had taken place. This was an unusual decision for him: In the periods when children could choose what to do, he tended to prefer active physical play. Using the same kind of paper on which his mother had written his name earlier—computer paper with punched holes along the edge—he began to write. He produced a number of symbols, including some which were quite complex and resembled his mother's Thai writing (see Figure 4.1).

Billy remarked "I write like my mum" and "Mu-ang Thai" ("Thailand"). That afternoon, he returned to the writing table and began tracing the outline of some plastic alphabet letters, identifying "B" for "Billy" with the help of a classmate. I helped him to find each letter of his name, referring to his mother's writing of "Billy" as a resource, and Billy drew around each plastic letter with care. We then displayed all the texts written by Billy and his mother on the home corner wall. The recognition of Billy's mother as a bilingual writer in the nursery had enabled him to take up this role for himself, in both languages.

Billy's success had considerable further effects. Soon afterwards, his mother told us that Billy was writing a great deal more at home. We invited her to bring his writing into school, and several days later she came in with a carrier bag containing twenty-one different texts. Billy had used many materials to write on, ranging from notebooks and old letters from school to restaurant placemats. Some of his symbols were English alphabet letters (including a confident representation of the first three letters of his name, and others we had not seen him write before, such as the first letters of his

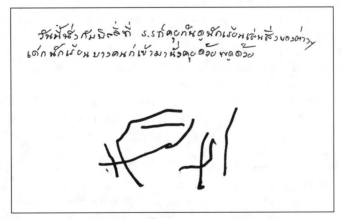

Figure 4.1 (above) Extract from Airletter in Thai, Written by
Billy's Mother in Nursery School
(below) Symbols Written by Billy Later That Morning—He said,
"I write like my mum" "Mu-ang Thai."

parents' and sister's names). There were also numbers, circles, and some complex characters which looked like Thai. Billy had drawn people too, and his mother told us that this was unusual for him. So he had been inspired to engage in different kinds of graphic representation.

I sat with Billy's mother in the classroom, looking at each of his texts, and Billy joined us to talk about his work. The teacher also praised him—another important acknowledgment of his writing. Three days later, Billy's mother came in with another plastic carrier bag, this time containing twenty-seven pieces of writing. Apparently Billy was writing prolifically, even at breakfast time! As well as developing his knowledge of English alphabet letters, he had worked with his mother to copy a whole line of Thai letters. Billy showed these to me and mentioned "Mu-ang Thai" ("Thailand"). His motivation for writing Thai at home seemed to have been increased by the attention given to the language in nursery school.

Meanwhile, Billy had also become a more confident writer in the classroom, continuing with his activity of drawing round wooden and plastic alphabet letters and producing his name. The links between home and school supported his literacy learning in both environments.

Recep: The Inspiration of Newspapers

Recep, from a Turkish-speaking family, was one of the children who participated in the multilingual newspaper workshops at the age of five. His teacher told me that whereas he was enthusiastic about participating in most classroom activities, he seemed less interested in writing. I decided to ask him about Turkish writing. To the question, "Does anyone in your family write in Turkish?" he answered, "My grandmother." When I asked if he could show me how she wrote, he covered a poster-sized sheet of paper with symbols. The teacher and I were struck by the energy of his response. When playtime arrived, Recep said that he did not want to go out yet because "I haven't finished." Clearly the idea of literacy in Turkish held important meanings for him, stemming from having seen his grandmother write at home.

Recep's mother and aunt came into the classroom to help with the Language Workshop, bringing Turkish newspapers from home. We soon realized that Recep was familiar with the contents of these. He cut out images and text in order to make his own newspaper, making comments as he did so. He found a photo of his favorite singer, Hülya Avsar, and wrote her name underneath with adult help, singing lines from some of her songs. Then he chose a picture showing the stars of a soap opera which he watched on Turkish satellite TV, and copied several lines from the accompanying text (see Figure 4.2). Turkish football was another passion of Recep's; he selected a photo of a dramatic encounter between two football players and again carefully wrote one of the words from the text underneath it.

As well as his cultural knowledge in Turkish, Recep also had some familiarity with news events and history, although he was only five years old. He cut out a picture of Tansu Çiller, then prime minister of Turkey, and placed it centrally on the front page of his own newspaper. He included the caption below the photo, which highlighted Çiller's name. Also, he recognized the drawing of Atatürk, founder of modern Turkey, which appeared alongside the banner headline of one of the newspapers, and asked his aunt to help him write the name "Atatürk" above the headline. He later told us that he had a book about Atatürk at home. For Recep, these were important reasons for producing his own writing.

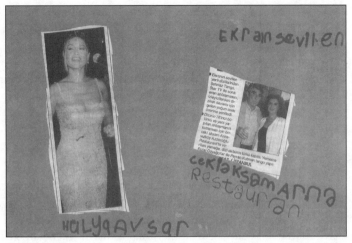

Figure 4.2 Recep's Turkish Newspaper: His Favorite Singer and
TV Soap Opera

Recep also wanted to represent his family in his newspaper—their names were an equally significant source for his writing. He drew his sister Gülten and wrote her name on the front page next to the photo of the prime minister (see Figure 4.3). And he wrote his mother's name, Halide, next to his writing of "Atatürk." He brought into school his family photo album about visits to Cyprus, talking about the pictures with his classmates and the other parents during the multilingual sessions. Using a map shown on a postcard in his album, he produced an accurate outline of the island of Cyprus, and below this he drew a picture of his grandfather in a coffin with flowers.

Figure 4.3 Recep's Turkish Newspaper: The Prime
Minister and Recep's Sister Gülten

According to Recep, his grandfather had died and gone up into the sky. Later his father told me that Recep had attended the funeral in Cyprus at the age of three, and that this had made a strong impression on him.

Thus, when given the opportunity to represent people, places, and events which were central in his life, Recep responded with a considerable amount of writing and drawing. If the multilingual sessions had not taken place, Recep's knowledge about Turkish life and culture would have remained invisible—and so, probably, would his desire to write.

Conclusion

The research described here demonstrates that teachers can successfully make links with children's home literacy experience, and that parents are key partners in this enterprise. Bilingual learning can add an important dimension to children's literacy learning in the classroom. Previous action research projects have also shown that where mother-tongue literacy is encouraged by schools, this has contributed to children's understandings in English. The National Writing Project (1990), for instance, included examples of the use of materials such as bilingual newspapers to promote writing. Sneddon (1993) reports on the results achieved by a dual-language book-making workshop for families at an East London school.

Many schools run brief activities around writing in other languages: for example, workshops on calligraphy for Chinese New Year. The challenge now is to achieve more lasting results by sustaining an ongoing multilingual literacy environment throughout children's school lives. Bilingual writing and reading need to be integrated into all policy initiatives concerning literacy. For example, Gravelle (2000) shows how a teacher using the National Literacy Strategy in England explored a traditional West African story with eight- and nine-year-olds in other languages as well as English. The children's learning was enhanced by being able to compare their different pieces of writing and discuss how each was constructed. Work of this kind could be at the core of the National Literacy Strategy, with its emphasis on the explicit analysis of written language.

To take their place as global writers in a multilingual world, children should be given the chance to develop their literacy abilities in more than one language. For bilingual children, there is already a great deal to build on from their literacy experiences in homes and communities. These experiences are also the mainspring of their early connections with writing and reading. If teachers approach their pupils as bilingual writers with varied language and literacy histories, this will give children "a place to write from," providing both source and motivation.

References

Baker, C. (1995) *A Parents' and Teachers' Guide to Bilingualism*. Clevedon: Multilingual Matters.

Cummins, J. (1991) "Interdependence of first and second language proficiency in bilingual children," in Bialystok, E. (ed.) *Language Processing in Bilingual Children*. Cambridge: Cambridge University Press.

DfEE (1998) *The National Literacy Strategy*. Annesley, Notts: DfEE Publications.

Gravelle, M. (2000) *Planning for Bilingual Learners: An inclusive curriculum*. Stoke-on-Trent: Trentham Books.

Gregory, E. (1996) *Making Sense of a New World: Learning to read in a second language*. London: Paul Chapman.

Hall, N. (1987) *The Emergence of Literacy*. Sevenoaks: Edward Arnold.

Hall, N. and Robinson, A. (1995) *Exploring Writing and Play in the Early Years*. London: David Fulton Publishers.

Kenner, C. (1999) "Children's understandings of text in a multilingual nursery," *Language and Education* **13**(1), 1–16.

Kenner, C. (2000) *Home Pages: Literacy links for bilingual children*. Stoke-on-Trent: Trentham Books.

Luke, A. and Kale, J. (1997) "Learning through difference: Cultural practices in early childhood socialisation," in Gregory, E. (ed.) *One Child, Many Worlds: Early learning in multicultural communities*. London: David Fulton Publishers.

Martin-Jones, M. and Bhatt, A. (1998) "Multilingual literacies in the lives of young Gujaratis in Leicester," in Durgunoglu, A. and Verhoeven, L. (eds.) *Literacy Development in a Multilingual Context: Cross-cultural perspectives*. Hillsdale, NJ: Lawrence Erlbaum Associates.

McWilliam, N. (1998) *What's in a Word? Vocabulary Development in Multilingual Classrooms*. Stoke-on-Trent: Trentham Books.

National Writing Project (1990) *A Rich Resource: Writing and language diversity*. Walton-on-Thames: Nelson.

Neuman, S. and Roskos, K. (1991) "Peers as literacy informants," *Early Childhood Research Quarterly* **6**(2), 233–48.

Ochs, E. and Duranti, A. (1982) "Change and tradition in literacy instruction in a Samoan American community," *Language and Society* **11**, 49–76.

Rashid, N. and Gregory, E. (1997) "Learning to read, reading to learn: The importance of siblings in the language development of young bilingual children," in Gregory, E. (ed.) *One Child, Many Worlds: Early learning in multicultural communities*. London: David Fulton Publishers.

Reese, L., Balzano, S., Gallimore, R., and Goldenberg, C. (1995) "The concept of educación: Latino family values and American schooling," *International Journal of Educational Research* **23**(1), 57–80.

Saxena, M. (1994) "Literacies among Panjabis in Southall," in Hamilton, M., Barton, D., and Ivanic, R. (eds.) *Worlds of Literacy*. Clevedon: Multilingual Matters.

Sneddon, R. (1993) "Beyond the National Curriculum: A community project to support bilingualism," *Journal of Multilingual and Multicultural Development* **4**(3), 237–45.

Taylor, D. (1983) *Family Literacy: Young children learning to read and write*. London: Heinemann.

Part II
Different Ways into Fiction and Poetry

Chapter 5

Responding to Poetry Through Writing

Gervase Phinn

For much of the last century, poetry has been the poor relation of fiction. It has been hardly noticed, often completely ignored, and has had little relevance in mainstream society. It has frequently received a cool welcome in schools with inspector's reports confirming that, for many children and for some teachers, poetry mattered very little. Thankfully, in this new century, poetry is rediscovering its place in society and in schools. In the English Literacy Strategy, children are expected to read poetry, aloud and silently, talk about their preferences for particular poems, and write in a range of verse forms.

This chapter aims to alleviate some of the anxiety about how to handle poetry in the classroom. It offers some suggestions and strategies for teachers to help children see that poets are people like themselves, speaking to other people about common human experience, but in words that make such experience come alive. It also offers suggestions for helping children to respond to poetry through writing and shares some wonderful examples of very sensitive poetry written by young children.

> Poetry needs to be at the heart of work in English because of the quality of the language at work. If language becomes separated from the moral and emotional life—becomes merely a trail of cliches which neither communicate nor quicken the mind of the reader—then we run the risk of depriving children of the kind of vital resource of language which poetry can offer. (DES 1987)

This statement was in relation to teaching poetry in the secondary school, but the same sentiments are applicable to younger children. Reading and writing poetry is a crucial part of the language curriculum. The current educational climate in England charges teachers with introducing to all their pupils the great range of verse, encouraging them to enjoy and appreciate the rhymes and rhythms of the language and helping them achieve good standards in their own writing. Children for their part are entitled, from the very earliest age, to a range of material which is rich and varied. They should be exposed to poems of intensity and excitement where the language is crisp, clear, and forceful; poems awash with exciting, vigorous language and saturated with reflective, thoughtful messages. Sadly, they are not always exposed to this richness nor are their responses to poetry always allowed to be as refreshing and original as they could be, as the following piece of writing indicates:

> My story on Monday began:
>> *Mountainous seas crashed on the cliffs*
>> *And the desolate land grew wetter . . .*
> The teacher wrote a little note: *Remember the capital letter!*
>
> My story on Tuesday began:
>> *Red tongues of fire licked higher and higher*
>> *From Etna's smoking top . . .*
> The teacher wrote a little note: *Where is your full stop?*
>
> My story on Wednesday began:
>> *Through the dark, pine scented woods*
>> *There twists a hidden path . . .*
> The teacher wrote a little note: *Start a paragraph!*
>
> My story on Thursday began:
>> *The trembling child, eyes dark and wild,*
>> *Frozen midst the fighting . . .*
> The teacher wrote a little note: *Take care, untidy writing!*
>
> My story on Friday began:
>> *The boxer bruised and bloody lay,*
>> *His eyes half closed and swollen . . .*
> The teacher wrote a little note: *Use a semi-colon!*
>
> Next Monday my story will begin:
>> *Once upon a time . . .*

This poem, entitled *Creative Writing* (Phinn 1996), parodies the kind of situation one sometimes feels is happening in elementary schools, whereby children are trying their very best to write effectively while their teachers are on different wavelengths with completely different agendas in mind.

Raising the Poetry Profile

Poetry must be read, talked about, appreciated, and responded to before it is analyzed. Furthermore, children model their writing on what they have previously read and talked about, hence they should be encouraged to read as much poetry as possible and take all the help they can get from what they read. This is the point that Rosen (1996) makes in his work looking at why we write poetry; he states, "The history of poetry is one of plunder." Rosen feels that we need to "create situations in which children know they can be in control of language, can mould and change it at will" (p. 14). This exact point, whereby children write words and phrases they have previously heard and talked about, can be seen in two poems written by Amy and Mark, aged 7 and 10 years, respectively (Figures 5.1 and 5.2). They had read some poems about grandmas which had spurred them on to talk about what their grandmas were like. They had then discussed their appearance, their personalities, what they smelled like, and what they said and did. Many of the ideas which emanated from their poetry readings and subsequent conversations were used in their poems, which both show a real sensitivity through the words used and the charming images.

Of course, for children to read poetry, adults, in the form of parents, teachers, and caregivers, must read poetry, too. Three very important factors in fostering children's poetry reading and writing in the school years are teacher influence, the provision of a wide range of material, and the opportunity to "have a go." So, teachers themselves must be readers of poetry. They need to have read the poetry anthologies they present to children, select them with care and knowledge, and be skilled in judging how and when to use them. The importance of these points was clearly seen in a conversation I had with Helen, a very enthusiastic, confident seven-year-old child whom I met when visiting a school (four- to seven-year-olds) to look at the range of writing undertaken by the children. Helen initiated the conversation:

"I'm very good at writing, you know. Would you like to see my poems?"
"I would love to," I replied.
She smiled, *"I'll fetch my portfolio."*

My Grandma

I loved my Grandma.
She was very thoutgull.
Her hair was like silver
And her face like gold
Eyes like emerolds
That glinted in the sun.
She was very preicious.

Amy.

Figure 5.1 "My Grandma"

My Nan

I like my Nan.
She's raund and rinkly and powdery
And smells of flowers and soap.
She's as comfy as a cushen to sit on.
When my Mom shouts at me
I go to my Nan.
She cuduls me and says
Never mind love
Your Mum was like that
When she was a littel girl
A real grumpybum.

Mark

Figure 5.2 "My Nan"

Helen was right, she was good at poetry. Her folder contained poems relating to the local environment; her holiday memories; shopping in the local supermarket; and the thoughts of a Roman soldier—part of the history theme they had just been studying. Helen was very clear about what had helped her to become a poet—as her continuing conversation showed:

> *"Do you write poetry?"*
> *"Yes, I do,"* I replied.
> *"Do you get the rhythms?"*
> *"Yes."*
> *"And the rhymes?"*
> *"Sometimes."*
> *"Do you illustrate your poems?"*
> *"No, I'm afraid I don't."*
> Helen smiled. *"I do,"* she said, *"I think it makes them look nicer on the page."*

When Helen was asked why she was so good at writing poetry, she verbalized the three above-mentioned factors—she stated that there were lots of poetry books in her classroom, she referred to her teacher who loved poems and read them to the class everyday, and she said there are lots of opportunities to write different kinds of poems.

Teachers might heighten children's awareness of poetry by using a range of strategies. These could include:

1. Reading a wide selection of poems to children. For example, each schoolday might begin with a poem—not to be analyzed, just enjoyed. There does not always have to be follow-up work. Simply reading poetry to children "beds their ear" with the richest kind of language.
2. Compiling a list of poems suitable for different age groups and making a collection of poetry posters and cards to go in a poetry browsing box.
3. Inviting poets into schools to work with children and share their experiences of the process of writing: where ideas come from, the research they have to undertake, how they draft and revise, proof read, and submit for publication. Listening to popular poets reading and interpreting their own work will fascinate and inspire children.
4. Displaying a wide selection of different types of poetry and asking the children to browse and then from an anthology select just one short verse, perhaps a limerick or a haiku. Ask each child to copy out the selected poem and decorate it, commit it to memory, and then recite it to others in the class. A collection of these short poems could be put together into a poetry booklet or form part of a colorful display.
5. Mounting displays of poetry anthologies, book jackets, and posters in school corridors and classroom. Publishers will often provide material.
6. Organizing an evening for teachers, parents, school officials, and children when a speaker such as an author, adviser, or member of the local School Library Service talks about the importance of poetry. As part of the event, the children could be asked to read or perform a selection of poems (including their own) accompanied by music and mime. This could include a dramatic reading or a group choral presentation.

7. Spending a little time each week reading and discussing a longer, more demanding poem. When studying a poem, do so sensitively. Appreciation comes before analysis.
8. Enlarging short poems and hanging them from ceilings or decorating classrooms and corridors with them. A range of colorful and varied pictorial charts and poetry posters will brighten up any classroom or corridor and raise the profile of poetry in school.
9. Placing a poem screen saver on the classroom computer—change the poem daily.
10. Integrating poetry into any class topic work. Poetry text sets might be formed based on themes: *Food, Animals, Places, Traditions, Light and Dark, Friends and Enemies, Magic and Mystery.*

Four- to Seven-year-olds Responding to Poetry Through Writing

When they first arrive at school, many children will have already had some experience of poetry. They will have heard television jingles, pop songs, rhymes, and snippets of verse. Some will be familiar with the traditional rhymes and rhythms of familiar nursery rhymes:

> *Humpty Dumpty sat on a wall,*
> *Humpty Dumpty had a great fall.*
> *All the king's horses and all the king's men,*
> *Couldn't put Humpty together again.*

While other children might even know variations on original themes, making use of clever, quirky words leading to a multitude of pleasures and surprises:

> *Humpty Dumpty sat on a wall*
> *Eating black bananas*
> *Where d'you think he put the skin?*
> *Down his silk pajamas.*

In school, children should be introduced to and encouraged to join in with the lively rhythms, strong rhymes, choruses and repetitions of modern as well as traditional material. Teachers draw on the children's early experiences and encourage them to perform the little rhymes they know: *Humpty Dumpty, Miss Polly Had a Dolly, Georgie Porgie, Simple Simon, Jack and Jill, The Grand Old Duke of York,* and *Mary, Mary, Quite Contrary.* They read to the children regularly, encouraging them to hear the rhymes and clap to the rhythms. They present a wide range of verse, which relates to what children see and hear around them, stimulating their imaginations, enriching their vocabulary, and building listening skills. They also introduce the children to the poetry of new and inventive poets and delight them with poems about mummies and daddies, big sisters and baby brothers, snowflakes and sunshine, sand and sea, caterpillars and cats, toy soldiers and teddy bears.

In these early stages, the teacher's aims should be to:

- encourage the children to listen attentively to the rhythms and rhymes of poetry;
- make poems important and enjoyable for them;
- use their knowledge of alphabet letters and simple words;
- encourage them to actively participate in the reading when they feel confident to do so;

- stimulate their own spoken language, encouraging them to speak with clarity, confidence, and expression;
- teach them about some of the surface features of writing, such as spelling and punctuation, stressing high-frequency words like *said, see, make, come, because, him, her, when, where, with, will, look;*
- help them understand how successful poems work;
- learn the terminology of poetry: rhyme, rhythm, theme;
- foster their voluntary independent reading of poems.

Children should be introduced to nonrhyming verse at an early stage and come to appreciate that not all poetry rhymes. It was with this thought in mind that I took some stuffed animals into a class of six- and seven-year-old children. I wanted these children to write poetry related to the animals, but prior to this we began to talk about the creatures: They included a mole, badger, rabbit, hedgehog, and a dormouse. We looked at each animal in turn and talked about how they had died (many of these animals had been road accident victims, and this in itself was a talking point), the colors of their bodies, their shapes, features, and anything else the children wanted to raise. Prior to starting the collaborative part of our writing, I read some poems and short descriptive extracts from stories which featured these animals. I then began to list the parts of one animal's body on the board; the children chose to focus on the dormouse:

eyes   ears   nose   mouth   tail   fur

The children suggested adjectives to add some description and, with me acting as the scribe, they came up with some words which were very descriptive of the dormouse—two adjectives were added to each noun:

black round eyes
soft flappy ears
wet little nose
small whiskery mouth
thin pink tail
soft brown fur

From further discussion, which emerged after adding *like* at the end of each line, a class poem was created:

Dormouse
Black round eyes like shiny beads,
Soft flappy ear like a crumpled purse,
Wet little nose like sticky tar,
Small whiskery mouth like a tiny cave,
Thin pink tail like a lazy worm,
Soft brown fur like a carpet.

Support had been offered, but the children had effectively composed the poem themselves. They then began to work in pairs, once again helped and supported by myself, and they produced other detailed, descriptive little poems based on this approach (Phinn 1995).

Mole
Fat black little body like an old kid glove,
Shiny fur as soft as silk,
Sharp little nose like an ice cream cone,
Big flat paws like pink spades,
Eyes that cannot see.

Rabbit
Big big eyes as round as the moon,
Soft soft fur as grey as the mist,
White whiskers like bits of cotton,
Round little tail as white as the sky.

Badger
Bristly fur like a doormat,
Fat round body like a dog's,
Long sharp teeth like icicles,
Glistening eyes like marbles,
Black and white in the night.

Hedgehog
Round, spiky body like a ball of spikes,
Crinkled pointed face like an old man,
Long long whiskers like spiky grass,
A carpet of spines, a bristly brush.

A very supportive start, making use of stimulating artefacts and giving the children the chance to talk and discuss, had moved through shared writing into guided and finally independent writing. Some very creative poems to be proud of had been the final product of this piece of work.

In order to help children enjoy and respond to poetry through writing, teachers can select a particular poem and:

- read it in different ways, using different voices and intonations, varying the pace and rhythm;
- record the reading and leave a taped version for further listening;
- ask the children to talk about the theme of the poem and relate it to their own experiences;
- mount a copy next to pictures and photographs of the theme;
- explore how sounds of words reflect their meaning;
- encourage the children to mime actions described;
- encourage the children to think up new rhymes and word pairings;
- ask different kinds of questions about the poem—factual questions, speculative questions, and questions to elicit personal responses;
- discuss word patterns, unusual spellings, interesting rhymes from the poem;
- provide copies of the poem for the children to work on their own readings in pairs or groups;
- use drama activities: improvisation, tableaux, hot seating, and readers' theater to explore the theme;
- encourage the children to illustrate it (or part of it) and use this as a basis for further discussions of the verse;
- cover words or short sections of the poem and ask the children to suggest other suitable words and phrases.

These activities will all help to shape children's oral responses to poems in readiness for their written responses.

Seven- to Eleven-year-olds Responding to Poetry Through Writing

Encouraging older children to read and respond to poetry is not dissimilar to working with younger children; one must hold onto certain tenets, one crucial one being not to slog tediously through a poem, explaining words and phrases, before the poem has had a chance to breathe—appreciation comes before analysis. Children should be given the opportunity of hearing the full poem read, re-read, and appreciated prior to any discussion.

With a group of eleven-year-old children we looked at a range of poetry over a six-week period. I wanted to encourage them to read, prepare, and present a selection of poems, to encourage them to share their opinions about the poems both orally and in written form, and to compare a range of poetry and recognize the key differences between prose, poetry, playscript, and nonfiction writing.

First, we looked at the poem *Night* by Richard Pasco, aged eleven (1990):

Night

Gently laps the sea.
The black rocks glisten wet.
Moonlight silvers the sand,
And the gulls are quiet.

Night. Ice in the air.
Trees silhouetted, stark, straight.
Branches like ragged birds,
So still, so black.

Beyond the dark rocks
Stretching shingle to the sea,
Patches of blue mud
And pools of silver.

Night. Ice in the water.
Great Neptune sleeps
And in the cold, cold deep,
All is still, all is black.

The children were asked to read the poem quietly to themselves. We then read it slowly together. A general discussion followed, using four question prompts:

1. What, in one sentence, is this poem about?
2. What parts of the poem do you particularly like? Can you say why?
3. What parts of the poem do you find difficult to understand? Can we see if we can get to the meaning?
4. Have you any other comments to make about this poem?

These general questions opened up the discussion and we focused upon some of the features of this poem: the creation of atmosphere, the four-lined stanzas, the lack of rhyme, the gentle quiet rhythm which reflects the tranquillity of the scene, the frequent use of the letter "s" (*sea, silvers, sand, silhouetted, stark, still, stretching, shingle, silver, and sleeps*), the contrasting colors, the choice of certain words and phrases, the use of significant detail, the repetition, and the figures of speech. As the discussion was taking place, I tried to convince these children that when responding to poetry there is "no right answer." I constantly challenged them to justify their points of view by referring to the text and I ensured that I valued each and every contribution as it was made by making comments such as, "That's a good contribution," "It's interesting you should say that . . ."

After our class discussion in relation to *Night,* the children were grouped according to ability and asked to respond to a particular poem. The material was differentiated so, for example, the most able group was asked to consider a complex, free-verse poem, *Bonfire Night* (Phinn 1998), and the least able group was to read and study the more accessible poem, *If You Go Down to The Woods Today* (Phinn 1998).

Bonfire Night

I remember my first Bonfire Night.
It was cold and clear and the air smelled of smoke.
My father sat me high on his shoulders to see the dancing flames
And the red sparks spitting in the air.
My face burned with heat.
And then I saw him—
The figure sitting on the wigwam of wood.
I screamed and screamed and screamed.
"There's a man on top," I cried, "a man in the fire!
Oh help him, daddy, please!"
And everyone laughed.
"It's just the guy," my father said.
"He's made of rags and paper.
He's not real."
But I was sad and scared to see
Those clinging fingers of fire
Scorch the stuffed body, crackling the arms,
Those searing tongues of flame lick round the bloated legs,
And swallow up the wide-eyed, smiling face.
Now, as I stand around the bonfire,
My own child perched high on my shoulders,
I recall my father's words:
"He's just a guy. He's made of rags and paper.
He's not real."
Yet, still I shudder at the sight of the blazing figure
Burning in the night.

If You Go Down to The Woods Today

If you go down to the woods today,
You're sure of a big surprise.
We're chopping down the trees you see,
Before your very eyes.
The pines and ash and poplars,
They all are coming down,
To make a smart new ring road,
To circle round the town.
The cedar, cherry, chestnut,
The beech and elm and briar,
We're going to pile them all up high,
And set them all on fire.
The willow, maple, alder,
The silver birch and oak,
We're going to make a great big blaze,
And they'll all go up in smoke.
The sycamore and mountain ash,
Yes, everyone must go
To be replaced by motorway,
That's progress, don't you know.
So if you've nothing else to do,
Well, why not grab a saw,
And help us build a bonfire.
Isn't that what trees are for?

The children had to consider the poem allocated to their group, using the four prompt questions they had previously used; each child was then asked to work independently and write a paragraph about the poem s/he had studied. From the simple act of reading the poem several times, then discussing the four questions in a collaborative group fashion, the children were able to respond to the poems in writing. The fact that these children were used to talking about all types of writing (poetry, prose, and nonfiction) in terms of structure, layout, imagery, and use of particular language to create effect helped them to respond to the poems in their own personal ways.

Bonfire Night was one written response to the original poem from an able girl. This response was a third draft, written after corrections:

Bonfire Night is supposed to be an exciting time. It is full of noise and colour and interesting smells. There are bangs, crackles, whooshing rockets, whizzing fireworks, sparks, flames, reds and yellows, woodsmoke, sausages sizzling, steaming soup, chewy toffee. It's a time for families and fun. But it's not like this for one little boy who goes to his first bonfire and sees a man on the top of the pile of wood burning in the night. Everyone seems to be taking no notice. It's like a nightmare for him. The figure is only the guy (Guy Fawkes) but no one has told him that it is not real and he screams to see the body smouldering and eaten by the flames. The memory has stayed with him all his life. Now when he is a father himself and takes his own son to the bonfire he shudders at the sight of the burning guy. The poem is about the fears of childhood and how adults sometimes do not understand.

I like the way the poem uses words to paint a picture of the bonfire with its dancing flames and the red sparks spitting in the air, those clinging fingers of fire and the description of the burning figure with the scorched, stuffed body, crackling arms, round the bloated legs and the wide-eyed, smiling face.

If You Go Down to The Woods Today was written by a boy with special educational needs and his work is once again a third draft, written after corrections and teacher intervention:

This poem is about chopping down trees to make way for a road. It reminds me of the children's song called The Teddy Bears' Picnic. *It begins in the same way. I think the writer wants you to think this. I think he wants to make you think it is a silly little song and when he has got our attention he describes something serious. He says if you've nothing else to do why don't you join everyone to chop down the trees and help burn them. What I think he really means is that we should all do something to stop the cutting down of the forest and stop people ruining the countryside by building roads.*

Using the four question prompts is one way of encouraging children to respond to poetry, but they can also be helped to focus on the structure of the verse and on aspects of the language by doing activities which involved reorganizing, completing, or adding something else to a piece of text. Sometimes words are omitted (cloze procedure), paragraphs re-ordered (sequencing), or a text broken into installments to aid prediction. These techniques involve drawing on the full range of reading strategies and can also be used with narrative and nonfiction material. Searching for clues in order to complete a piece of text, re-ordering jumbled sentences, segmenting (marking off key groups of phrases or sentences), labeling, grouping (putting sections of text into different categories), and rewriting the information in the form of tables, diagrams, and flow charts, encourages careful reading and develops the children's comprehension skills.

I wanted to try some of these techniques with a class of eleven-year-old children and decided to use a poem written by Dominic, also aged eleven. The poem was presented with certain words and phrases missing and the children, working in groups, were asked to complete the two verses.

It was _____
The sun shone down on ground that was _____
Tall trees _____ like _____
_____ a _____ sky,
And the pond in the park _____

It was _____
The _____ fell on pavements that were _____
A _____ woman splashed through _____ ,
Pushing a _____
Past shops which were _____ and _____

One completed poem which was typical of the children's response overall was:

> *It was hot.*
> *The sun shone down on ground that was dry and dusty.*
> *Tall trees drooped like tired runners,*
> *Beneath a summer sky,*
> *And the pond in the park shimmered.*
>
> *It was wet.*
> *The rain fell on pavements that were silvery.*
> *A young woman splashed through puddles,*
> *Pushing a pram*
> *Past shops which were warm and dry.*

Each group presented their version of the poem, the differences and similarities were discussed, and, finally, the original version was read:

> *It was cold.*
> *The sun shone down on ground that was iron hard.*
> *Tall trees stood like sharp straight pencils,*
> *Pointing to a cloudless sky,*
> *And the pond in the park glistened.*
>
> *It was cold.*
> *The snow fell on pavements that were steely-grey.*
> *A cold woman splashed through slush,*
> *Pushing a supermarket trolley*
> *Past shops which were warm and bright.*

This activity really showed the children that there is no one particular response to poetry and there is certainly no right or wrong response; the reader responds to the text in the way that is appropriate for him or her at that moment in time. As Rosen (1996) states: "Writing is a very democratic form of language because it hands so much over to the reader" (p. 14).

Another activity which encourages children to discuss and examine a poem's structure is sequencing; this is where children are given jumbled-up verses, couplets, or lines, then asked to place them in an order which is understandable and interesting. Some ten- and eleven-year-olds were given the lines to the poem, *I Am* (Phinn 1990). Much discussion ensued and the children eventually realized that with this particular poem the meaning was not lost, whichever way the lines were organized.

The original version:

The different, resequenced version:

I Am

I am small for my age: Hi Titch!
Thin as a beanpole: Oi Skinny!
I wear glasses and get spots!
Look at spotty four eyes!
I always come top in maths!
Listen to the Professor!
I am me: I can't help it!

I Am

I am me: I can't help it!
I wear glasses and get spots!
I am small for my age: Hi Titch!
I always come top in maths!
Look at spotty four eyes!
Thin as a beanpole: Oi Skinny!
Listen to the Professor!
I am me: I can't help it!

Conclusion

There are many other ways of responding to poetry and of using poems to help to develop a positive attitude in the classroom situation; teachers committed to the teaching of poetry will know and use these ideas already. If, as teachers, we try to encourage children to turn to poetry as a source of enjoyment, we must ensure that this is matched by our own professional commitment. We must know the range of anthologies available and what kind of poems interest individual pupils, and be in a strong position to advise and help in the choice of reading material. If we provide children with a variety of stimulating poems that fascinate, excite, intrigue, and amuse; that give them fresh insights; that open their minds and imaginations; and that introduce them to the wonderful richness and range of language, then we produce avid, enthusiastic, and discriminatory readers and offer them the very best models for their own writing. James had been exposed to these kinds of models. He swam in a pool of poetry at home and at school and was just eleven years old when he presented his teacher with this remarkably moving poem about his sister:

My Sister

My little sister died last night
In the hospital.
She was four days old,
Only four days old
And when I saw her for the first time
I don't think that I had ever been as happy.
She was so small and crinkled
With big eyes and soft, soft skin,
And a smile like a rainbow.
Her fingers were like little sticks
And her nails like little sea shells.
And her hair like white feathers.

Now she's gone.
And my mum can't stop crying
And my dad stares at nothing.
I loved our baby.
And I'll never forget her.

References

Department of Education and Science (DES) (1987) *Teaching Poetry in the Secondary School.* London: HMSO.

Pasco, R. (1990) "Night," in Phinn, G. (1990) *Lizard Over Ice.* Surrey: Thomas Nelson.

Phinn, G. (1990) *Lizard Over Ice: A poetry anthology.* Surrey: Thomas Nelson.

Phinn, G. (1995) *Touches of Beauty.* Doncaster: Roselea Publications.

Phinn, G. (1996) *Classroom Creatures.* Doncaster: Roselea Publications.

Phinn, G. (1998) *Bonfire Night.* Unpublished.

Phinn, G. (1998) *If You Go Down to The Woods Today.* Unpublished.

Rosen, M. (1996) "Into the red brick factory," in Powling, C. and Styles, M. (eds.) (1996) *A Guide to Poetry 0–13.* Reading: Books for Keeps and The Reading and Language Centre.

Chapter 6

Writing as a Response to Literature
David Hornsby and Lesley Wing Jan

PART I: RESPONDING TO LITERATURE

The Importance of Literature

The literature strand is the *heart* and *soul* of your literacy program. Other strands (such as shared reading, guided reading, shared writing, independent writing, language experience, and so on) are all very important strands; some of you may even refer to them as the *guts* of your program. However, without a significant literature strand, the heart and soul of your program is missing.

Recent trends emphasize the *guts* of the literacy program. At the systemic level, there is an obsession with cognitive aspects of literacy learning, and an almost total exclusion of the essential affective aspects from thinking about literacy. This obsession with the cognitive is evident in the results of a survey conducted by the International Reading Association. The topics identified as "hot topics" included early intervention, phonemic awareness, phonics, and so on. Topics identified as "not hot but should be" included comprehension, family literacy, literature-based instruction, multicultural literature, and Reading Recovery. The authors of the survey report wrote: "This contrast between what is 'hot' and what 'should be hot' might suggest that forces other than leaders in the (literacy) field are determining the literacy agenda" (Cassidy and Cassidy 2000). It seems that the literacy experts (including many teachers) have little say in the current climate. Rather, those who have political power or other positions of influence are determining the literacy agenda despite a lack of knowledge about literacy learning.

We make a passionate plea for teachers to maintain their rich literature programs, since literature is one of the most powerful ways of tapping into children's emotions, and research over many years demonstrates conclusively that emotions influence learning.

Five-year-olds pick up the pattern in books like *The Very Hungry Caterpillar* by Eric Carle (1974). They often join in spontaneously and make comments about how much the caterpillar eats. One child said:

> *How does he eat so much? I couldn't eat all that! What would happen if I ate that much?*

Seven-year-olds pull extraordinary faces and laugh with delight when they are listening to *When the Wind Changed* by Ruth Park (1980). One child wrote:

> *I'm glad it's not true that your face changes when the wind changes because my dad pulls faces all the time.*

Nine-year-olds in Grade 4 identified with the main character in *The Pow Toe* by N. L. Ray (1985). Rory had to contend with Bionic Barlow, the school bully.

> *I was glad when Rory threw up all over the bully, because I know how it feels to be bullied. Last year, I was bullied all the time. Bullies need to know how it feels. Maybe the author knew what it was like to be bullied too.*

Eleven-year-olds responded to the prejudice shown by Phillip in *The Cay* by Theodore Taylor (1973).

> *I think that the author was trying to tell people that there is no difference between black and white people. Timothy said, "It's all the same beneath the skin." You love somebody for who they are, and not what they look like. I don't understand why people are prejudiced.*

Memorable, lasting experiences of literature help children to become life-long readers. Today, more than ever, we need a commitment to sharing quality literature with children and a program that helps them to develop personal response. The examples already used show how powerfully literature can influence children and their responses.

The Importance of Response

Children Respond Naturally

Children respond naturally to what they have read. However, reading itself can be a fairly solitary activity, and much of the response that occurs *during* reading may not be expressed or explored unless sharing times are arranged as an important part of daily classroom practice. When you meet with small groups of children, you provide opportunities for expression and *exploration* of personal response.

C. S. Lewis has argued that it is the *quality of response* which differentiates literary readers from nonliterary readers. Helping children to develop the quality of their response is an important aim for all teachers. We *must* organize time in our program for this to happen.

Different Forms of Response

We respond to literature in many different ways. Children respond naturally by laughing, talking, asking questions, acting out, requesting that the book be read again, drawing, and even by becoming quiet or sitting with tears in their eyes.

We also respond by writing. However, writing is not usually a *natural* response to reading. We may keep a diary, and in a letter to a friend, we may write about a favorite book. But if writing is not a natural response to reading, even for adults, why do we want children to respond in written form? What does written response help them do?

The Importance of Written Response

Many writers and researchers believe that writing enhances children's response to reading (Hansen 1987; Tiedt 1989; Tierney *et al.* 1989). In fact, when children are given opportunities to respond in written form, the process they go through helps to develop a stance toward reading that may not be developed in any other way (Calkins 1983).

Unlike oral response, which can often be "all over the place," written response can lead to more focused thinking. It allows the writer to follow a line of thought more carefully and to persevere with that line of thought. It also allows scribbling and doodling and drawing, which, among other things, allow exploration and expression of feelings.

However, a final written response is only a part of what we're looking for. Equally, if not more important, are the *thinking, feeling,* and *reflecting* that occur as a result of reading and before a final product is even considered. The thinking, feeling, and reflecting are more important than the final written product. In a personal communication, Grant (1985) has reminded us that children must be given opportunities to "reflect upon the experience of reading before it evaporates, or is forgotten."

When something is written down, it becomes a record that the writer can read and re-read. This allows the writer to reflect upon what has been written, to scribble in new thoughts, to try different ways of arranging the words, to use more precise vocabulary in the hope that it comes closer to what is intended, to formulate new questions. The opportunity to read and reread what has been written helps the writer to see connections that weren't seen before, and to clarify meaning in his or her own head. In other words, "we write to learn" (Atwell 1990; Mayher, Lester, and Pradl 1983; Smith 1982). A written response can also be revisited on a following day and seen with a new pair of eyes. It can be shared with others, and the feedback from others can help to clarify or extend the meaning the writer intended.

Writing as a form of response to reading allows children to:

- take the time to consider things they wouldn't have considered otherwise;
- "discover" further questions as they think through their response;
- develop private thoughts in their heads before they have to share them publicly;
- recapture an experience as well as think through a line of reasoning;
- re-read their responses and reflect about how these have changed over time;
- appreciate their reading more for the insights gained into the meaning of the text;
- gain a greater awareness of the way the text has actually been crafted.

Aspects of Response

What Are We Looking For?

Response is an interactive product of the text, the experiences of the author, and the experiences of the reader. Response involves

> the total learning experiences of the individual reader . . . the whole person's life-project, personality, style or identity is involved. Thought and feeling, the affective and the intellectual, unite in the process of representation and interpretation of experience that informs the reader's and writer's contributions. (Grant 1990, p. 213)

Since response includes both subjective and objective elements, children will respond to the same material in different ways. We will help children discover shared or public meanings, but we will also encourage diversity. Rosenblatt refers to both an "efferent stance" to reading when readers attend to the shared or public meaning that can be carried away from the text, and to "an aesthetic stance" when they choose to focus "primarily on what is being personally lived through, cognitively and affectively, *during* the reading event" (1985, p. 102). Efferent and aesthetic readings refer to the reader's choice of stance and not to the text. The two stances are at opposite ends of a continuum, and Rosenblatt reminds us that most of our reading lies somewhere between the two. When we are helping children respond to literature, we are concerned with both the shared or public meaning of the literature, as well as the aesthetic responses they "thought and felt" during reading. Obviously, we are looking for individual, personal responses as well as the development of shared meanings. "Competency in literacy should encompass the development of both stances, as appropriate to personal and impersonal purposes, texts, and tasks. Yet an efferent bias clearly predominates (in current practice)" (Rosenblatt 1985).

While the children in our classrooms will be given many opportunities to share their responses, they will also be given the right to keep some of their responses private.

> Some stories or poems are too special, too personal to be shared. The child may want to savor them, to read them again and again in order to hold their thoughts close to him. A teacher should know the children in the class well enough to know what will help each student have memorable experiences with books. (Huck *et al.* 1987, p. 678)

As we work with children, we have opportunities to monitor the development of their responses. We will look for evidence of different elements of response as described in the next section.

Elements of Response

There are *elements* of response rather than *stages*. Harding (1967) and Grant (1985, 1990) have written that a mature or considered response will include the six elements described in Table 6.1. The first three show that the reader has established a relationship with the *text*; the second three

Table 6.1 Elements of Response

	Elements	
Dimension 1	1. Attending willingly (accepting reading as valuable, interesting, or enjoyable) 2. Elementary perception and comprehension of the scene 3. Empathizing with characters, problems, or action	establishes the reader's relationship with the text
Dimension 2	4. Drawing analogies with life and searching for self-identity (learning and feeling things that help one's own life and self-understanding) 5. Detached evaluation of the characters and what they do and suffer 6. Reviewing the whole work as a social convention and accepting or rejecting the author's stated or implied values	establishes the reader's relationship with the author

(Adapted from Harding 1967 and Grant 1985, 1990)

indicate that the reader has now established a relationship with the *author*. It is convenient to identify these levels of response as "Dimension 1" and "Dimension 2."

We must remember, however, that a reader may respond differently, depending on the text being read, the reader's related background knowledge, the reader's familiarity with the genre, and the purposes and contexts for reading.

For example, a child may include all elements of response to a very simple, familiar text. However, when reading a much more difficult text, the same child may attend willingly (Element 1) but be unable to grasp the full meaning (Element 2), and certainly unable to empathize with characters, problems, or action (Element 3). In other words, the full range of elements of response may not be demonstrated.

Without explicit modeling by the teacher, many children will fail to move into Dimension 2. But this second step is decisive. It is decisive because it indicates that the reader has an awareness that fiction is a social convention and that he or she can view a text as one form of communication used by the author.

The more recent work of Lo Bianco, Luke, and Freebody has helped us to appreciate the four "practices" of effective readers (Table 6.2). Children's written responses to reading can help to show us whether the children are applying all practices effectively.

When we read children's written responses, we get valuable information about the practices they are applying as readers. But it is important to remember that the nature of the text itself influences the children's reading practices and their written responses. For example, if the children are reading relatively simple text, and the genre is familiar, their responses may include many different elements. There will be evidence to show that there has been a mature reading of the text. However, if the text is difficult, and the genre is unfamiliar, the children will read it with different levels of competence. They may be involved in code-breaking practices, and making partial meaning, but may be prevented from being text users or text analysts. And, of course, a reader may respond in different ways to different sections of the one text.

Table 6.2 Four "Practices" of Effective Readers

Practices	What the reader does
code breaker (coding competence)	• understands and applies knowledge of the written script (i.e. relationship between spoken sounds and the ways they are represented as written symbols)
meaning maker or text participant (semantic competence)	• makes meaning • draws upon and applies knowledge of the topic, text structure, and syntax to make sense of a text
text user (pragmatic competence)	• draws upon knowledge of the role of written texts within the society in order to use them to participate in social activities in which texts play a central part • knows that purpose of the text influences its format and how it is read
text analyst or text critic (critical competence)	• draws upon awareness that all written texts are crafted objects; they are not neutral • understands how the text is "positioning" the reader; is able to read it "critically"

(Lo Bianco and Freebody, 1997; Luke and Freebody 1999)

Selecting Appropriate Texts

As teachers, we have a vital role to play. Children will often be selecting their own texts, and it will be important to provide opportunities for the children to respond to those. However, we also want to select and provide texts that *extend* children's opportunities to respond in written form.

We will select texts that provide the greatest opportunities for children to go beyond a relationship with the text to a relationship with the author. We will select texts that help children to apply reading behaviors related to all four *practices* described by Luke and Freebody. When we provide suitable texts, the code-breaker practices become automatic, meaning is established more easily, and attention can be given to text-user and text-analysis practices.

Suitable texts are written in a familiar genre, they have familiar content, and they are at an independent reading level. If we want children to experience the social purposes of texts, and to experience the nature and variety of written discourse, then we are obliged to provide texts that are written by "real authors" for "real purposes." "Real books" can never be replaced by contrived texts "written by no one for no one" (Grant 1990, p. 216).

Meek (1988) also reminds us that the texts we provide teach their own lessons! "The most important single lesson that children learn from texts is *the nature and variety of written discourse*, the different ways that language lets a writer tell, and the many and different ways a reader reads" (p. 21).

The Teacher's Role

As a result of what has been discussed so far, we could say that our role involves us in helping children to:

- explore suitable and varied texts;
- explore feelings, thoughts, reactions, emotions, and memories;
- make connections to their own experience;
- think about themselves as readers and what they do when they read;
- see the relationship between reading and writing;
- capture the "spontaneous, lived experience";
- encourage creative response and validate the multiple meanings that readers develop as they read.

Development of Written Responses

Patterns of development can be observed. The elements of response described in Table 6.1, the different kinds of reading practices described in Table 6.2, and similar descriptions of reading behaviors help us to see these patterns of development.

Even though there is a continuum of more and more sophisticated response to reading, development occurs along different dimensions simultaneously. Consequently, individual children follow different pathways. We should not expect regular, linear development.

To assist children along their pathways, we certainly encourage their thinking and feeling, but we must also help them know how to *express* their thinking and feeling. Huck reminds us that "The process of the interpretation is more important than the interpretation itself; both are of greater value than the content of the book or the craft of the writing" (1979, p. 738). Opportunities to express responses, to explore and restate them, and to reflect upon them are essential for development.

When children first write as a response to reading, they may write something as simple as, "I liked the book because I liked it." Gradually, simple retellings will be written, but they can be quite boring repetitions of the story. Later, children may start adding personal comments, reactions, and feelings (Hansen 1987, p. 134). The examples of children's written responses in the following tables may help you to glimpse some of the indicators or signposts of development described by Harding (1967) and Grant (1985, 1990). Written responses from children in the first three years at school are shown in Table 6.3, and from children aged eight to twelve years in Table 6.4. (Refer to Children's Literature in the References for details.)

We can't expect children to write sophisticated responses with "felt-thoughts" from the start. It takes time to reach the place when responses enter "Dimension 2" (see Elements of Response—Table 6.1), and it takes time for readers to become more consciously aware of different reading "practices" (Four "Practices" of Effective Readers—see Table 6.2). It takes even more time for this awareness to influence children's written responses.

Because writing makes more demands upon thinking than simpler forms of response, such as drawing or talking, children need to be supported in their development toward considered

Table 6.3 Sample Written Responses from Children Ages 5 to 8

One possible pathway	Sample
Child attends to story but response is immature. A simple observation and/or comment may be made.	I liked Rosie's Walk because it was good. (Lee, 5 years) "Mr McGee" is funny because he falls on his head in the bed. (Sophie, 6 years)
⇩	
Child provides a simple retelling (often incomplete).	**Bruce the Goose** Bruce let himself get pushed around and bullied by Barge. But in the end he became friends with Barge. (Emma, 8 years)
⇩	
Child retells with personal comments or reactions. Comments show empathy with characters, problems, actions.	**Harry the Dirty Dog** Harry didn't like having a bath, so he buried the scrubbing brush and ran away. I think I should do the same thing. But then Harry got dirty on the road and he got dirty in the truck and everywhere. When he went home, they didn't know who he was so he ran upstairs and jumped in the bath and then they knew who he was. I was worried when they didn't know who he was. (Sam, 7½ years)
⇩	
Child draws analogies with own life; includes evaluation of characters and what they do or experience.	**Bruce the Goose** If I were Bruce, I would be feeling angry and upset. But I would also feel outsmarted and dumb. I would be sad because I have been teased. I know what it feels like to be teased. As they were all closing in on me, I would stop and say, "I am not a goose!" Like Bruce, I would want to have a good day, not a sad day. (David, 8 years)
⇩	
Child is able to see the text as something crafted by the author; child accepts or rejects the author's stated or implied values.	**The Lonely Troll** The Troll thought no one wanted to be friends with him, but the goats didn't realize that he was trying to be friends. It was interesting to see how the author told the story how the Troll saw it. But I didn't think Trolls really wanted friends. (Donna, 8 years)

Table 6.4 Sample Written Responses from Children Ages 8 to 12

One possible pathway	Sample
Child attends to story but response is immature. A simple observation and/or comment may be made.	**Tales of a Fourth Grade Nothing** I felt sorry for Peter because Fudge was a pain. (Beccie, 8 years) It was funny when Peter had to go to the dentist. I laughed because Peter had to show Fudge what to do. (Sophia, 8 years)
Child provides a simple retelling (often incomplete).	**Voices in the Park** Different people went to the park with their dogs. There was a bossy mother, a different father, and some kids too. The boy and the girl became friends. (Viet, 9 years)
Child retells with personal comments or reactions. Comments show empathy with characters, problems, actions.	**The Burnt Stick** This book was very emotional. It was about a young aboriginal boy who was taken away from his parents by the government. It shows how hurt a mother can be when a child is taken. I felt sorry for her, and ashamed of the government. (Chris, 10 years)
Child draws analogies with own life; includes evaluation of characters and what they do or experience.	**Goodnight Mr Tom** I was happy for Willie when he was finally with Mr Tom and other friends. But I was trying to stop the tears rolling when Willie had to go back to his London home and the violence and cruelty … Imagine knocking your own son unconscious. If my mother did that to me, boy would she be in trouble—but she wouldn't do it! But Willie's mum is mentally disturbed. The tension is building up, and if I write much more, I'm sure I'll become affected too! (Andre, 11 years)
Child is able to see the text as something crafted by the author; child accepts or rejects the author's stated or implied values.	**The Burnt Stick** The author, Anthony Hill, taught me so much about the Stolen Generation of aboriginal children. He had to know about our history, and he explained some of it through characters in his story. He was able to show how they felt by using just the right words. He believes that today's government should apologize for wrongs in the past. I agree. If the white people who took the aboriginal children were my ancestors, I would feel really bad. Anthony Hill's story has convinced me that we should say "sorry" and work for reconciliation. (Victoria, 11 years)

response. They need to become more aware of the similarities and differences between the social, shared responses and their personal responses. They also need to discover how the different kinds of response are constructed.

Development in written response will be greatly enhanced as a result of modeling, experience (including other forms of response), social interaction with other readers, and practice.

PART II: CLASSROOM PRACTICES THAT SUPPORT DEVELOPMENT OF WRITTEN RESPONSE

Part I of the chapter has outlined some of the issues that we think are relevant to helping readers respond to literature in written form. A consideration of these issues has guided our beliefs about the classroom practices that are relevant for helping children develop written responses to literature.

We can't describe all relevant classroom practices. They include both teaching procedures and child activity. We describe four teaching procedures which we believe are essential in your teaching repertoire. These teaching procedures assist children in many of the activities that help them to develop considered responses.

Use of Prompt Questions

Prompt questions can be used to help children through *guided discussions*. Such guided discussions help children develop an awareness of the many ways in which we can respond to reading, and provide an experience necessary for writing as a response to reading.

Initially, guided discussion can be used during read-aloud sessions. As you read, you may stop occasionally and invite the children to comment, but more often you will ask prompt questions *after* reading. Cianciolo reminds us that "the story should be read, first and foremost, for the pleasure it has the potential to offer each student and for the impact of the gestalt on the reader's involvement and identification with the literary elements" (1995, p. 146).

We ask questions to stimulate higher-order thinking, to raise awareness of feelings, and to explore both. We also ask questions to help children learn how to ask the same kinds of questions *for themselves* as they read privately and as they write personal responses.

We must remember that, while prompts can be supportive as children first learn to verbalize or write considered responses, they are a temporary crutch. When children are reading familiar text types that are at an independent reading level for them, the questions should be carefully withdrawn so that the children develop their own voice and take increasing control over their exploration of responses to reading. If the children are reading more complex texts, you may find that you need to use *prompt questions* again. The art of teaching is knowing how much support to provide, and how much learner responsibility to expect. Providing too much support can take away opportunities to learn!

The prompt questions are *not* asked to have the children arrive at an answer you have in your head. Neither are they intended to lead the children to a common response. In fact, they must know that people respond to literature differently, and that it is even desirable that they do! They also need to learn that their own response to a piece of literature can change when they have re-read the piece, or had additional experience with it.

The best *prompt questions* are open-ended and grow out of your interaction with the children and the text as you read together. However, *general prompt questions* can help you get started. The following sections show how we can use certain "frameworks" for constructing general prompt questions. Considering the different frameworks helps you to expand your questionning repertoire and to develop the more important higher-order questions that stimulate thinking and feeling.

Harding-Grant Dimensions

The Dimensions of response described by Harding (1967) and Grant (1985, 1990) provide one framework for the generation of a range of questions that help children explore their relationship with the text (Dimension 1) and with the author (Dimension 2) (see Table 6.5).

Table 6.5

	Dimension 1 (Relationship with the Text)	Dimension 2 (Relationship with the Author)
Characters (people, animals, toys, . . .)	• How do you think the character felt when . . . ? Why? • What do you think the character will do when . . . ? Why? • What would you have done in the same situation? Why? • Is the main character believable? Why/why not?	• What similar (or different) experiences have you had? How did that help you to understand the character? • Why do you think the author decided to give . . . (the character) this kind of personality? • How did the author help you get to know the main character? (Through actions? What he/she said? Description?)
Setting	• Where does the story take place? • What was the place like? • Have you ever been to a place like it? Tell us about it. • When did the story take place? (Is it in the future? Is it happening now? Did it happen long ago?) • Why do you think the setting was appropriate?	• How do you think the author was able to describe the setting in that way? • Why do you think the author chose this setting? • Do you think the author may have lived in or known a place like this? Why?
Plot	• What were the main things that happened in the story? • How did you feel when . . . happened? • Were you able to guess what was going to happen? What helped you to guess that? • What do you think was the most important part of the story for you? Why?	• Why do you think the author left this information until the last chapter? • Why do you think the author decided to . . . (sequence the events in that way? Use a "flash-back"?) • Why do you think the author chose . . . (particular event) as one of the key events in the story? • Do you think . . . (experience) might have happened to the author? Why do you think so? • What did the author have to know in order to write about that? *(continues)*

Table 6.5 Continued

	Dimension 1 (Relationship with the Text)	Dimension 2 (Relationship with the Author)
Theme	• Is there one "big idea" in this book? What is it? • What does the book tell us about... (prejudice, equality, humor, family life, relationships, survival, personal journeys, ...)? • This book is about..., but what else is it about?	• Do you think the author had suffered as a result of ... (prejudice, inequality, etc.) Why do you think so? • Why do you think the author chose to write about this theme? • What message was the author wanting to communicate?
Mood/style	• How did you feel while reading the book? Why? • How did your feelings change as you read the book? • What do you think was the funniest (saddest) part? Why? • What special words does the author use to help you hear things in the story? ... see things in the story? ... feel things in the story? • What pictures has the book left in your mind?	• How was the author able to make you feel ...? • Why do you think the author wanted to make you feel that way? • What kind of a person do you think the author is? Why? • Why do you think the author chose to write in this ... (mood, style, genre)?

Generic prompt questions such as the ones already provided as examples may look quite complex, but they can be adapted for use with children at different developmental stages and for texts of different levels of sophistication. For example, many of the above questions could be adapted for use even in the first year or two of school.

For six-year-old children responding to *Elmer* by David McKee (1990), the questions could be adapted as shown in Table 6.6.

Table 6.6

	Dimension 1	Dimension 2
Characters	• How was Elmer different from the other elephants?	• Have you ever felt "different"? In what way? • How do your feelings help you understand Elmer?
Setting	• Where does Elmer live?	• David McKee also illustrated this book. • Do you think he might have lived in a place like this? Why/why not? *(continues)*

Table 6.6 Continued

	Dimension 1	Dimension 2
Plot	• When Elmer felt tired of being different, were you able to guess what he was going to do? What helped you to guess that? • What happened after Elmer looked like any other elephant?	• Why do you think David McKee decided to have a rain storm? Why wouldn't he have Elmer go for a swim, or something like that?
Theme	• Do you think the story about Elmer tells us anything about people? • The book is about elephants, but what else is it about?	• Do you think David McKee used the story about elephants to tell us something about people? What do you think he was trying to tell us? • What did David McKee want you to know about being different?
Mood/style	• When did you feel happy for Elmer? • When did you feel sorry for him? Why? • Are there any special words used in the story? Why were they special?	• Why do you think David McKee used such colorful illustrations? • What kind of a person do you think David McKee is? Why?

For ten- and eleven-year-old children responding to *People Might Hear You* by Robin Klein (1983), you could choose prompt questions from Table 6.7:

Table 6.7

	Dimension 1	Dimension 2
Characters	• How do you think Frances felt when she realized that she would not be allowed to go back to school or see her friends? Why do you think that? • What would you have done if you were Frances when she was let out at night to do some exercise? • What do you think will happen to Helen now that she is with Frances?	• Do you know of any other people who had experiences like Frances had? • Were there any aspects of Frances' personality that reminded you of yourself or someone you know? • Were there any of the experiences that Frances had that reminded you of things that you or other people have done? • Were you able to understand how Frances felt about being in the sect? Why?
Setting	• Where does the story take place? • What was Mr. Tyrell's house like? • Why do you think the house needed to be like this?	• Do you think she described what some sects might be like? What makes you think this? • What would she have needed to know to write about this? • Could she have developed the same story line if it were set somewhere else? Why? *(continues)*

Table 6.7 Continued

	Dimension 1	Dimension 2
Plot	• What was the story about? • Which part made you realize what Aunt Loris was involved in? • What might have happened if Frances had accepted Mr. Tyrell's rules?	• Why do you think Robin Klein wrote about this? • Why do you think she chose this topic? • What do you think were the significant events in this story?
Theme	• This book is about Frances' experience in a sect. But what other "big idea" is it about? • What does the story tell us about tolerance?	• What message do you think Robin Klein gave in this story? • How did Robin Klein keep your interest in the story? • What do think Robin Klein thinks of sects? • What was she telling us about sects and the people in them? What makes you think this?
Mood/style	• What did you think of the story? • What type of story is it? • How did you feel about Mr. Tyrell/Aunt Loris/Frances as you read the story? How did Robin Klein do this? • What do think about now that you have read the story?	• What did you think of the way Robin Klein created the characters? • Do you think she made each character believable? How? Why? • What feelings did you have as you read the story? What did Robin Klein do to make you feel this way?

Generally, responses may be sought and provided during the reading of the text (at the completion of significant sections), but the sample questions provided here would be relevant after reading the whole text. They are examples only of different types of questions.

Luke and Freebody's "Four Practices" Model

This chapter is about responding to texts that are used in the literature strand of your program, so we discuss the "four practices" in relation to *literature*. (The four practices model will also be relevant when using different kinds of texts in the other strands of your literacy program.)

In general classroom practice, and certainly in our literature program, we prefer to start with questions that lead children to be "Meaning Makers," since our focus is always on reading for meaning. We then use questions to help children become "Text Users" and "Text Analysts." When helping children to respond to *literature*, there will be less emphasis on code-breaking practices. We are more likely to help children become "Code Breakers" through other teaching procedures (such as guided reading). In our literature program, we want to focus on the quality of the literature and the children's responses to it. However, there will be times when it is appropriate to tackle code-breaking practices. For example, if you were enjoying a nursery rhyme together, it would be appropriate to have the children identify and play with the rhyme, and you could use this to help their development of phonemic awareness.

The balance between the four reading practices will also vary according to the type of text being read and the readers' purposes. For example, when reading narrative, readers may adopt more of the "Meaning Maker" (text participant) practices and the "Text Analyst" practices. When reading nonfiction, readers may be most concerned with "Text User" practices. "Code Breaker" practices will usually only become obvious when the reader is having difficulty with the text. (As noted above, the teacher may nevertheless focus on "Code Breaker" practices in other strands of the literacy program.)

Luke and Freebody's four practices model can also help us to develop a range of generic prompt questions. The sample questions shown in Table 6.8 will help you see the possibilities. No single model should be used to generate prompt questions, but they all help us to expand our questionning repertoire.

Table 6.8

Practice	Questions That Will Help Children Develop Oral and Written Response

Meaning Maker (Text Participant)	*Literal questions*
	  • What did (character) do?
	    • What happened after . . . ?
	Inferential questions (referring to implied meaning; meaning not obvious in the text or the illustrations)
	  • Do you think (character) liked the house? Why?
	  • How do you think she felt? Why?
	Critical questions (exploring the "truth" or accuracy of the text)
	  • Why did the man *really* do that?
	  • What was the bigger issue in that chapter?

Text User	*Questions focus on the purpose of the text and its consequent structure. In this chapter, we are focusing on fiction, but there are many different forms of fiction. Questions also help children develop a language about texts.*
	  • What kind of fiction is this? (retelling, traditional tale, poem, legend, realistic story, fantasy, cartoons, science fiction, . . .)
	  • What do we know about this kind of fiction already?
	  • How do we read this kind of fiction?
	  • Why do we read this kind of fiction?
	
	Other questions will be related to specific forms of fiction.
	
	Realistic story:
	  • What is the problem?
	  • How do you think it will be resolved?
	  • Why do you think that will happen next?
	Fantasy:
	  • How does the author make that seem possible?
	  • Where do you think the author got the idea for that?
	  • What picture do you imagine in your head?
	                                                                (continues)

Table 6.8 Continued

Practice	Questions That Will Help Children Develop Oral and Written Response

	Traditional tale:
	  • How did you know this was going to be a traditional tale?
	  • What did you expect when you read "Once upon a time . . ."?
	Fable:
	  • Knowing this is a fable, what do you expect?
	  • What was the author's purpose in writing this fable?

Text Analyst	*Text Analysts or Text Critics evaluate the author's purpose. They also evaluate the author's decisions about the information that is presented and how it is presented. They evaluate the author's values. They ask about the intention of the text and how the text influences them.*
	  • How does the author want me to read this?
	  • What does the author want me to understand here?
	  • What is the author's real message?
	  • What did the author have to know to write this?
	  • Why do you think the author used a "flashback" there?
	  • Do you think the author left that information out on purpose?
	  • Why do you think the author kept that information until now?
	  • How is the author trying to influence me?
	  • Has the author been convincing?
	  • Why do you think the author chose to write about (honesty, independence, prejudice . . .)?
	  • Would that happen in most families in that situation?
	  • The author chose to write the book as if Lonnie were speaking. How did that influence you?

Code Breaker	It won't always be appropriate to ask questions that require children to use "Code Breaker" practices when reading literature. However, when the literature contains text that highlights certain features of the graphophonic cueing system, it might be appropriate. For example, you might use questions to help the children "tune in" to alliteration or assonance. Or, when reading rhyming text, children could be asked to identify the rhyming words and the spelling patterns for the rhyming parts of those words. You will use prompt questions to encourage "Code Breaker" practices mainly in other strands of the literacy program (and especially during small teaching groups).

Another Framework for Generating Questions

We can adapt the idea behind De Bono's *Thinking Hats* (1982) to formulate prompt questions. "White questions" help children focus on facts from the text, "red questions" on their emotional view, "black questions" on their negative or gloomy interpretation, and "yellow questions" on their positive or optimistic interpretation. "Green questions" encourage creative, lateral thinking, and "blue questions" encourage broad interpretations that take in the "big picture."

    De Bono's idea was used to formulate the following prompt questions (Table 6.9) for *George's Marvellous Medicine* (Roald Dahl) and *Sadako and the Thousand Paper Cranes* by Eleanor Coerr.

Table 6.9

	George's Marvellous Medicine by Roald Dahl	*Sadako and the Thousand Paper Cranes* by Eleanor Coerr
White	• What did George do to his grandmother?	• What did you learn about Hiroshima as a result of reading this book?
Red	• How would you feel if you were George/George's grandma/father/mother when...?	• How do you feel as a result of reading this book?
Black	• What would be the disadvantages of having gigantic farm animals?	• What couldn't Sadako change or control?
Yellow	• What would be the advantages of having gigantic farm animals?	• What positive things may have resulted from Sadako's terrible illness?
Green	• If you had to create a marvellous medicine, what would it be? • If the grandma had been able to do something to George, what do you think she might have done?	• What could you do to help pass on the message of peace?
Blue	• What do you think of the way Roald Dahl portrayed the grandmother? • Why do you think he did this? • What do you think of the way he had George treating the grandmother? • What do you think of this book? Why?	• What do you think the author's purpose was in writing this book? • Do you think she achieved this purpose? How?

Cianciolo's Generic Questions

Cianciolo (1995) has also provided a set of generic questions that you could use as a guide to expand your repertoire.

A. Initial affective and cognitive response to literature:
1. What did you notice about this story or poem?
2. What do you think or feel about this story or poem?
3. What ideas or thoughts come to mind due to (or were suggested by) this story or poem?
4. Did you feel a part of this story or poem, or did you feel you were watching (observing) what was happening in the story or poem? Describe, explain, elaborate, etc.

B. Focusing on aspects of the story or poem or illustrations without ignoring the role of the reader while reading the selection:
1. What got your attention? What part of the story did you focus on (concentrate on)? What words, phrases, images, ideas, or illustrations do you think caused you to focus on that part of the story or poem?

2. If you were to write (or tell someone) about this story, what would you focus on (emphasize)? For example, would you choose a memory or association it triggered, an aspect
(part) of the story, something about the illustrations, something about the author or illustrator, or something else about the selection? Describe, explain, elaborate, etc.
3. What in this selection (the story line, the illustrations, or your reading of it) pleased you?
upset you? caused you the most trouble?
4. Do you think this is a good piece of literature? Why or why not?
5. If you were an illustrator, what aspect of the story would you select for illustration in order
to interest someone in this book?

C. Direct attention to the context in which the selection(s) is (are) encountered—a context of
other readers, other texts, and personal history:
1. What memories do you have after reading this story or poem (memories of people, places,
sights, events, smells, feelings, or attitudes)?
2. What sort of person do you think the author is? the illustrator?
3. How did your reading of this selection differ from that of your classmates or professional
reviewers? How was your reading of it similar?
4. What did you observe (notice) about the others in the class as they read or discussed this
story or poem?
5. Does this selection remind you of any other literary work—such as a poem, story, television program, or commercial film? If it does, what is the name of the other work? What
connection do you see between the two works?

Modeled Writing

When teachers share their own personal responses to literature, the effect on children is powerful.
Through modeled writing (for example, using an overhead transparency or an easel with large
sheets of paper) we are able to demonstrate to the children how we write to express our response,
how we support our response with examples from the text, and how we relate what we have read
to personal experiences. We are able to show children how a response is composed. While we are
modeling, we are demonstrating how we ask *ourselves* the prompt questions. We are letting the
children hear us "think aloud."

Journal Writing

We help children to use all kinds of journals for writing. Using such notebooks, children are able
to keep and organize their written responses, but when they are used properly, they provide a
powerful means for *developing* written response. *The Journal Book* (Fulwiler 1987) continues to be
a valuable guide for teachers. The contributing authors describe many different kinds of journals,
and provide evidence for the power that journals have to stimulate thoughts and feelings. As noted
in the foreword, journals help to "free" the children's minds and "counter the tendency of school
to freeze the mind."

Different Kinds of Journals

Different authors refer to many different kinds of journals for different purposes. Terminology is not used consistently. You will see references to diaries, journals, dialogue journals, reading-response books, literature logs, learning logs, and so on. Any one of these terms can be interpreted differently. For example, a "learning log" is often about learning in the content areas (science, social education), but it can also be a record of a child's learning about reading or writing or any other process area.

Lindberg (1987) describes the use of a "double-entry" journal. The right-hand pages are used for readers' personal entries as they react and respond to texts *as they read*; the left-hand pages are used to comment on the original entries and to "make something of them."

In our own classrooms, we used the term *journal* as a broad term to cover all kinds of notebooks used to respond to literature, including dialogue journals, double-entry journals, reading-response books, and literature logs.

Helping Children Discover Purposes

It doesn't matter what the journals are called; it's more important to help the children work out the purposes of the journals or other notebooks they use. If children have not used journals before, you need to introduce them with patience. Teacher modeling helps children know how to use journals and to develop appropriate purposes. Providing opportunities for the children to share their journals with each other will also help.

You will need to help the children discover that journals can be used to record their thoughts, feelings, questions, drawings, sketches, half-formed ideas, snippets of information, revelations, things they didn't "see" earlier, unexpected or surprising events, confusions, links with their own lives, and so on. André, a 10-year-old boy, used his journal most effectively. The excerpts below show how he used it.

18 Oct (8:30 pm)	*The introduction of* The Silver Sword *captures my attention. . . . Zakyna must have been terrifying for Joseph and anybody else. If I was there for that long with that treatment, I would have gone crazy.*
19 Oct (1:15 pm)	*Joseph was lucky to find two warm people from his own country. It was nice of the old folk to give Joseph food and a warm bed. When the German soldiers came into the room, I was on the edge of my seat!*
24 Oct (3:00 pm)	*Terror must have overwhelmed Edek on his cold and dangerous escape under the train. I wonder what Jan feels like now?*
25 Oct (7:30 pm)	*. . . The last bit of Chapter 17 thrills me a lot and compels me to read on. Jan was finally brought to tell the truth, for Edek's sake, for Captain Greenwood blamed Edek for the train robbery. The case was a fair one, but in Jan's view it was a rotten one.*
27 Oct (1:40 pm)	*The discussion between Frau Wolff and the children helped me understand that it was only the leaders of the countries who were enemies, not the people. . . . I'm sure the children will escape, but what will happen to the helpful couple?*

28 Oct (2:00 pm)   *Edek is getting close to death and the whole family knows it. I hope he lives to see his parents. . . . But what puzzles me is that the book says the dangerous part of the journey has not begun? . . .*

When the family was reunited my heart jumped for joy. All the children's efforts paid off in the end. . . .

This story tells me that when somebody believes in something hard enough, nothing can stop them. It also tells me how lucky I am not to be an orphan. This book has taught me hundreds of things. I hope a lot more people enjoy the pleasure of reading this book like I have.

The impressions, ideas, feelings, and snippets of information collected in a journal can be used later by a child who wants to write a connected, more continuous piece—a considered response.

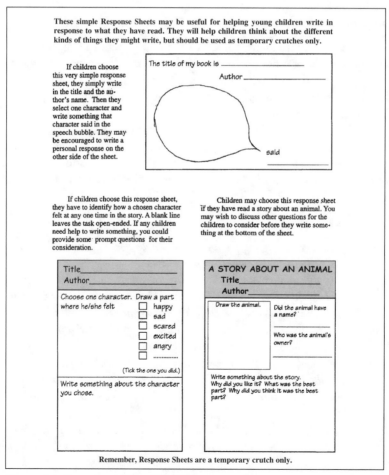

Figure 6.1 Response Sheets (Set 1)

Writing Response Sheets

Children can get stuck in a narrow way of responding, but they can also be helped to experience different elements of response by using proformas that require them to think and reflect in different ways. As they become more aware of the different elements of response, you will see the influence on their "freely written" responses.

Writing-response sheets should be varied and used only as temporary crutches. Any prompt questions they contain should promote higher order thinking and reflection. You will generally introduce specific response sheets by modeling their use as you write shared responses to a shared reading of a whole-class text.

With young children, you may introduce very simple writing-response sheets (like those shown in Figure 6.1) just to help them become aware of the kinds of information that may be recorded. They may not promote higher order thinking, and may only require minimal reflection, but they will get the children started. They will help to develop the habit of responding to reading in written form.

Response sheets can become more sophisticated over time. Those shown in Figure 6.2 were adapted from many excellent samples provided by Daniels (1994). They are open-ended, and they certainly help children take a step towards higher order thinking and reflection.

Over time, different response sheets may be introduced, and a wide selection will become available. The children will be free to write their own responses, but they will also be free to choose occasional response sheets if they are relevant to the books they have read and if they support the kinds of response they wish to make.

CONNECTOR

Name: .... Group: ....
Book: ....

Your job is to find connections between the book and the world outside. This means connecting the reading to your own life, to happenings at school or in the community, to similar events at other times and places, to other people or problems that you are reminded of.
You might also see connections between this book and other writings on the same topic, or by the same author. There are no right answers. If the reading connects YOU with something, it is worth sharing!

Some connections I found with other people, places, events, authors

....
....
....
....
....
....
....

DISCUSSION DIRECTOR

Name: .... Group: ....
Book: ....

Your job is to develop a list of questions that your group might want to discuss about this part of the book. Don't worry about details; your task is to help people talk over the big ideas and to share their reactions.

Possible discussion questions or topics for today:

....
....
....
....
....
....

Adapted from: Harvey Daniels, *Literature Circles*, Stenhouse 1994 (p. 77)

Figure 6.2 Response Sheets (Set 2)

Conclusion

There is a long path of development in reader response. To extend this response in writing is a further challenge for students. However, responding in writing helps students to interact with the text and the author in significant ways. It helps them to develop a stance toward reading that may not be developed in any other way. It allows them to focus their thinking and explore their feelings. It helps them "write to learn." It also helps them to reflect upon, and rethink, their earlier responses.

To develop response through writing, it is essential that we use high-quality texts with students; the power of literature, in particular, can not be overestimated. Literature, and the teacher's use of it, must stir students to the point where they *want* to respond. In fact, quality literature is an essential prerequisite for developing quality response, tapping as it does into children's emotions and dramatically influencing their desire to respond.

References

Atwell, N. (1990) *Coming to Know: Writing to learn in the intermediate grades.* Portsmouth, NH: Heinemann, and Toronto: Irwin Publishing.

Calkins, L. (1983) *Lessons from a Child: On the teaching and learning of writing.* Exeter, NH: Heinemann.

Cassidy, J. and Cassidy, D. (2000) "What's hot, what's not for 2000," *Reading Today,* January 2000, p. 28.

Cianciolo, P. (1995) "Teaching and learning critical aesthetic responses to literature," in Sorensen, M. and Lehman, B. (eds.) *Teaching with Children's Books: Paths to literature-based instruction.* Urbana, IL: National Council of Teachers of English.

Daniels, H. (1994) *Literature Circles: Voice and choice in the student-centered classroom.* York, ME: Stenhouse Publishers.

De Bono, E. (1982) *Six Thinking Hats Resource Book.* Cheltenham: Hawker Brownlow.

Fulwiler, T. (ed.) (1987) *The Journal Book.* Portsmouth, NH: Boynton/Cook Publishers, Heinemann.

Grant, A. (1985) "Young readers reading: A study of personal response to the reading of fiction based on five case studies of students at the upper secondary school level," Doctoral thesis, University of Melbourne.

Grant, A. (1990) "Towards a transactive theory of the reading process and research in evaluation," in Legg, S. and Algina, J. (eds.), *Cognitive Assessment of Language and Math Outcomes,* Volume XXXVI in the Series "Advances in Discourse Processes," Norwood, NJ: Ablex Publishing Corporation.

Hansen, J. (1987) *When Readers Write.* Portsmouth, NH: Heinemann.

Harding, D. (1967) "Considered experience: The invitation of the novel in English," *Education* **1**(2), pp. 7–15.

Huck, C. (1979) *Children's Literature in the Elementary School.* 3rd ed., updated. New York: Holt, Rinehart and Winston.

Huck, C., Hepler, S. and Hickman, J. (1987) *Children's Literature in the Elementary School.* 4th ed. New York: Holt, Rinehart and Winston.

Lindberg, G. (1987). "The journal conference: From dialectic to dialogue," in Fulwiler, T. (1987) (ed.) *The Journal Book*. Portsmouth, NH: Boynton/Cook Publishers, Heinemann.

Lo Bianco, J. and Freebody, P. (1997) *Australian Literacies: Informing national policy on literacy education*. Language Australia (Commonwealth of Australia).

Luke, A. and Freebody, P. (1999) *Further Notes on the Four Resources Model*. Reading Online. www.readingonline.org

Mayher, J., Lester, N. and Pradl, G. (1983) *Learning to Write/Writing to Learn*. Portsmouth, NH: Heinemann, Boynton/Cook Publishers.

Meek, M. (1988) *How Texts Teach What Readers Learn*. Exeter, England: Thimble Press.

Rosenblatt, L. (1985) "Transaction versus interaction—a terminological rescue operation," in *Viewpoints* **19**(1), pp. 96–107.

Smith, F. (1982) *Writing and the Writer*. Portsmouth, NH: Heinemann.

Tiedt, I. (1989) *Reading, Thinking, Writing: A holistic language and literacy program for the K-Classroom*. Written with the National Writing Team Consultants. Boston, MA: Allyn & Bacon.

Tierney, R. *et al.* (1989) "Writing and reading working together," in Haas Dyson, A. *Collaboration Through Writing and Reading*. Urbana, IL: National Council of Teachers of English.

Children's Literature

Allen, Pamela (1991) *Mr McGee*. Ringwood, Australia: Picture Puffins.

Blume, Judy (1981) *Tales of a Fourth Grade Nothing*. London: Pan.

Browne, Anthony (1999) *Voices in the Park*. London: Picture Corgi Book.

Carle, Eric (1974) *The Very Hungry Caterpillar*. Middlesex, England: Picture Puffins.

Coerr, Eleanor (1977) *Sadako and the Thousand Paper Cranes*. London: Hodder & Stoughton.

Dahl, Roald (1982) *George's Marvellous Medicine*. Puffin Books.

Hill, Anthony (1994) *The Burnt Stick*. Ringwood, Australia: Penguin Books.

Hutchins, Pat (1970) *Rosie's Walk*. Middlesex, England: Picture Puffins.

Jones, Shelley (1999) *The Lonely Troll*. St Leonards, NSW, Australia: Horwitz Martin.

Klein, Robin (1983) *People Might Hear You*. Ringwood, Australia: Puffin.

Magorian, Michelle (1981) *Goodnight Mr Tom*. Harmondsworth: Puffin.

McKee, David (1990) *Elmer*. London: Red Fox Edition, Random House Children's Books.

McPharlin, P. (1996) *Bruce the Goose*. Sydney: Angus & Robertson.

Park, Ruth (1980) *When the Wind Changed*. Sydney, Australia: Angus & Robertson.

Ray, N. L. (1985) *The Pow Toe*. Melbourne, Australia: Nelson.

Serraillier, Ian (1956) *The Silver Sword*. Harmondsworth: Puffin.

Taylor, Theodore (1973) *The Cay*. Harmondsworth, England: Penguin.

Zion, Gene (1968) *Harry the Dirty Dog*. Middlesex, England: Puffin.

Chapter 7

From Reading to Writing:
Using Picture Books as Models
Maureen Lewis

Ask any gathering of primary teachers to name a picture book they have used successfully with their class and the titles quickly start flowing. Ask the same question of a group of teachers with a special interest in language and literacy and the flow turns to a flood. Research studies have confirmed that one of the characteristics of effective teachers of literacy is they know about, and are enthusiastic about, children's literature (Medwell *et al.* 1998; Ruddell 1995). Effective primary teachers use picture books for a wide range of reasons. Chief among these is often the sheer pleasure of sharing a good story which is well illustrated, and all teachers know the power of those moments when stories and their pictures engage and enthrall the listeners. But there are many other ways in which a picture book can enhance the experiences of the listener or reader. Via the pleasure of good picture books—fiction or nonfiction—children can be motivated to persevere at the act of reading; books play a role in increasing the reader/listener's knowledge about stories and how they are structured and how nonfiction texts are organized; books help children learn about new experiences, places, and people; they take the reader/listener away from their everyday world to realms of fantasy and imagination and—most importantly, for the purposes of this chapter— they can provide models of what it is an author and illustrator do as they create a text.

The strategy of using a picture book as a model for children's own writing is well established. In story texts picture books model how stories are structured; give experience of the many ways stories can begin, develop, and end; demonstrate how writers keep the reader's interest; how words are chosen with thought and care; how the pictures can carry some of the story or give additional information; and how the reader may have to bridge the spaces between words and pictures. Writers draw on their experiences as readers to help them develop as writers. Teachers often make this reading/ writing link explicit to children by asking them to create a written piece based directly on a picture book they have just read. The use of models for children's own writing is one of the strategies identified as effective by Hillocks in his meta-analysis on research into writing (Hillocks 1984). Although they may not know the research, many teachers know and use the strategy.

Another strategy used successfully by many teachers is that of "innovating on text," that is, taking a well-known story as a base and adding a new dimension to it. Thus, many teachers read a story to their class using an interesting picture book and then ask their children to concentrate on one aspect of story making in retelling the same tale. Hence, they may ask their children to:

- place the story in a different setting (e.g. placing Red Riding Hood in the town rather than the country);
- place the story in a different time (e.g. placing Red Riding Hood in current time rather than in "fairy tale" time);
- provide an alternative ending (e.g. having Red Riding Hood recognize and outwit the wolf);
- provide an alternative beginning (e.g. having Red Riding Hood refuse to take the cakes);
- retell the story from a different viewpoint (e.g. from the wolf's point of view);
- alter the main characteristic of the hero or anti-hero and see what impact that has on the story (e.g. making the wolf a vegetarian).

Teachers also provide picture books that demonstrate these activities for children, for example *Snow White in New York* by Fiona French, which places Snow White in a different setting and era, or *The True Story of the Three Little Pigs* by Jon Scieszka, which tells the story of The Three Little Pigs from the wolf's point of view.

Such activities are excellent ways of drawing children's attention to how different aspects of the story affect the whole, but they do little to help young writers see explicitly how the events of the story are structured. The *overall structure* of the story is already provided for the writers in such retelling tasks. Learning how to plan the structure of a whole story is a writing skill many teachers feel unsure how to teach and pupils are given limited opportunities to learn. Bereiter and Scardamalia have pointed out how our more familiar speech "texts" rarely demand that we pay attention to the overall structure of a conversation before we begin it. It is therefore not surprising that children's writing often lacks "attention to the whole, and the backwards and forward-looking analyses that are the hallmark of compositional planning" (Bereiter and Scardamalia 1982, p. 23).

The analysis of the SATs writing sample each year provides an interesting insight into what it appears children can and cannot do. These analyses confirm Bereiter and Scardamalia's claim that children's writing shows little evidence of planning at the level of the whole text. In the 1997 analysis, for example, it was reported that a key difference in children's writing (and the levels they scored) was "the way the writing was structured" (p. 8). It was noted that some of the texts "were based on *well-defined structures* with which children were evidently *familiar*" and that

where children did not have this kind of support, they had more difficulty in producing an *appropriately organized* piece of writing. This was particularly the case with stories where unshaped rambling pieces contained undeveloped events following one another in rapid succession and lacking a conclusion. (SCAA 1997, p. 8)

In this chapter I outline two case studies which show how, using picture books as models for children's own writing, we can help them develop their explicit understanding of how writing is structured. I will argue that in these case studies books provide models that enable children to overcome the kind of planning problems identified by Bereiter and Scardamalia mentioned above. I will aso argue that by making children explicitly aware of the "shape" of the model they are using, we help them to become more aware of the processes involved in creating a completed piece of writing.

What Do Children Know About Textual Structures?

Fiction Texts

Throughout the 1970s and early 1980s cognitive psychologists examined individuals' mental representations (schema) of story components and how these components fitted together (Mandler and Johnson 1977). They argued that as we listen to and read stories, so our knowledge about stories grows, and we can draw on this knowledge to help us predict and understand what is happening, and likely to happen, in new stories (Mandler and Johnson 1977; Rumelhart 1978; Stein and Glenn 1979). This accumulating knowledge of stories texts, they believed, develops in us a set of expectations for the structure of a story, helps facilitate our understanding of stories, and improves our memory/recall of a story.

This work gave rise to several classroom strategies, such as story mapping (Benton and Fox 1985), story comparison charts (Worthy and Bloodgood 1993), and story structure charts (Newman 1989).

Nonfiction Texts

In the 1980s and 1990s attention turned to generic structures of nonfiction texts. Linguists such as Christie (1985) and Derewianka (1990) argue that in any society there are certain types of text—both written and spoken—of a particular form because there are similar social encounters, situations, and events which recur constantly within that society. As these "events" are repeated over and over again, certain types of text are created over and over again. Our lives are full of occasions when similar purposes and situations produce similar texts. These authors argue that such texts have "a high degree of internal structure" (Kress 1982, p. 98) which largely remains invisible to the reader, because when texts have become conventionalized (with recognizable rules and forms), they appear to have an existence of their own—they appear "natural." Genre theory looks at these larger textual structures of a whole text—what Kress calls the "linguistic features beyond the sentence" (ibid., p. 97)—as well as the language features within these larger structures. From this work, certain categories of non-fiction texts (such as recounts, reports, explanations, and so on) and their typical generic structures and language features have been identified. The practical classroom outcome of these ideas has meant that more explicit attention is now being paid to how nonfiction texts are created.

The case studies I will now describe will draw on insights from the research outlined above.

The Classroom-Based Work

Case Study 1

Parody, picture books and text structures

In a series of classroom writing sessions, parody picture books were used as models for children's own writing. Picture books that parody familiar text types are popular with children. They invite laughter by the humorous mimicking of other genres, and they provide a perfect vehicle for making children aware of what it is that is being parodied. Parodies make clearer to us what it is we know about particular texts. As David Lewis (1994) puts it:

> Parody is innately metafictive. That is, the subject of a full-scale parody is never the apparent subject of the text. Take for example *How Dogs Really Work*. No-one in their right mind would actually believe what the book tells you. The real subject of a parody is the nature of the text parodied. Parodies present readers with a distorted but recognisable image of the genre in question. This foregrounding of text-type makes the parody an excellent vehicle for text study. (p. 58)

One of the aspects parodies can make clearer to us is the structure of the overall text.

There are many well-known picture books that parody traditional tales, but in this case study I want to briefly describe some work undertaken with picture books that parody nonfiction genres. Such books include parody "guide" books such as *School* by Colin and Jacqui Hawkins or *Dr Xargles Book of Earth Mobiles* by Jeanne Willis; parody informational reports such as *Vampires* and *Spooks* by Colin and Jacqui Hawkins, which itemize different species in the manner of bird identification books; parody work manuals such *How Dogs Really Work* by Alan Snow; and parody information books such as *The Worm Book* by Allan and Janet Ahlberg, which makes fun of the simple, single line plus picture, nonfiction texts for children.

Some common nonfiction text types, their typical generic structures, and their language features are now included in the Framework of Teaching Objectives (DfEE 1998). Helping children recognize and use nonfiction textual structures in their own writing is recommended. Strategies such as writing frames can be used to support this (see Chapter 10). Ideally, work on textual structures arises from a rich experience of texts but at its worst can be a mechanistic, didactic teaching of structure. Using books that parody typical nonfiction structures encourages the children to articulate what it is *they* know implicitly (i.e. why is this funny?) and make it explicit. Two examples illustrate this process.

How Dogs Really Work by Alan Snow

This parody comes complete with diagrams (with fatuous labels), cut-away pictures, table of contents, index, and so on. The text purports to explain dogs and their behavior. As one would expect in a manual, everything is shown in the greatest detail. There is a double-page spread devoted to the workings of each part of the dog, such as "Legs and Getting About" or "Communication." The book created great excitement and laughter when it was used with a class of ten-year-olds and led to a long discussion about its features. As they talked about the significance of the headings on each page, the children articulated that "that was how those kind of books were organized." They compared it to car manuals, manuals for electrical machinery, and to DIY manuals and talked themselves into an understanding of the logical structure of such books. Going on to create their own parodies, page by page, led to a discussion as to the order in which the pages should be assembled into a book. Did the order matter? Should it move from the whole to the parts? Should the parts be in any order and, if so, why? By the time their books were finished, these pupils had a firm understanding of how and why manuals are structured as they are. Figure 7.1 shows a page from one of the completed pupils' books.

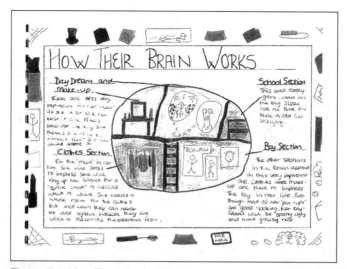

Figure 7.1 How Their Brain Works

School by Colin Hawkins

Parody guidebooks are usually forms of nonchronological reports—they begin with a definition of the items being described and then go on to itemize their characteristics. Figure 7.2 shows the teacher identification chart produced as the opening spread in the own "true guide" book created by a group of nine-year-old children. Their book was called *The True Guide to Teachers*.

This opening page was followed by the characteristics of teachers, i.e. pages on "What teachers say," "The teacher's desk," "The teacher's brain," "Teacher's clothes" and "The teacher's briefcase." The finished book is very funny and the pupils enjoyed writing it, but they also learned how to structure the text by drawing on the parody model they had read. As with the previous example, it was the comparative discussion of the parody against "straight" versions which enabled pupils to articulate knowledge which, until that moment, they barely knew they knew. But once articulated, the knowledge of text structure they had expressed was used by the pupils as they made decisions about how to structure their own texts.

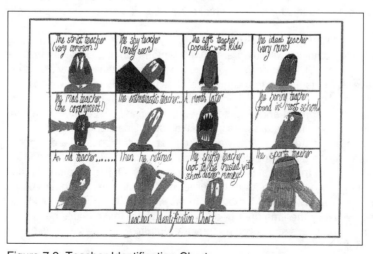

Figure 7.2 Teacher Identification Chart

Case Study 2

Using picture books with common story structures

The work described in this case study took place over one term with a class of eight-year-olds but can be adapted for older or younger children, depending on the texts selected. Working as a participant observer, alongside the class teacher, we helped children plan and write coherent and structured stories during an extended reading/writing session, which took place weekly. The sessions contained six steps and followed a process approach of gathering ideas, planning, drafting, revising, editing, and publishing. At the ideas, planning, and drafting stages, explicit attention to the overall structure of the whole story was emphasized.

1. Selecting a story structure

Stories often share a similar structure. A selection of picture book stories, narrative songs, and poems were collected under the following groupings:

- ***Cumulative stories***
  new events or physical features being added on consecutively, such as the traditional rhyme, *There was an old woman who swallowed a fly*

- ***Reverse cumulative stories***
  new events or physical features taken away, such as the traditional, *Ten Green Bottles*

- ***Journey stories***
  – linear journeys, from A–B, such as *Rosie's Walk* by Pat Hutchins
  – return journeys, from A–B–A, such as *Where's Spot?* by Eric Hill
  – circular journeys, from A–A, such as *Where the Wild Things Are* by Maurice Sendak

- ***Turning-point stories***
  character, circumstances, or physical characteristics changed by a significant event, such as the story of *King Midas and the Golden Touch*

- ***Three wishes/gifts stories***
  Characters are awarded three wishes or gifts in return for a good deed, and these are then used to help them overcome difficulties and gain a final reward. There are many traditional tales that follow this structure

- ***Wasted-wishes stories***
  In these stories, wishes are granted in return for some good deed, but these are wasted due to some flaw (greed, stupidity) in the character and they end up back where they started, such as in the traditional tale, *The Old Woman who Lived in a Vinegar Bottle*

- ***Simple problem/resolution stories***
  A very common structure. Best first introduced in a simple form—one problem which is solved, such as *Alfie Gets in First* by Shirley Hughes

- ***Days of the week stories***
  The days of the weeks are gone through sequentially and on each day, a same but different event occurs (e.g. the caterpillar eats each day but different food); on the final day a climax is reached and something new happens, such as in *Mrs Lather's Laundry* by Allan and Janet Ahlberg.

- ***The treatment of strangers stories***
  Characters meet a stranger in need. Different responses receive different rewards, with good being rewarded and unpleasantness being punished. There are many traditional tales that follow this structure.

A different story structure from the above list was used each week.

2. Enjoyment of story/experience of a particular story structure
At the start of the session the children were told that they were going to hear some stories and that although all these books/stories were different, there was something the same about them. They were asked to pay particular attention to the "pattern" of the story. Later, this terminology was changed to "structure" of the story. Two or three of the selected books were read to the whole class (or sometimes this activity was undertaken as oral storytelling) and the children encouraged to enjoy and respond to the stories. Picture books are ideal for this purpose, for not only are they appealing texts, but they offer a complete text in brief and so allow children to sample several examples in a relatively short space of time (Lewis 1997).

3. Explicit discussion of structure/graphic recording of the structure
The children were then asked about the structure of the story and in what ways it was similar in all the examples they had enjoyed. The structure was explicitly discussed, and this was followed by whole-class mapping/pictorial representation of one of the shared books. This visual representation of the story structure was drawn/scribed by the teacher on the flip chart, and the links between the representation and the story were also articulated as teacher "think-alouds" (Palincsar and Brown 1984) as the drawing progressed. This move, from recognition into a visual representation of the structure, was important for many of the children and seemed to help them fix the structure in their minds by moving it from an internal/abstract concept to an external/explicit object.

4. Independent recording of the structure
From this supported, whole-class work, the children then worked in pairs to read and map a further example of a story which had a similar structure to that shared in the whole-class activity. Here books could be differentiated according to reading ability, e.g. *Rosie's Walk* and *Hail to the Mail* both provide models of a circular journey text but make very different reading demands during their use in independent activities. Figure 7.3 shows an example of a mapping of an "A to B journey," story structure. This structure is:

• start of journey,
• events en route (either people or physical landmarks met. The events en route usually represent problems encountered and overcome),
• reaching destination,
• concluding act.

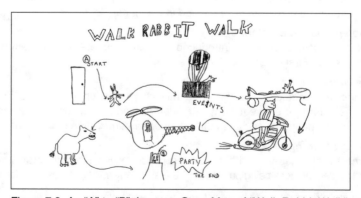

Figure 7.3 An "A" to "B" Journey, Story Map of "Walk Rabbit Walk"

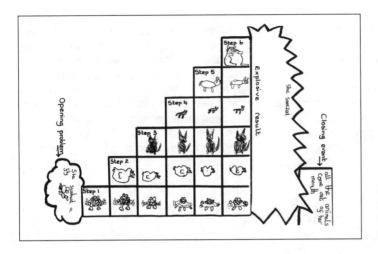

Figure 7.4 A Cumulative Story Map for "There Was an Old Woman Who Swallowed a Fly"

On other occasions, the children were given a preprepared mapping frame on which to record the structure of the story they had read. These mapping frames provided a visual prompt to the story structure. Figure 7.4 shows a completed cumulative story structure, mapping frame. The design of this frame helps the child recognize the elements of the structure:

- opening event or problem,
- addition of one new element each time,
- explosive climax when overload is reached,
- concluding event to close the story—or start the sequence again.

Graphic mapping frames were designed to reflect the story structures for turning-point stories, circular stories, and "take away" stories, and children who needed extra support rather than composing their own mapping structures used these. A further example of a preprepared mapping frame is shown in Figure 7.5.

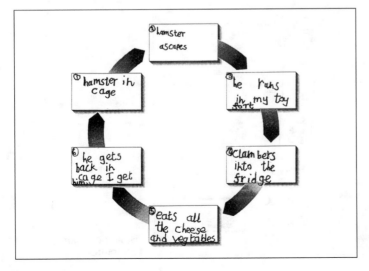

Figure 7.5 A Circular Story Map

5. Using the structure to plan their own story

From independent recording of the story structure, the children then moved into planning their own story, using the same structure. For some children, this involved moving straight into a written story plan, but for many children, it involved some kind of pictorial planning frame to help them. This planning frame was often a further blank version of the mapping frame they had just used, enabling them to see the links clearly. Several researchers have written about the link between drawing and writing in the planning phase of children's writing (Norris *et al.* 1998; Olsen 1992; Atwell 1990; Graves 1983), and the use of drawing as a pre-writing activity has been recommended, especially with children who have problems expressing themselves in written forms. Figure 7.6 shows a child's mapping of *Mrs Armitage on Wheels* (a cumulative story), using a structure recording frame. Figure 7.7 shows the subsequent planning frame for a story using the same frame.

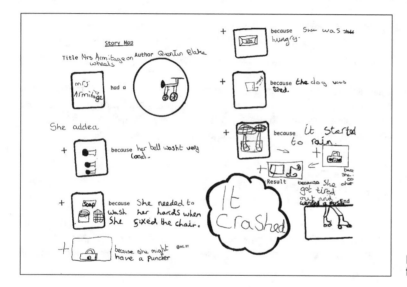

Figure 7.6 Story Map for Mrs Armitage

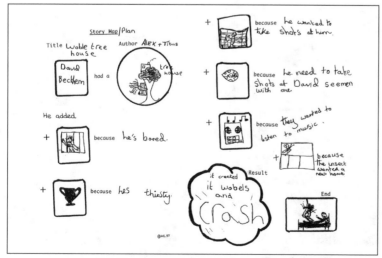

Figure 7.7 Story Plan Based on Same Structure

6. Drafting the story/sharing the drafts in a plenary

The pictorial plans were then used to write a first draft of a story. Norris *et al.* (1998), in their research on using drawing as a pre-writing activity, found significant differences between groups of children who drew before writing and those who did not do so. Their data indicate that "drawing became an effective planning strategy for the children who appeared to rely on their drawings as a reference point to prompt them towards what should come next in their writing" (p. 73).

Figure 7.8 shows the first draft of a cumulative story based on the mapping/planning structures shown in Figures 7.6 and 7.7. The close link between the "drawn" story and the writing is clear.

The story drafts were shared in a plenary session, when the rest of the class listened and commented on whether the structure was clear, and the story coherent.

Collaborative discussion

Throughout the sessions, time was given over to talk (between the teacher and the children and between pairs and groups of children) about the books being read and the stories being written. The whole-class discussion during the class mapping of the structure, the paired discussion in undertaking further mapping/drawing of another example, and the discussion engendered by joint, pictorial planning of their own story all enabled children to articulate their ideas and understandings.

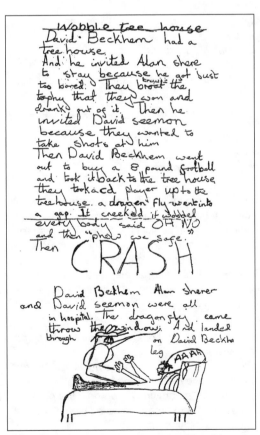

Figure 7.8 Story Written from the Plan Shown in Figure 7.7

However, it was the talk during the revising of the first draft which appeared to have the most impact on the writing these children undertook.

One group of four children, for example, first produced a well-structured but fairly ponderous and lengthy "take-away" story. The finished book, however, was very different. It was their discussion at the revising stage that led them to articulate the importance of letting the repetitive and predictable story structure "do some of the work." In the final text, each spread has the text on the left and, on the facing page, a picture of the dining table set with the meal. The dog is under the table. Under these pictures are written the words, "the dog smiled." As each page is turned, an item is missing from the table, the dog's tummy is fatter, and the dog's smile broader. In the final picture, however (a single page as opposed to the double spreads so far), we see mom for the first time, looking very cross; the dog has a huge tummy; his smile has turned to a sad expression and the usual refrain is missing. A speech bubble coming out of mom's mouth says, "You naughty dog."

The book reads as follows:

> *The Vanishing Dinner*
>
> *Mum laid the table and left the room.*
> *The dog smiled.*
> *"Where's the turkey?" said mum when she came back into the room.*
> *The dog smiled.*
> *"Where's the peas?" said mum.*
> *The dog smiled.*
> *"Where's the chocolate pudding?" said mum.*
> *The dog smiled.*
> *"Where's the wine?" said mum.*
> *The dog smiled.*
> *"Where's the potatoes?" said mum.*
> *The dog smiled.*
> *"You naughty dog!" said mum.*

The paring down of their original text to make full use of the repetitive, take-away story structure and the use of the pictures to carry some of the meaning were achieved after considerable discussion between the four children working on the book. The discussion was prompted by the teacher asking how the length of their story compared to the books they had shared. The group was then left alone to ponder this comment. During subsequent discussion they returned constantly to the picture books they had on the table before them, their pictorial map of a take-away story, and their pictorial story plan. Gradually they talked themselves into an understanding of the importance of the structure for "carrying" the reader through the text.

Kylie: *We don't need to explain it all. Look, look (pointing to some of the books on the table).*
         The pictures can explain.
Lewis: *And you can tell the story from the plan. It's not long. The writing doesn't have to be long.*
         Our plan's not long. Those books aren't long.
Kylie: *Yeah! People know what's coming. They know the pattern of the story. They know it's*
         the same but different. That something gets taken away.
Sam: *And add-on. The dog's belly. It gets big . . .*
Kylie: *We can cross this out.*

Following this discussion, the children went back over their text, crossing out their written descriptions of what the dog did, until the story given above remained.

Talk at this stage of the process was clearly effective for these children, but Beard (1988) quotes research that suggests that the effect of preparatory talk before beginning to write seems "to lessen the maturity of the subsequent writing on five out of six measures of linguistic factors" (p. 79). It may be that focused discussion around a specific aspect of writing, once the writing is underway, is more effective in supporting writing development than lengthy pre-writing discussions. Such focused discussions can be a feature of writing conferences in classrooms.

The impact of the work

In evaluating the impact of focused work on story structures outlined above, we must look closely at what the pupils said and wrote. There was much evidence to suggest that these children became more explicitly aware of story structure, with many examples of them spontaneously commenting on structures outside the writing session. For example:

John:	*When I was hearing my little brother read. The end bit of the Gingerbread Man. That's kind of a "take-away" story isn't it? Not all of it. The bit where the fox eats him bit by bit. And it's "add-on" too—all those people who chase him.*
Class teacher:	*Kylie said that she went home and read, after we'd done our session together. She then went home and looked for the same kind of patterns. So she was clearly up and away.*

Many of the children, when interviewed some weeks after the writing sessions, were able to recall and talk about story structures they now knew. They were thinking about structure as they planned stories, and they expressed keen interest in what they had done and how they wanted to continue. Ellie's comments are typical.

Ellie:	*Those story patterns. They were really interesting. It made me want to write a story. I thought my "take-away" story was really good. It was funny. When we write now my teacher always reminds us to structure our story. He tells us to know where we're going when we start.*

The class teacher felt the work had had an effect on the quality of the written work of many of the children and was particularly pleased with its effect on the quality of the writing of the less able children.

Class teacher:	*To start with, they did find it a bit difficult—when they were doing that first one some of them found it difficult . . . but last weekend I took all their books home and went through the last story and most had got a structure—some sort of pattern—and the less able children too. They didn't ramble or fizzle out. They had really got better during those weeks we were working on it.*

The work had also had an impact on the teacher's own explicit awareness of textual structures.

Class teacher:	*When we did stories (before), the plans for stories were character and setting. But I could never get my head around finding some sort of structure to base the story on because I always believed it was up to them to actually think of the structure themselves. Whereas now I can see far better how to guide them, and the results are definitely better just reading what they've come up with.*

Conclusion

Knowledge of how to structure an extended text (be it narrative or nonnarrative) is only one piece of the complex web of knowledge children need to create successful writing of their own, but it is an important and often neglected aspect of crafting a written text. In the case studies outlined above, pupils' rich experience of good picture books was always the starting point. On each occasion, they experienced the same text structures being used in individual ways while retaining a generic similarity. One of the criticisms that can be leveled against making textual structure explicit is that it can create formulaic writing, which stifles individuality and creativity. There was little evidence of this within the work produced. The wide variety of individual stories the class wrote each week showed children still using very different characters, settings, and ideas within the structures they were using. The nonfiction parodies they created are models of creativity and individuality. The class teacher in the first case study felt strongly that, far from stifling creativity, explicit teaching within the context of quality texts was a step to greater creativity.

Interviewer:	*Can it stifle children's creative initiative?*
Class teacher:	*I don't think you do stifle that. Because I remember way back to when I qualified, we weren't allowed to teach them how to paint, were we? They had to express themselves. I rarely got anything good in art, whereas now art is quite structured. You do drawings from life or whatever. You do looking at other artist's work—all those sort of things and the quality of art is much better. You see those 3D things, in the class (indicates). I long since realized that you've got to teach them something, because people only actually can be expressive when they can build on some inner knowledge...I think with structures for stories in English we're doing the same thing...They can be as imaginative as they like because they have the tools with which to build...we owe it to them to give them the groundwork...that's what primary education is about. We give them the groundwork and then, when they are able, they can take off. They can fly. There are children now who I am sure can write without the mapping or frames any more, but can use the knowledge that they now know is their own.*

References

Atwell, N. (1990) *Coming to Know: Writing to learn in the intermediate grades.* Portsmouth, NH: Heinemann.

Beard, R. (1988) *Children Writing in the Primary School.* London: Hodder & Stoughton.

Benton, M. and Fox, G. (1985) *Teaching Literature 9–14.* Oxford: Oxford University Press.

Bereiter, C. and Scardamalia, M. (1982) "From conversation to composition: The role of instruction in the developmental process," in Glaser R. (ed.) *Advances in Instructional Psychology.* London: Lawrence Erlbaum Associates.

Christie, F. (1985) *Language Education.* Oxford: Oxford University Press.

Department for Education and Employment (DfEE) (1998) *The National Literacy Strategy Framework of Teaching Objectives.* London: HMSO.

Derewianka, B. (1990) *Exploring How Texts Work.* Newtown, New South Wales: PETA.

Graves, D. (1983) "We won't let them write," *Language Arts* **55**, 635–40.

Hillocks, G. (1984) "What works in teaching composition: A meta-analysis of experimental treatment studies," *American Journal of Education* **93**(1), 133–70.

Kress, G. (1982) *Learning to Write*. London: Routledge.

Lewis, D. H. (1994) "Some recent picture books and their use in the primary classroom," in Lewis, M. and Wray, D. (eds.) *Aspects of Extending Literacy*. Papers presented at the first EXEL Conference, 1993. University of Exeter: EXEL Project.

Lewis, D. H. (1997) "Working with picture books in the primary classroom." Unpublished Conference Paper. Manchester: UKRA Conference.

Mandler, J. M. and Johnson, N. S. (1977) "Remembrance of things parsed: Story structure and recall," *Cognitive Psychology* **9**, 111–51.

Medwell, J., Wray, D., Poulson, L., and Fox, R. (1998) "Effective teachers of literacy." A report commissioned by the Teacher Training Agency. London: TTA.

Newman, J. M. (1989) "Online, The Flexible Page," *Language Arts* **66**(4), 457–64.

Norris, E., Kouider, M., and Reichard, C. (1998) "Children's use of drawing as a pre-writing strategy," *Journal of Research in Reading* **21**(1), 69–74.

Olsen, J. (1992) *Envisioning Writing: Towards an integration of drawing and writing*. Portsmouth, NH: Heinemann.

Palincsar, A. and Brown, A. (1984) "Reciprocal teaching of comprehension-fostering and comprehension-monitoring activities," *Cognition and Instruction* **1**(2).

Ruddell, R. B. (1995) "Those influential literacy teachers: Meaning negotiators and motivation builders," *The Reading Teacher* **48**(60), 454–63.

Rumelhart, D. E. (1978) "Understanding and summarizing brief stories," in LaBerge, D. and Samuels, S. J. (eds.) *Basic Processes in Reading; Perception and Comprehension*. Hillsdale. NJ: Lawrence Erlbaum.

SCAA (1997) *Standards at KS2. English, Mathematics and Science. Report on the 1996 National Curriculum Assessments for 11-years-olds*. Middlesex: SCAA Publications.

Stein, N. L. and Glenn, C. (1979) "An analysis of story comprehension in elementary school children," in Freedie, R. O. (ed.) *New Directions in Discourse Proceeding*. Norway, NJ: Ablex.

Worthy, M. J. and Bloodgood, J. W. (1993) "Enhancing reading instruction through Cinderella tales," *The Reading Teacher* **6**(4), 290–301.

Children's Books

Allan Ahlberg, illustrated by Janet Alhberg (1986) *The Worm Book*. Picture Lions. ISBN 0006633617.

Allan Ahlberg, illustrated by Janet Alhberg (1981) *Mrs Lather's Laundry*. Puffin. ISBN 0140312439.

Quentin Blake (1987) *Mrs Armitage on Wheels*. Jonathan Cape. ISBN 0224024817.

Fiona French (1987) *Snow White in New York*. Oxford University Press. ISBN 0192798081.

Colin and Jacqui Hawkins (1992) *Vampires*. Picture Lions Collins. ISBN 0006625754.

Colin and Jacqui Hawkins (1992) *Spooks*. Picture Lions. ISBN 0006625762.

Colin and Jacqui Hawkins (1994) *School*. Collins. ISBN 0001938576.

Eric Hill (1983) *Where's Spot?* Puffin. ISBN 0140504206.

Shirley Hughes (1997) *Alfie Gets in First*. Bodley Head. ISBN 0370324455.

Pat Hutchins (1970) *Rosie's Walk*. Picture Puffins. ISBN 0140500324.

Samuel Marshak, illustrated by Vladimir Radunsky (1992) *Hail to the Mail*. Bodley Head. ISBN 0370317335.

Jon Scieszka, illustrated by Lane Smith (1989) *The True Story of the Three Little Pigs*. Kestrel. ISBN 0670827592.

Maurice Sendak (1992) *Where the Wild Things Are*. Picture Lions. ISBN 0006640869.

Alan Snow (1993) *How Dogs Really Work*. HarperCollins. ISBN 0001937030.

Jeanne Willis, illustrated by Tony Ross (1993) *Dr Xargles Book of Earth Mobiles*. Red Fox. ISBN 0099881500.

Chapter 8

The Magic of Writing with Computers

Dawn Nulty

From the moment children realize that print conveys meaning, they are on a magical journey. When they reach their destination, they will have become masters of the language arts. It is the privilege of any adult sharing this journey with children to witness the development of these skills and the delight the children show in their mastery of them. It has been my immense joy to work with children at the beginning of this journey through the early years of school and to be allowed to contribute to the development of their language skills.

In this chapter I focus on the work of some young children writing with the aid of a computer. The study highlights the differences in writing and in attitudes to writing at the beginning and at the end of a two-year period. It also offers a model for school-based language work using a word processor, identifies some of the benefits of using information technology to aid the developing writer, and provides an insight into the development of children's writing ability in the early years of school.

The children who are the focus of this work were in a class of twenty-six and were mostly five years old at the beginning of the study. They were of varying abilities and many of them had entered school with very low language skills. Despite, or perhaps because of, the fact that many of the children did not have ready access to the world of books at home, they particularly enjoyed the experience of story time, when the teacher would select a picture book and read it with them. Without exception, they would sit transfixed by good-quality children's literature.

Building on this tradition of story reading came the class practice of oral story telling to stimulate the children's imaginations and also as an aid to creative writing. I would begin a story and invite the children to continue. The children had created several stories in this manner. One particular story began:

> *One day a house appeared on the playground, and although it looked like a very ordinary house it soon became clear that there was something special about it . . . It happened to be a magic house . . . and it could fly.*

Table 8.1

Magic House Story Plan (title)
Beginning—How will your story start?
Middle—What happens in your story?
End—How does your story finish?

Many written adventures ensued from this simple beginning, and I decided to exploit the children's massive enthusiasm through a language lesson on story structure that concentrated on the development of beginning, middle, and end in narrative (Table 8.1).

As an aid to the creative process and also to fulfill our information technology objectives, the children spent a one-hour session in the computer room, using a paint package to draw their magic houses. Illustration is often added as an afterthought or embellishment in the directed work of young children, but I found that to have an illustration on which to base the story is often a powerful aid to the creative process.

The children's pictures (see Figures 8.1, 8.2, and 8.3) were typical of the work produced. The houses appeared very ordinary; however, it became evident through questioning that they

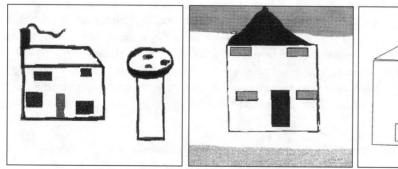
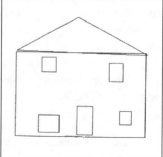

Figure 8.1 Daniel, age 5   Figure 8.2 Terry, age 5   Figure 8.3 Carly, age 5

were anything but ordinary in the imaginations of these children. Daniel's house had a smoking chimney, and yet he lived in an area where coal fires are a thing of the past. The reason his had one is that he had drawn a house from a story he heard on an earlier occasion about an empty house that needed a fire. Terry's house looked rather conventional, but, on closer examination, it was clearly set in the middle of a beach; his story was set in Turkey, where his family had recently spent a holiday. Carly's house looked the most ordinary of all, no color or scenery, but her story was very imaginative and included a genie and the concept of magic powers. It was almost as if she wanted her picture to add to the element of surprise, because, after all, aren't the most ordinary of things allowed to be magical? Remember Jack's beans that grew into a magical beanstalk!

The initial session using a paint package was followed by a further session where the children were shown how to incorporate their artwork into a document. With their computer-generated pictures and written story plans from the first language session, they began the process of using the computer to write their stories using a word processor.

In agreement with many renowned educators (Calkins 1986; Graves 1983; Smith 1982), it has long been my view that children need to realize that a piece of writing will not be completed in one session. As a result, I have always advocated that children prepare a plan, from which the process of drafting and redrafting begins.

McFarlane (1997) points out that "children don't begin the process of drafting and redraft-ing spontaneously"; she advocates the importance of teaching this process.

In order to help develop the concept of a piece of work as something to reflect on and revisit, it is important that children realize at the beginning that this is part of the task. The importance of this process can not be overemphasized; literacy is about more than decoding and encoding text. It is important that children understand that writing is a process where each stage has a part to play in shaping the whole. Writing is a means by which children can develop and communicate their ideas and feelings.

Using a word processor helps children understand that text is something to be experimented with, and, just as importantly, it makes the task of redrafting so much easier. The Kingman Report (DES 1988) noted that, "the word processor, with its ability to shape, delete and move text around provides the means by which pupils can achieve a satisfactory product" (p. 37). This is only true if the word processor is used correctly as the powerful, enabling, flexible tool it is. Statistical bulletins from United Kingdom government reports (DfE 1995) suggest that the word processor is the most used information technology tool in schools today. Unfortunately, it is also documented that while teachers do plan for the use of the word processor, it is often used as "an intelligent typewriter" (Adams 1990). Children are asked to copy type work they have previously composed using pencil and paper, and therefore fail to utilize the powerful editing capabilities of the software and come to view it merely as an aid to presentation.

As a teacher of young children, I am aware of the difficulties children have with the mechan-ics of writing, in particular with letter formation, and feel most strongly that a lack of mastery of the mechanics should not deprive the child of the writing experience itself. Children who struggle to form letters and words often know what they want to write and the ability to organize their thoughts and ideas into a piece of writing is just as important as being able to write the ideas down on paper. In an ordinary classroom situation, the teacher or classroom assistant may act as a scribe for the children. For some children, this use of a scribe is also necessary at the point of composition when using a computer. The real magic of using the computer to write is not to be found solely in the child's initial drafts, or in the teacher's guidance, or in the use of the computer itself. It is the powerful combination of all three: allowing the child the freedom to compose, allowing for sensitive teaching intervention, and alleviating the problems associated with the technical aspects of the writing process, that creates the magical achievement of a child's published story.

Hunter (1988), in his work analyzing the writing process, described a hierarchy of writing development which begins with the pencil stroke to form a letter and proceeds through the creation of words, sentences, and paragraphs, to chapters and an overall structure, intention, and plot of a book. While not everyone would agree with the finer details of Hunter's analysis, it matches quite accurately that of Carly, age seven, who, when asked how she learned to write and how the computer helped her, stated:

> First day I came to school the teacher showed me how to hold a pencil, a day after that I could write letters, then I went into the computer room and could write words with the computer and then stories.

Sadly, it doesn't happen that fast, not even for Carly, who at five years old struggled enormously with letter formation and even now at the age of seven, experiences difficulty structuring her writing to present a story. The important thing is that she is positive about her writing development because she has not experienced some of the technical problems related to writing outlined in Hunter's work (1988). If she had, then she may not have moved much beyond the first two steps of handling a pencil and forming letters; she certainly could not talk of writing stories with such ease. The computer removed the technical barriers and allowed Carly to "write," without worrying about the mechanics, thereby developing her understanding of the writing process as a whole.

The draft stories were full of the usual errors experienced within a class of five- and six-year-olds; not even a word processor can change that. Children presented me with a printout of their work and together we discussed the errors. Common errors were:

- semantic errors
- spelling errors
- punctuation errors.

In terms of the first of the three, I would read the work with the child and generally s/he would spot that the writing did not make sense, something was missing. It was then relatively easy for the child to return to his/her on-screen work and make additions to complete the work. Errors of punctuation and spelling were marked on the printouts and discussed with children. They then had to return to their on-screen work and make the corrections; in the case of punctuation, by editing the work to include capital letters and periods and with spellings by using a dictionary/word book to select the correct spelling.

Having their work on-screen meant that corrections could be made right away rather than having to copy out the whole story, making corrections as they went and possibly making errors of transcription. Loveless (1995) noted that when the classroom practice is for children to re-write work in best handwriting, they often write less to begin with so that there is less to copy out. The word processor removes the need for laborious copy writing, and this could encourage children to write at greater length.

The resulting writing was short; some children managed no more than a sentence, while others attempted to introduce setting, character, and sequence.

The old house had no curtains no beds and no fire but one day some people came into it. The people wanted the house. They moved into the house. The house was happy.	When I was in Turkey and I woke up I was in a place that wasn't my house. I went in it. It got bigger. I saw a monster and he gave me tea and then I went home.	There was a magic house that could fly in the sky. One day I found out that there was a genie in that house. The genie gave me magic powers. I could turn people into ants! Be careful!
Daniel, age 5	Terry, age 5	Carly, age 5

These early attempts at narrative writing were significant for these children, and using the computer had several benefits. The children recognized that:

- It is "funner." Daniel, age 5
- When I make a mistake I don't get a black mark on the paper from rubbing out. Terry, age 5
- The computer doesn't hurt my hand. Carly, age 5

For Daniel, the key element was fun; he was motivated by learning that contained an element of fun and excitement. Daniel liked anything new and sought to find out all he could about it. The computer added another dimension to his learning, and in his eagerness to have "fun," he actually learned a great deal about its use and developed his writing ability in the process. For Terry, the computer was a great enabler; the ability to delete his errors was magical; once he had backspaced, no evidence of the original error was left to cause comment. For Carly, the implication was that she wrote less with a pencil because her hand hurt and she had to keep stopping to rest it. This invariably meant having a chat with whoever else was "resting" their hand, consequently using up all the available time—a good excuse for talking in class, or a child's honest perception of the writing process?

The children had learned and knew intuitively what a powerful presentation tool the computer was. Within any class there is variation in ability, and most teachers work hard to achieve a consistent standard, valuing children's work and the progress they make. In this particular class there were several children whose ability to form letters was poor; consequently, there was a need to help them improve their handwriting. Using the computer in this instance did not have any direct bearing on the development of their ability in either of these areas, but it did allow them the luxury of composing their story without the worry of letter formation and other associated problems. Furthermore, in terms of raising their self-esteem, these children's final compositions were equally as well presented as their peers. Obviously, there were different levels of ability evident in the content of individual pieces of work, but the computer-generated work meant that each child's work was neatly presented and, perhaps most importantly, much admired by the children themselves. Several children who needed guidance to develop a consistent style and standard of handwriting could be quite harsh in their self-criticism, but on this occasion they were immensely proud of their work.

As stated at the beginning of the chapter, this study was conducted in two parts. Two years after the initial work was completed, I once again had the opportunity to work with the same children, now mostly aged seven. It was interesting to see how they had developed in terms of both computer and writing skills. I retold the original *Magic House Story,* and the children discussed their initial pictures and stories which I had brought along to share. Before inviting them to compose new stories, I asked them to draw another magic house, once again using the same paint package on the computer.

The original magic house pictures had been almost traditional in style—just ordinary houses—but the second batch contained many different elements. The latest drawings were more imaginative and elaborate than the originals, having wings, faces, portals, feet, aliens, and other magical features (see Figures 8.4, 8.5, and 8.6).

Daniel, who at five borrowed his ideas from an existing story, felt able at seven to draw purely from imagination, and his house had a face and arms. Terry, who had used his experience of a holiday in Turkey to draw his first house, once again placed his house in a particular setting; this time, the theme was space age and his house resembled a rocket. Carly, who at five had drawn the most ordinary of all the houses, now drew a house full of color, with a face and legs.

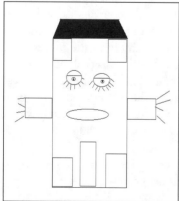
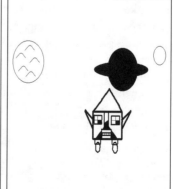

Figure 8.4 Daniel, age 7   Figure 8.5 Terry, age 7   Figure 8.6 Carly, age 7

The children were asked to plan and compose a story once again. Upon reading these stories, it was noticeable that they, too, like the second set of illustrations, contained many magical elements that had not been present in the originals—and—they showed a greater grasp of story structure.

One day I woke up on an ordinary Wednesday. I had my breakfast and went to school but there was a weird-looking house in the middle of the playground. My friends Dylan and Thomas knocked on the door. It opened and we all went inside. Thomas invited everybody in the playground to come in and then people began to shout that the house was taking off. Luckily it was out of fuel and we could all get back to the playground. Mr Heaton came out and said to the house "You are expelled." The house told him it was out of fuel so Mr Heaton decided it was safe to let the house live in the playground and play with the children and that's just what it did. Even now you can come to our school and find the house in the playground.

Daniel, age 7

One time long ago there was a house. It was no ordinary house because it had magical powers. It landed at our school and we all got in. When we looked out of the windows the land was black and fireballs were crashing into electricity lines. The house flew us away from there and we went to live in space. One day a dragon came and was throwing flames at the house and so the house flew back to earth and landed in our playground again. When we looked out of the window, everything was back to normal so we left the house, waved goodbye and went to school. "Terry, time for school, wake up!" "Mum, I had a brilliant dream, I wonder if there will be a house in the playground today." "Get dressed Terry, you and your dreams." The End

Terry, age 7

One day I was walking in the park when I saw a strange little house that had never been there before. I knocked on the door and it opened by itself. I walked in and a voice said, "Don't be afraid, I won't harm you. My name is ET. Would you care to join me for a cup of bug tea?" "Thank you" I said. ET asked me to sit down and then told me how he got to the park. He said the house was a flying one and it had flown him from Mars but crashed and fell to earth and now it wouldn't start. He asked me to help him fix it. We worked hard to fix the house and I didn't go home until 11pm. The next day I went back and we worked some more. By 9pm the house was fixed and ET went back to Mars, I waved him off and we both lived happily ever after.

Carly, age 7

The children's imaginative writing abilities had clearly developed over the past two years. In addition, each child was able to write in more depth and showed greater awareness of setting, character, and descriptive language. So whereas a child at age five years might have written, "I saw a house," the same child at age seven years was more likely to write, "I saw a weird-looking house in the field."

Daniel at seven didn't need to borrow ideas from other authors and wrote at length about his magical house, setting it within his own experience, incorporating the element of surprise, and bringing his story to a satisfactory conclusion. Terry sets his story in the familiar surroundings of the school playground but rapidly transports us into space, encounters a fire-breathing dragon before returning us to earth and the realization that he had been dreaming. Carly at seven has developed her use of setting and descriptive language; her opening is now much more thoughtful and her story follows through a series of events, with a happy conclusion.

The children's writing had shown much improvement over a two-year period, but it was evident from their stereotyped openings and resolutions that more work would be needed in these two areas.

Regular computer teaching meant that the children's computer skills were also more fully developed and for many this made the editing process a more independent activity. The children were working with Microsoft Word 97, which gave them access to some quite sophisticated software tools. Most children were familiar with the concept of a spellchecker and employed this to good effect in their first draft, essentially performing some self-editing before presenting their work to me.

Ciaron, a seven-year-old, with well-developed computer skills, used the spelling/grammar check to assist him with the drafting process (Figure 8.7).

Ciaron knew that the wiggly lines were there to show him that something was not quite right. Often, the wiggly line was enough to make him reassess his work and work out the correction. However, if he needed help, by selecting the "spelling and grammar" option on the word processor, he received on-screen help in the form shown in Figure 8.8.

The text appears in the upper window with the misspelled word highlighted. The bottom window offers suggestions for what the word may be and the child selects the correct spellings by clicking the mouse and selecting the change button.

The Magic House

One day I saw a wierd looking house. I knocked on the strange looking door. I seen a switch and I fell into a portal.
I was transported to a very big room. I saw a wierd looking person he turned round and chased me into another portal this time it took me to my bedroom. I opened my eyes and I found out it was only a dream.
BOOM!!! I saw it again "here it goes again" I said. I looked out of the window It was only Dad building a shead.

Ciaron

Figure 8.7

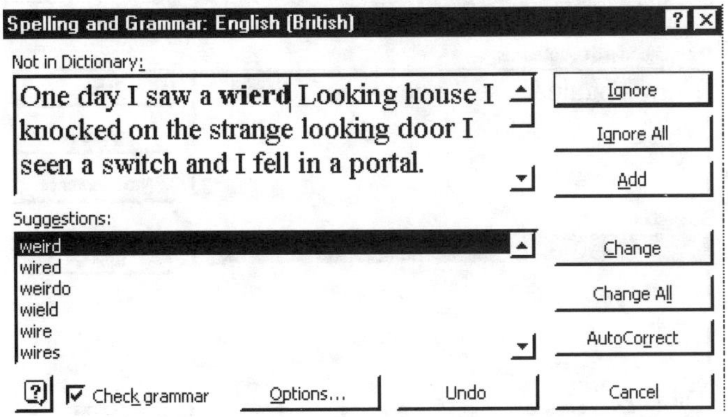

Spelling and Grammar: English (British)

Not in Dictionary:

One day I saw a **wierd** Looking house I knocked on the strange looking door I seen a switch and I fell in a portal.

Ignore
Ignore All
Add

Suggestions:

weird
wired
weirdo
wield
wire
wires

Change
Change All
AutoCorrect

☑ Check grammar   Options...   Undo   Cancel

Figure 8.8

Ciaron's second error was identified as one of punctuation by the software (Figure 8.9), however, Ciaron knew it was customary to use only one exclamation mark. He used several as a presentation technique, in much the same way as he enlarged the font size for the word *Boom*. He was experimenting with using the appearance of text for dramatic effect and so could ignore the advice offered by clicking the "ignore" button.

The third error was one of speech punctuation (Figure 8.10). Ciaron omitted the comma before closing the speech marks. This facility was particularly useful to the class, as punctuating speech was one of the language objectives we had been working on. Once again, the software highlights the error and gives the correction; Ciaron accepted this by clicking on the "change" button.

The final error was identified as a spelling mistake and again suggestions were given (Figure 8.11). Ciaron's spelling errors had been so close to the original word that each time the correct spelling was the first on the suggestion list. Again he just had to click the "change" button and the error was corrected.

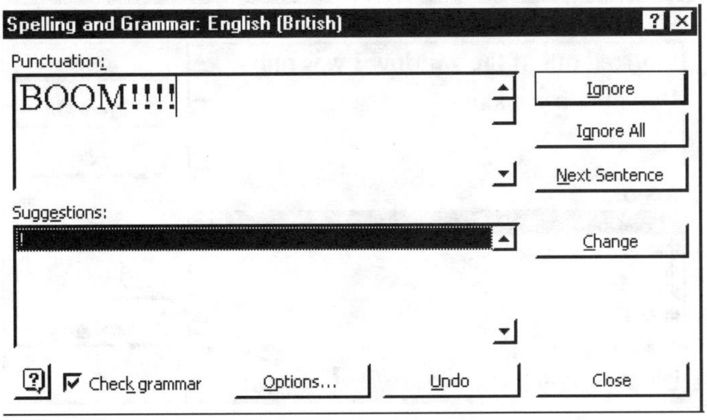

Spelling and Grammar: English (British)

Punctuation:

BOOM!!!!

Ignore
Ignore All
Next Sentence

Suggestions:

!

Change

☑ Check grammar   Options...   Undo   Close

Figure 8.9

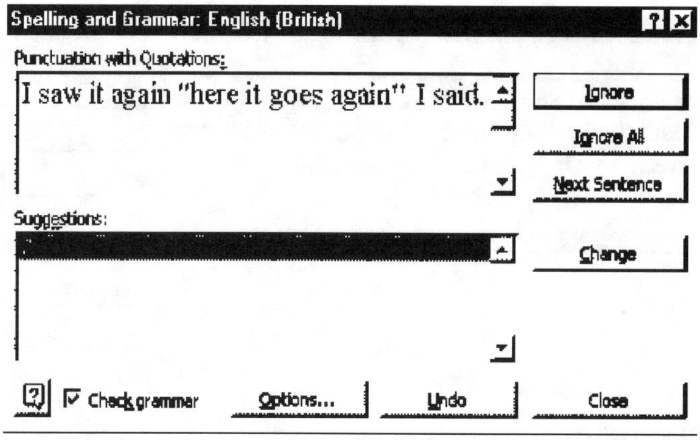

Spelling and Grammar: English (British)

Punctuation with Quotations:

I saw it again "here it goes again" I said.

Ignore
Ignore All
Next Sentence

Suggestions:

Change

☑ Check grammar   Options...   Undo   Close

Figure 8.10

The use of these software features meant that I spent less time correcting errors of punctuation and spelling and was therefore able to spend more time working with children to develop their drafts in terms of composition. When I first read Ciaron's work, it was error-free in terms of spelling and punctuation due to his ability to utilize the spelling/grammar check; however, it still required a lot of work in terms of structure and character development.

At the start of the study, the children were still beginning writers and had many skills to develop; by the second phase of the study, two years later, they had all made significant progress with their writing and many had begun to develop a consistent writing style; they were more aware of issues of presentation and audience. Using the word processor provides a forum for discussion, as identified by the Kingman Report (DES 1988), and encourages children to discuss the nature and likely impact of their writing. Furthermore, children begin to talk about appropriate structure, correct punctuation and spelling, and vocabulary suitable for their audience. The thesaurus facility of

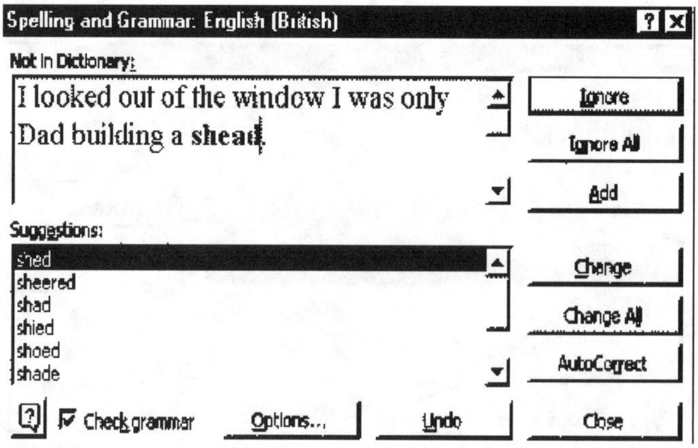

Spelling and Grammar: English (British)

Not In Dictionary:

I looked out of the window I was only
Dad building a shead.

Ignore
Ignore All
Add

Suggestions:

shed
sheered
shad
shied
shoed
shade

Change
Change All
AutoCorrect

☑ Check grammar   Options...   Undo   Close

Figure 8.11

the software encouraged children in their consideration of language use and fulfilled another of our language objectives, that of understanding the purpose and organization of a thesaurus.

Children were particularly eager to present their work well and enjoyed experimenting with the presentation features of the software, such as alignment of text and the whole layout of their work. When asked how the computer helped them with their writing, there was no shortage of answers. The children identified four of their favorite features:

- You don't have to sharpen a computer.
- You can make your writing look different.
- You can write with any color.
- You can change the font.

The first comment referred to the time-wasting chore of sharpening pencils when writing. What the children were saying was that the quality and clarity of the computer font never alters—the pencil is always sharp. The second feature admired by the children was the selection of available fonts, so that they could experiment with the "look" of their work. Carly, who liked her work to be well presented and neat, enjoyed using the computer because, "Their handwriting (the computer's) is better than mine." However, the more adventurous Daniel, who used fonts to good effect, said "The fonts are good because I can't draw those letters." Daniel liked to use intricate and fancy fonts to match the content of his stories. The third and fourth features identified by the children were again to do with presentation, the use of colors, and the size of text.

These children usually wrote using black lead pencils and were encouraged towards a consistent size and appearance of letters as laid down by school policy. The magic of word processing took them away from this ordered and colorless land and allowed them to paint their stories in whichever colors and shapes seemed most appropriate to them. It was interesting to note that what the children had identified were all technical aspects and none related to the composition of their work.

The children were clearly motivated to use the computer as an aid to the writing process. It has been said that children who are good at handwriting are not motivated to use the computer (Stradling *et al.* 1994), but this was not the case here. All children expressed a preference to compose at the computer, valuing the assistance it offered them in terms of editing aids and versatility of fonts, size, and color. Indeed Cassie, one of the more able writers in the class, commented that, while using the computer is not faster, it is preferable because it makes you slow down and think. She went on to explain that "I rush with a pencil but not with the computer." This "rushing" caused her to make many minor errors of punctuation and spelling, which didn't happen when she used the word processor, because the on-screen spelling/grammar checker highlighted her mistakes and allowed her to self-correct.

Using a word processor as an aid to the writing process, with careful teacher intervention, was certainly an extremely positive learning experience for these children. It provided the motivation necessary to stimulate some of the lower attaining children and provided the higher attaining children with enough scope to stimulate their learning even further. "Being able to capture and represent our thoughts in the form of written text and have them available for further scrutiny is an important ingredient in thinking and learning" (Jessel 1992, p. 23). To encourage children to reflect on their writing, it is important to encourage them to view it as something that can be changed, something to be experimented with in the process of learning.

The word processor offers us a medium which makes such change and experimentation more accessible to all, especially children and adults who lack basic literacy skills. "The computer can remove some of the obstacles and open up new areas of learning. Young writers become more adventurous because the word processor allows them to make changes easily" (NCET 1994, p. 9).

Information technology, like time, never stands still, and it is worth noting that future developments will enhance the use of computers in the classroom even further. This study has concentrated on how the computer removes some of the technical aspects of writing, allowing children to concentrate more on the compositional aspects. However, most children will still require teacher intervention to model and guide their ideas into coherent text. The development of voice-recognition software means that children will no longer need to dictate their stories to the teacher but will be able to speak directly into a microphone and see their composition appear on the screen in front of them. Certainly such software would have speeded up the drafting process for some children and, more importantly, would have led to greater feeling of independence. More teacher time would then have been available to work with children to develop their drafts.

The benefits and the necessity of incorporating the use of computers into language work cannot be overstated. A basic word processor, sensitive teaching, and a knowledge of the process of writing can lead to great things, but it is the enthusiasm of the children for this medium that is the real magic of writing with computers.

References

Adams, A. (1990) "The potential of Information Technology within the English Curriculum," *Journal of Assisted Learning* **6**, pp. 232–38.

Calkins, L. (1986) *The Art of Teaching Writing.* Portsmouth, NH: Heinemann.

Department for Education (DfE) (1995) *Statistical Bulletin: Survey of Information Technology in Schools.* London: HMSO.

Department for Education and Science (DES) (1988) *Report of the Committee of Inquiry into the Teaching of English Language, Kingman Report,* London: HMSO.

Graves, D. (1983) *Writing: Teachers and children at work.* Portsmouth, NH: Heinemann.

Hunter, P. (1988) "The writing process and word processing," *Microscope Special: Writing,* pp. 3–8.

Jessel, J. (1992) in McFarlane, A. (1997) *Information Technology and Authentic Learning.* London: Routledge.

Loveless, A (1995) in McFarlane, A. (1997) *Information Technology and Authentic Learning.* London: Routledge.

McFarlane, A. (1997) *Information Technology and Authentic Learning.* London: Routledge.

National Council for Educational Technology (NCET) (1994) *IT Works.* Coventry: NCET.

Smith, F. (1982) *Writing and the Writer.* London: Heinemann.

Stradling, B., Sims, D., and Jamison, J. (1994) *Portable Computers Pilot Evaluation Report.* Coventry: National Council for Educational Technology.

Chapter 9

Aspects of Gender: How Boys' and Girls' Experiences of Reading Shape Their Writing

Elaine Millard

Reading seems to me to be the essential fundamental source of knowledge about writing from the conventions of transcription to the subtle differences of register and structures in various genre.

(Smith 1982, p. 177)

Issues of Gender

In this chapter, I intend to draw out from a range of writing accumulated over the past ten years (a period which coincides with the establishment of a National Curriculum in England and Wales) some differences in approaches to writing, which I have observed in boys and girls undertaking similar writing tasks. The pieces range from early work produced in the primary grades (ages five to seven) to others completed during the first term of secondary education. These latter are used to provide some indication of what young writers may appear to have learned about the writing process by the time they enter the secondary phase of their education.[1]

Before looking in detail at particular examples, it is important to state that, although I will be making broad distinctions between the writing interests and achievements of boys and girls, my intention is not to suggest that all boys and all girls fit neatly into the categories I describe. Gender differences stretch across a broad continuum, and there are many boys who excel—indeed delight—in writing, just as there are girls who find it "boring" and who choose to do as little as they can. When I recently canvassed a group of thirty-six student English teachers about what had convinced them that they were "good at English," it was one of the eight male students who put a love of writing as the key motivation to his choice of subject, citing Terry Pratchett and the writers of the Blackadder series as his early models. Most of the women students reported variations on a theme which linked personal experiences of family, relationships, and career to the central themes of books they had encountered at home and in school, naming for the most part classic texts like *Little Women* and *Jane Eyre*. Similarly, I have found that boys who achieve in the subject have many strengths, including greater technical audacity and a more adventurous vocabulary.

With this in mind then, it is essential to stress the importance of asking which boys and which girls require most support rather than making blanket judgments about whole classes. Nevertheless, I have found repeatedly that there are sufficient observable differences in the writing of boys and girls which, when recognized, will not only help the teacher guide an individual's progress, but also suggest ways of introducing and differentiating writing tasks within a whole class. It is the identification of such differences which forms the subject of the next part of this chapter.

I have argued previously that boys and girls see aspects of their literacy as reflections of their developing sense of identity, and this is intimately bound up with what is considered appropriate behavior for boys, and what is acceptable in a girl. Reading and writing in school become inextricably caught up in this gender game (Millard 1994, 1997, 1999). And so, despite the importance of acknowledging the areas where boys do perform well, whenever I test out the thesis developed in *Differently Literate* (1997) that more girls than boys relate positively to the language curriculum in school, I find collaborative evidence. Before writing this, I revisited the Nottinghamshire primary school where had I completed a research project in 1992, to ask six Year 3 children (ages 8–9), Year 5 (ages 9–10) and Year 6 pupils (ages 10–11) about their writing. At the same time, I asked a teacher in a Northampton primary school to ask pupils to report on the aspects of their current writing which they enjoyed most.

The Role of Review

In order to form an opinion of individual pupil's writing interest, I am in the habit of asking pupils to review carefully the work they have completed so far in the year and to extract a piece of writing with which they feel pleased, alongside one that they have found less satisfactory.[2] I taped writing conferences with the eighteen Nottingham pupils and received short written reports from the pupils in the Northampton class. On this occasion I found enthusiasm from a number of the boys about specific aspects of some of their writing. In the Nottingham group, for example, all three boys from a Year 6 group showed me pieces of work which they had contributed to a news page on their school web site. The use of laptop computers and the privilege of being allowed out of their own, into other classes, to interview pupils, had provided a strong motivation for their work. In the written reports from the Northhampton group, I also found three out of fifteen boys who indicated that they really enjoyed some aspects of their schoolwriting. In this case, they had sent me copies of imaginative stories they had been producing, some of them relating to a science topic describing the effects of bacteria on the teeth and bowels.[3] This is a narrative genre I had already found to be popular with eleven-year-old boys, from stories called *Pat the Particle*, collected as part of the evaluation of a Secondary literacy project, and *A Day in the Life of Sam Sperm* displayed on the walls of one school I visited. The more scatological references that can be sneaked in, it seems, the more interesting the boys find the writing task!

However, in both groups, there were many more girls who expressed a keen delight in writing and far fewer who described the task of writing as "boring." From the Northampton school, six out of ten girls told me that they positively enjoyed writing, and all but two of them chose narrative as their favorite piece of work. Further, only one of these girls said she found writing completely boring, compared with six of fifteen of the boys in her class. Of the Nottingham pupils, five girls said they wrote for their own pleasure at home, in comparison with only one of the boys. In addition, the boy reported that the main impetus to write at home came from his father, a schoolteacher, who set him little writing tasks to do on their shared computer. Boys who openly admitted to enjoying writing remained in a minority.

This is not the place to discuss in detail reasons why many girls see themselves as successful writers at an earlier age than most boys; however, in previous research I have pointed to ways in which early experiences may shape such gender preferences. It remains the case that girls are often provided with writing materials and experiences of writing earlier than boys, a tendency which acts to reinforce a predisposition to choose writing activities in early learning situations, both at home and in school. As Sue Pidgeon has shown, young children use differences in early reading both "to reflect and confirm gender identity" (1993, p. 34), and the same can be argued for their writing.

In Table 9.1, I have recorded the written comments collected from the Northampton group in response to the question: I think writing is... Where more than one pupil has made the same comment, I have included the number in parentheses.

Table 9.1 I Think Writing Is . . .

Boys' Comments	Girls' Comments
Really boring (3 pupils)	Writing is boring because we do it every day and it's just boring.
Boring or Quite boring (3)	OK (2 pupils)
OK, but it makes my fingers hurt. OK, but it is hard to think of ideas. (2)	It is both fun and stupid—stupid when we do adjectives, fun when we do stories.
OK because it is a practical skill. (2)	It is good—you get to express your feelings and emotions.
Writing is helpful because it helps your ability to write neater and tidy.	Writing is imaginative. I love writing stories
OK—you get to use long words and increase your vocabulary.	It's good you get to use your imagination.
All right because I am good at stories and can use my imagination.	It is fun.
OK—I come up with good things to write about.	Good. I like story writing best of all because you don't have to be realistic and you get to make new people up, which is great.
I think handwriting is good because it improves my writing and I get a bigger vocabulary.	Writing is active love.
Total 15 pupils	Total 10 pupils

It is clear from these comments that writing is something that more girls than boys in this class relish as a matter of personal choice. This is a finding which has been repeated wherever I have sought pupils' views. Although I always encounter a small number of boys who enjoy writing in school, I have rarely encountered boys who admit to writing at home. The finding is also not in any way new. A quarter of a century ago, Carolyn Steedman recorded *The Tidy House*, a narration of working class domestic life as perceived by a group of eight-year-old girls, contained in a long collaborative story which they composed spontaneously during a single week in the summer of 1976. She commented:

> Every instinct possessed by those who grew up in the culture that produced *The Tidy House* insists that it must have been written by little girls and that it could never have been written by little boys. In the classroom where Linda, Melissa and Carla (the writers) worked, little boys did write, certainly not with the alacrity displayed by the girls, but sometimes at great length producing episodic, epic adventures with lone male heroes moving through time and space. As a group, the boys in this particular classroom (as in many others) demonstrated far less competence in reading and writing than did the girls. Several of them were only just beginning to read at the age of eight and did not have the means to produce extended pieces of writing. (Steedman 1982, p. 135)

I want to discuss the differences in boys' and girls' choice of story theme, and its implications for the developing writer, in more detail below.

Readers into Writers

As an advisory teacher with responsibilities for the introduction of the National Curriculum, I first began collecting samples of writing at the end of Key Stage 1 and 2 (ages 7 and 11) in order to make preliminary judgments of how teachers could be supported in arriving at their own assessments of pupils' work. Once the writing had been collected and levels agreed, other issues arose, and it is one such issue I want to consider first.

It concerns the importance of understanding the kinds of prior knowledge that pupils bring to any written task they are given in school. Models of what is appropriate to writing are acquired in many ways, but one of the main sources in the early years is familiarity with stories (Wells 1987; Weinberger 1996). In the piece (Figure 9.1) written by Hugh Pascall, which I have used as illustration in an earlier book (Millard 1994), it is, I think, quite easy to see the source of the young writer's inspiration. Although he was set the task of writing after having heard a story, called *Alistair's Time Machine* (Sadler 1986), read in class, his version is powerfully influenced by recollections of another children's picture book, Maurice Sendak's (1963) *Where the Wild Things Are*. Sendak's is a text full of suspense in which Max, dressed in a wolf suit, is sent to bed without supper for acts of mischief of one kind or another. Max is transported in a small boat from his bedroom, over an ocean, to a land where huge monsters "roll their terrible eyes and gnash their terrible teeth." He becomes king of these wild things and leads them in a wild rumpus which he thoroughly enjoys, but which he chooses to leave in order to return to the security of his own home. When he returns "he found his supper waiting for him and it was still hot." This last clause is printed memorably at the bottom of an otherwise blank page, at the end of the book.

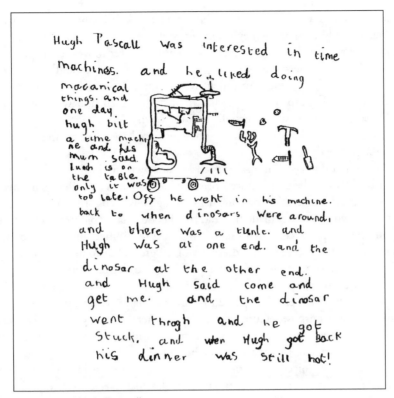

Figure 9.1 Hugh Pascall

Hugh's story ending, however, is not directly copied from Sendak, but rather adapted to serve his own purposes. Teachers who have marked endless children's stories which find no better conclusion than "he awoke and it was all a dream," will instantly recognize Hugh's originality. Perhaps less readily noted, but just as remarkable in a writer of this age, is his consistent use of the third person as the omniscient narrator.

Compare Hugh's story with this story opening written recently by a ten-year-old boy practicing for a national writing test:

One day Jay said to his mum: "Can I have the keys to the shed please?"
"What do you want them for?"
"I want them so I can get the shovel out"
"OK."
Mum got the shed keys off the high hook and gave them to me. I walked up to the shed and got out the spade

The teacher comments:

This story is good but you made the big mistake of writing "I" instead of "he." Remember who you are writing about.

On the contrary, I would argue that the writer did know whom he was writing about, intending a version of himself as the key character of the story, but slipped out of his role in the text as omniscient narrator. The key moment is when the writer moves from speech to narrative description. At this point, he completely forgets his narrative stance and reverts to a personal recount of events, something which Australian research has shown is common in inexperienced writers who have a weak grasp of genres other than those which deal with personal experience (Education Department of Western Australia 1994).[4] In the light of many pupils' preference for first person narrative throughout the primary phase, we are better able to appreciate Hugh's skill in sustaining a narrative distance.

Hugh's early reading has clearly supported his story writing in three ways. He incorporates drawing into his text, as all the best picture stories do, he sustains a consistent narrative stance, and finally, he brings his story to a satisfying conclusion. Hugh has been fortunate enough to have been a member of a class whose teacher made the reading of good-quality picture books an essential part of all her pupils' early experience. Hugh's school was next to a public library, and on the occasions I visited his classroom to observe the children at work, I grew accustomed to finding them poring over new picture books, supporting each other's reading and sharing opinions.

Teachers can encourage a similar influence in all stages of schooling by choosing books to present to their pupils which embody powerful forms of narrative and which offer models they can adapt for their own purposes. Currently, many teachers are using pupils' interest in horror, gothic, and "chiller" stories to help develop an understanding of setting. There are, however, many other kinds of narrative that may act as a holding form.

Figure 9.2 shows two pieces of writing done in the same year as Hugh by an eleven-year-old boy in his first week of the first term of secondary school, which I have selected to show how pupils benefit from being given literary models.

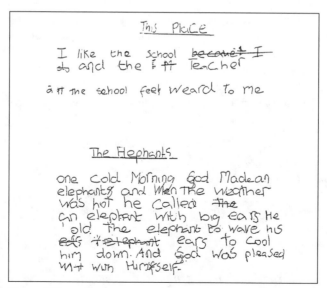

Figure 9.2

The older boy has some learning difficulties, and his first piece of work for his secondary English teacher clearly shows how little understanding he has of how to accomplish the written task that has been set. He has managed to complete only a title and two unconnected lines. Prior to the teacher's invitation, "Write about what you think of your new school," there had been a class discussion and "brainstorm" about the features of the new school which were different from life in the primary school. The teacher endeavored to guide the pupils by writing a series of questions on the board, and this particular writer has attempted to "answer" them as if they were a comprehension task. This has prevented him from shaping a meaningful piece of work.

The task of moving from spoken language to a written report is too complex for him, and his writing would require a more sustaining structure in order for him to succeed. In surveying the writing of eleven-year-olds for an evaluation of a Key Stage 3 literacy project, I found a large number of examples of such pieces of writing from across the curriculum, whether they were aimed at outlining the collection of rainwater in the Sheffield area or describing the stages of a design project; many of the pieces were left incomplete. Teachers hope that their questions will prompt the writer's understanding, but often the written work that is produced is fragmentary when read without the worksheet and meaningless for later revision.

In the boy's second piece, written only a week later, there is a much stronger sense of an appropriate genre.

The Elephant

One cold morning God made an elephant and when the weather was hot he called an elephant with big ears. He told the elephant to wave his ears to cool him down. And God was pleased with Himself.

The narrative is a re-working of one of Ted Hughes's fables from *How the Whale Began* (1963). Again, the story is not directly copied from the model, but the writer has been able to pick up on the rather biblical tones of the text. A more able boy finds the story a stimulus to a vividly imaginative response.

WHY THE POLAR BEAR IS PURE WHITE

When God created the animals he created the polar bear first.

"My first animal shall be the greatest of them all, therefore he shall have the brightest colours," God said. He placed him carefully on the earth and set him off on his way. Five days later (when all the animals had been made) the polar bear saw how brightly coloured he was, compared to all the others. He stuck his nose up in the air and turned around as he said,

"I am not staying around with all of you lot. You're all too common and short of colours, whereas I'm bright and brilliant!" and with that he walked away. All of the other animals were shocked and annoyed at this, so the lion, the leader of them all decided to have a meeting.

"We are gathered here to discuss what to do about the polar bear," the lion said.

"He's so stuck-up!" squawked the parrot, and all the other animals agreed.

"I suggest," continued the lion, "that we play some kind of trick on him for his selfishness, but what shall we do?"

There was a short pause and then the monkey said,

"I've got it, we'll hide behind a rock with a sheet over us and then jump out at him, making horrible noises, that should scare him silly," and the animals agreed that was what they'd do; so, in the morning, as the polar bear was taking his morning walk admiring himself by the river, they all jumped out at him. The polar bear was so frightened, that he froze in shock and went totally white. God had seen all of this and called out with a boom,

"Polar bear you have been so snobby, selfish, immature and such a show-off, for that reason your punishment will be to be totally white for ever."

And that is why the polar bear is pure white to this day.

Examples of a more spontaneous use of models derived from private reading can be found in the work of both boys and girls. However, when left to draw on their own resources, many boys turn to different kinds of narrative pleasure for their inspiration. From the stories they invent in their earliest play to those they write in later English lessons, many boys favor narrative models which reflect a delight in action and conflict. Their stories derive more often from visual rather than written texts, and draw upon the conventions of comic books, television, and video for both plot development and dialogue.

Vivien Gussy Paley (1984) recounts two contrasting narratives from Chicago nursery children who are reporting back on the stories they have devised in a creative play area. Paley discovered that the patterns of activity and passivity found in the early play preferences of boys and girls were replicated in the more formal stories told after play—as in the following:

We sneaked up in the house. Then we put the good guys in jail. Then we killed some of the good guys. Then the four bad guys got some money and some jewels.

Once there were four kittens and they found a pretty bunny. Then they went to buy the bunny some food and they fed the baby bunny and then they went on a picnic.

Not only are the contents of the boys' and girls' stories quite different, with the girls' narrative located firmly in childhood tales of anthropomorphic creatures (such as *Peter Rabbit* or *My Little Pony*) and the boys in the tough world of cops and robbers, but the embryonic narrative structures differ markedly, too. The girls' story demonstrates the emergence of the early discourse markers of continuous prose fiction. There is a traditional story opener, "Once," and the connectives are used to signal both chronology and consequence: "then," "and," "and then"—though, as we would expect, they are the simplest ones. The boys' story, on the other hand, relies heavily on an account of one action following another rather like a storyboard for a film or television drama.

In a discussion on the differences in the play narratives she had recorded over time in her classroom observations, Paley comments:

During a two day period in May the boys tell eleven stories: three *Star Wars*, two *Mighty Mouses*, one *Superman*, one jailhouse, two Draculas, one *Woody Woodpecker* and one *Tom and*

Jerry. Except for *Star Wars*, the inspiration for all the stories comes from television. (The girls dictated eight stories on those two days and did not include a single television or movie character.) (1984, p. 106)

The next two stories were produced in the first term of secondary school, one by a boy, the other by a girl. On this occasion, the class had read Nicholas Fisk's story, *Grinny* (1973), in which a boy describes the arrival of a strange old aunt, as a guest in his family, who is found later to be an alien. The class had been asked to write their version of the arrival of an alien being to earth. The stories began:

> *The night was dark and cold. There wasn't a sound to be heard. Suddenly, there was a dazzling light in the sky, flashing. All this was happening above Cross Street, a small street. A little boy called Luke lived in one of these houses. He was looking out of his bedroom window and when he saw these bright flashes of light he ran down stairs and started shouting,*
> *"Look, look, mum and dad, look!"*
> *They all rushed outside, by which time most of the neighbours were already outside, staring up at the bright sky. People were amazed at what they saw. Some shouted out, "It's a UFO!"*
> *"No, it's a spaceship!"*
> *"Whatever it is I don't like the look of it."*
> *The dazzling light seemed to start drifting down to Earth. After ten minutes or so, the bright light was only about ten metres away from the people. It finally touched down.*

> ### Chapter One
>
> #### The Year 3045
> *Scorpion storm troopers led an attack against Goblin High Command, Krane war troopers led a frontal assault against the dreadlock troopers. They were massacred and only a few escaped. Only one managed to get to a ship. He abandoned the war-torn planet. He set course for a planet called Earth.*
> *After travelling a few light years the shuttle crash-landed on Earth. Suddenly he emerged from the hatch. He slowly prowled over to the bushes. Two boys were walking by the road—then he attacked!*

It is not difficult to decide which of the two pieces was written by the girl, which by the boy. In fact, the second piece reproduces the epic proportion that Steedman quoted above, attributed to younger boys' narratives. Yet each story can be said to succeed in its own terms. The boy has deployed a more challenging vocabulary, his story has a broad historical sweep and introduces universal themes of conquest; with sufficient care, it would lend itself to large-scale epic. In sharp contrast, the girl shows a keener interest in the small boy who is her narrative focal point and begins to build up a picture, not of the universe, but of the small community in which he lives. However, there is a difference in the value school usually places on each kind of work. Boys' narrative preferences often hinder the production of texts which satisfy broad criteria for success in school writing tasks in English. Their stories appear less well developed, more fragmentary, and rarely have a detailed account of setting or character, which are necessary for the higher levels of attainment. It is important then that the structures of different kinds of story are regularly discussed as part of the preparation for writing and that pupils are given tasks that help them to develop in greater detail specific aspects of narrative, such as the description of setting and the outlining of character.

The differences in the story themes chosen by both the younger and older writers I have quoted graphically illustrate the different ways story telling acts as a form of gender display. Jordan (1995) has described boys' cooperative fantasy play as re-enactments of "warrior" discourse, a discourse that informs epic narratives in a tradition which she suggests stretches from *Hercules* and *Beowulf* to *Superman* and *Dirty Harry* (p. 76). These plays, she suggests, are to determine the hero roles available to boys while creating a further masculine identity which is designated "not female." In each of the boys' stories there is the possibility of this kind of narrative pleasure, whereas the girls' stories encapsulate their interest in small domestic detail and the development of feeling.

To conclude this brief look at narrative writing, I want to consider two further stories written by ten-year-olds, one a fictional narrative, collected in 1994 in preparation for *Differently Literate* (Millard 1997), and the other a story which was written in 2000, as part of a science topic about bacteria.

ROBOCOP 4

"This is the News headline and yes, there is another Robocop out, but this time it's even better."
"Murphy, hold it, there he is."
"DEAD OR ALIVE YOU ARE COMING WITH ME!"
Crime in progress.
"Hey what are you doing in there, mister?"
"Book him."
"Why?"
"He's a cop killer."
"Hey, what are you doing in there, mister?"
"Gimme all your money, before I blow your brains to bits."
"Dream on tin head."
BANG!
"My arm, aargghhhh!!!"

Both the plot and the central character of this narrative have been derived from film. In particular, the use of the numeral in the title, places the writing firmly within the film genre. However, the narrative itself recalls news bulletins, another filmic device used frequently in superhero narratives, where journalists and news reporters are used to track the movements of the main characters. Further confirmation of its ties with visual narrative is in the abrupt change of scene, created as in film, by a direction, rather than through narration. The main action concerns a robbery but because the reader is given nothing more than the dialogue, it is difficult to follow who does what to whom. The writer has made the assumption that his reader will share the knowledge of the supporting film text.

The next story, produced more recently, is intended to explain a scientific phenomenon:

THE STORY OF BOB

Bob, the building bacteria, lived in a mouth that was so big that to Bob it was like the sun. Luke, the mouth's owner, was at his friend's party. Bob, back in Luke's mouth, was getting ready for a party too. Bob invited his family and friends over.
"Luke," shouted Edward.
"What do you want Ed?"
"Just want to know if you want some sweets?"
"Yes," said Luke.
Bob was counting down, "5,4,3,2,1 Whoooo!"
After both parties were over all of Bob's family and friends had to go to the toilet.
If you were in the mouth all you could hear was "phhhhhhhh, plop."
All day the acid was burning through the teeth and all of a sudden
"Arhhhhh!"

The story form shares many of the characteristics of the Robocop piece. Again, the dialogue is made to carry most of the action, and I would argue that the limitations of the narrative form has also limited the writer's ability to show what he knows about hygiene. Too much of the decay process is left to an implicit understanding, and the story rests on a visualization of the action in the mouth. A comic strip might have caught more of the information, and it is probably a comic format that lies behind the narrative.

I have spent some time discussing the construction of fictional stories because it is often story writing, rather than nonfiction, which children select when given a choice. There are now in most schools more developed frameworks for helping all young writers to think carefully about the nature of narrative, prompting them to include the depiction of the setting, the development of character, and the complication or reversal of fortune, which is essential to plotting (see, for example, Bearne 1998, pp. 101–5). However, as the examples above show, planning also needs to rest on wide access to good writers who model the range of strategies for opening, developing, and arriving at satisfactory narrative closure. Good writing is supported by good reading.

Teachers may form some idea of the influence of pupils' prior reading by conducting an audit of the kinds of stories they would choose to write for themselves. In an earlier piece of research (Millard 1997), I analyzed 80 eleven-year-olds' stories in terms of the genre chosen (see Table 9.2).

Table 9.2 Comparison of the Genres Chosen for Writing Stories

Genre	Boys	Girls
horror	7	14
adventure	9	6
teen fiction	0	8
children's story	1	5
war	4	0
sci-fi	3	0
detective	3	1
sport	4	0
anecdote/recount	3	0
school	2	2
folk tale	0	2
ghost	0	2
Western	2	0
parody	2	0
TOTALS	40	40

At first glance, Table 9.2 shows that the boys appear to draw on an equally wide range of genres as do girls, with some key differences. What the categories mask, however, is boys' much stronger reliance on televisual narrative forms, in which dialogue conveys most of the action, whereas the genres preferred by the girls are more often traced to continuous prose fiction, offering better models for written forms. It is important that teachers are able to recognize the sources of pupils' inspiration for writing and the limitations they can impose.

Writing Nonfiction

Figure 9.3 is the first piece of information writing that this little girl had been asked to do by her kindergarten teacher. The class had been making a book on mini-beasts, and she had been given

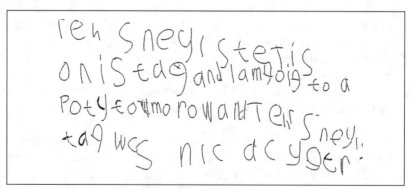

Figure 9.3 "The snail's teeth is on his tongue and I am going to a party tomorrow and the snail's tongue works like a cheese-grater." (Kate, age 4½)

the snail as her topic. She has written out the information she has been helped to find in an information picture book, but in the middle of the piece, her own purpose for writing has broken in on the task, taking her back to a personal recount. It is a pattern that is repeatedly found in developing writers throughout the primary school, though usually not quite as dramatically as in this piece. Most pupils find writing nonfiction more difficult than writing stories or accounts of personal experience and, without being given clear guidance about the structure that is appropriate for their task, frequently return to the forms with which they are most familiar. Kate slips back into personal account.

Here some Year 5 (age 9–10) boys' attempts at reports for a school newspaper also confound recounting with reporting.

SLIMBRIDGE STORIES

The Moorhen's Nest
While we were looking at the flamingos, Mr H spotted one of the hundreds of moorhens squatting down in a clump of grass. Peter Wood approached it and the bird walked off, revealing a nest of twigs with two large eggs in it. When we approached the nest the next day the mother got up and walked away for the second day running and this time there were three eggs. The eggs were a dirty white with brown speckles. As soon as we had left the nest the bird flew off.
By Paul and Michael

On Your Knees
Robert was in to bat and Paul hit the ball and Robert was running until he sprained his knee. Robert said, "It felt painful," but he began to walk back to the hostel.

Ball up a Tree
Mr H took us children to play football As he was playing, Andrew kicked the ball up a tree, then David got a leg up the tree to shake the branch to get the ball down then we carried on playing.
By Louis and Robert

In their separate sections, the boys have attempted to imitate the format of a newspaper by creating a headline and sub-headings. The first section is a pure recount of an interesting natural observation. In the next pieces, they attempt to write a report by discussing Robert's accident in the third person. However, they have difficulty in reporting speech and at the end of the piece revert to a recount—"then we carried on playing."

Pupils treat all kinds of reports in this way, from science experiments to newspapers, because they are unfamiliar with the syntactical structure of the genre required. The following is an early piece of secondary school work for design and technology from an eleven-year-old pupil:

What We Have Done So Far

First what we did is have a look at the machines. He told us how to behave and told us true stories of how the machines could kill you. One of the machines is called a pillar drive and it can drill through your hand if it gets nudged into it in a split second. A couple of safety rules are: if you have long hair tie it back, wear goggles and don't be silly with machines.

This piece is pure recount and has taken this form because the writer has not perhaps been given a clear enough idea of what is required. The teacher's concern was to impress safety, not to show how safety rules are written. Typically, what have impressed themselves on the writer are the "true stories" of danger.

In surveying pupils' nonfiction writing at the end of primary school and in the first term of secondary education, I have found that both boys and girls experience problems in using more formal genres for their nonfiction work. However, as when composing narrative, they again tend to fall back on the genres most familiar to them. This has different consequences for boys and girls, as can be seen in the following examples. Here, two equally able pupils attempt to construct a newspaper account of *The Battle of Hastings* for History.

Saxon Times

By early morning of the 14th of October, 1066, we were standing on the top of Senlac Hill, just outside Hastings, looking down at the Norman army. We stood behind a hastily built wooden fence. The Normans started to walk away from us. We thought we had won; we were all crying and we were all happy.

Harold started to walk down the hill and we followed. It was a stupid thing to do. They had only been gone ten minutes, not even that. Then we saw their cavalry coming. We were shocked, so we fought, but we had no chance against them. They had cavalry and we didn't. I thought we fought well against the Normans, but we lost lots of men to their cavalry. They got King Harold and killed him. We had no chance against the cavalry so we gave up and William became the king of England. People were upset, angry and unhappy that he had died, but to have some disgusting king like William.

In the war I was a foot soldier, King William thought they had a very hard army indeed, but they were on the wrong side, They should have been on our side. So, I say they are dirty and I feel a little sad that we lost, but I got over it and fought well.
Girl, age 11

Battle of Hastings

The 14th of October 1066 and I think the Normans are going to surrender, because they are soft. Their leader William is being protected by bodyguards. He's a wimp. Oh yes, they've retreated. I knew we'd win they're soft. "WE'VE WON." I ran down the hill shouting, "WE HAVE CONQUERED THEM." "Oh no, they're coming back with CAVALRY." We fought and fought, but they were too strong. I think he's weak. He had to use dirty tricks to win us over. He's only won because we were not ready for battle.

The fight was terrible. My best friend, John, was killed. I am really upset. He was my only friend. But I did hack the Normans to the ground. Two of the heads I took off and I stabbed one in the heart. I have run to the forest and am hiding in a bush. OH NO! I am hearing Normans coming through the forest.
Boy, age 11

This history task required an understanding of report writing, a genre with which both these pupils appear unfamiliar. As I have argued in discussing the younger pupils' newspaper activity, fewer children than we might anticipate read daily newspapers and they get their ideas of reporting more commonly from television or radio. In marking these pieces, the teacher awarded the boy's piece a higher grade because of his presentation (not included here), which included bold headlines, sub-headings, action photographs with captions, and advertising copy and conveyed many aspects of the visual construct of a newspaper front page. Yet both pieces contain about the same amount of factual information, and I would argue that the girl's work, though muddled at the end, which employs a diary or journal recount, comes closer to what is usually required by school tasks and is a better preparation for later writing. The boy's piece draws heavily on the conventions of spoken commentary, probably a football commentary. It serves less well as a basis for conveying what has been learned in a more formal setting, such as an examination.

Acting on the Evidence from Pupils' Work to Support All Writers

It is now two years since the introduction of the National Literacy Strategy in the United Kingdom, and preliminary findings suggest that creating a structured support for written tasks is proving especially beneficial to boys. In a number of schools, the use of the Extending Interactions with Text (EXIT) model (Wray and Lewis 1997) is being used to enhance pupils' experience of nonfiction texts. The model suggests three important stages of preparation for writing: teacher models the written form, class and teacher produce a text together, and then pupils write independently. In my own research, I have also found beneficial effects on boys' motivation, as they often selected pieces of nonfiction or analytical work, supported by formal structures, as the pieces they had particularly enjoyed completing. In addition, the use of computers greatly increased many boys' interest in writing, and a combination of a computer-based writing frame coupled to a clear purpose was particularly productive.

However, the key to properly engaged writing remains dependent on the teacher's ability to present a topic in a way that absorbs the pupil's attention and motivates each writer to want to explain ideas clearly, or to tell a story well. No amount of scaffolding, whether in the form of frames or individual support, can bypass the process of engagement with the topic.

Further, I want to emphasize that a focus on the purpose for writing and a habit of discussing what Sheeran and Barnes (1991) call each subject's "ground rules" will be as beneficial to an increase of girls' as well as boys' performance. Elsewhere (Millard 1997) I have argued that, while girls' disposition towards reading and writing in school, particularly English work, may help them perform in examinations, there is a need to consider whether these accomplishments will serve them equally well after school.

From Factual to Imaginative Writing

In a recent brief survey I made of pupils' writing interests, only boys expressed a particular dislike of any of the writing they had recently been asked to do, and the genre mentioned most frequently was poetry. In a class of ten- to eleven-year-olds, several boys whom I asked about their writing preferences suggested they did not like poetry at all. It was hard for them to pinpoint exactly why this was the case, except perhaps some of the ways they had been set the task appeared rather vague. Two boys in particular explained that they had been unable to think of anything "imaginative" when they were asked to listen, to close their eyes to listen to music and record the scenes and feelings conjured up while listening. However, displayed on the walls of the classroom was clear evidence of rich poetry work from both boys and girls, completed in the previous term. One way of overcoming the boys' initial barriers to poetry had been by beginning somewhere other than with a traditional "creative writing" task. The kind of description used in poetry to create a sense of a particularly object closely observed is a skill which is essential in all the sciences, particular to natural sciences

The poems set out below had sprung out of a factual scientific project on fungi in which a crop of inkcaps found in the school grounds had been investigated. As one boy explained in this procedural writing:

Mushrooms: How to make a spore print

1. Get a fungus
2. Pull off the stalk and skin
3. Get a plain piece of white paper
4. Place the fungus onto the paper so you can't see its gills
5. Leave overnight in a place without draughts.

Hot tips

1. For best results leave until morning
2. When you lift the cap off the paper be careful or it might smudge

Life cycle of a fungus
(Information found through computer search)

First a fungus starts its life underground. It eats all the goodness up. Then near to winter it could die, so it comes up from underground with a little cap on top. Under the cap are lots of lines called gills and this is where the spores are produced. When they are ready they will drop and be blown around and when they land and get trodden into the ground they will grow into more mushrooms.

This is a poem developed from this work:

FUNGUS
Fungus grow
Listen, at night
You might hear
Fungus speaking,
Speaking quietly.

Watch at night
You might see
Fungus opening their gills
Spreading, scattering their spores
Making new fungus.
They keep on growing;
They're invading us;
They're taking over.
Then they shrivel up,
Ink caps dissolving
Turning into ink.
Then they die
But more fungus grows.
By Ben

I was delighted by the imagery of stealth which permeates this poem, and which echoes that of Sylvia Plath's *Mushrooms* (Plath 1981, p. 139). Yet the latter is a poem which neither the pupils nor their teacher had read. The idea of the fungi taking over the environment had occurred spontaneously through exploring the inkcap's life cycle. Each pupil's poem had been given its own shape. A second boy's poem is structured quite differently:

MUSHROOM

A mushroom is growing by a tree
The field of mushrooms sway from side to side
The cap is white like a polar bear
The long fat stalk is growing fast
Spores drop from the mushroom and blow away in the wind.
It dies—all messy and black.
By Michael

Responding to Writing

One of the most important issues to take into account when considering how to support pupils' writing is the nature of the teacher's response. At the time of the National Writing Project (1989), the teachers involved were surprised to find that most children, no matter what their age, when asked about writing focused on technical aspects of the process, i.e. spelling, punctuation, and neatness of handwriting, rather than composition. The reason for this became clear when teachers' responses to writing were recorded. A far larger proportion of comments related to technical, rather than compositional features. Both pupils and teachers appeared to see good performance in writing as "getting it right" and "making few mistakes," rather than exploring ideas and certainly not feelings. The focus of the National Writing Project helped to develop a more thoughtful response (NCC 1990). One teacher reported how her experience of the project had changed her marking routine:

Since the beginning of the Writing Project I think the biggest change in my attitude to the children's writing has been in the approach I take to marking. I now try to approach the work with a much more positive way, looking for good points to praise rather than faults. (1990, p. 15)

The emphasis of the whole project on giving positive feedback was based on reading all work for its meaning. It is a message that needs to be reiterated frequently. In preparation for this chapter I again asked children to assess their writing and soon became aware that pupils were most aware of the features we might place under the heading "technical accuracy." In commenting on their work, both boys and girls pointed to surface features, citing neatness and good punctuation as reasons for selecting pieces as "good." It was also the case that the teacher selected aspects of layout, punctuation, and spelling to comment on. This is, of course, because it is far easier to comment on errors or small points of style than to find positive features of composition. However, superficial aspects of presentation may come to dominate pupils' thinking and reinforce a view of writing which overvalues technical accuracy and neatness at the expense of composition. This is usually at the expense of boys' sense of proficiency, as shown in Figures 9.4a,b.

Both of the pupils in Figures 9.4a and 9.4b had been asked to produce an acrostic, based on an animal, a task the girl was judged to have accomplished successfully, resulting in praise from

Figure 9.4a Hamster

Figure 9.4b Spitfire

the teacher in the form of a merit mark. The boy's piece, on the other hand, attracted only critical comments. It was "scruffy," he was told, he had not written about an animal, his illustrations were "inappropriate," and the upshot was that he was required to repeat the piece. Consider for a moment a word-processed version of the work:

Scramble the pilots race to their planes
Planes are fast like UFOs.
It's firing time,
Thrusting engines like blazing infernos
Fires roaring on the ground.
It's the "deadlock," says a pilot.
Ready to land.
Engines cool in the wind like ice,
Scramble, here we go again.

I would contend that this piece simply deserves the teacher's praise. As an initial response, the teacher might have congratulated the boy on the power of the imagery to create an atmosphere of fear and delight in combat and his clever return to the first word of the acrostic for its ending. To tackle presentation, I would ask the pupil to word-process the text for display and perhaps find a suitable image to cut and paste as illustration. Finally, I would want to discuss the boy's reason for choosing an inanimate object for his poem, the Spitfire, rather than a creature. My next suggestion would be to make use of the Spitfire as a metaphor for a bird of prey, e.g. "hawks come from the sky as spitfires..."

It is a sobering task to collect, as I have done recently, all the exercise books of those pupils who are not doing well in school and record the balance of positive to negative comments that they receive for their work. There are always many more boys than girls who fall into this category, and it is difficult to see how some of the comments they receive will help them to improve. I found many expressions of exasperation, such as: *Remember capitals! You must use full stops! Untidy! Scruffy work! Spellings!* Few which move the writer on: *It would be a good idea to describe this character in some detail. You need to give your reader more idea of what your characters do as well as what they say here.* It is particularly important to adopt a constructive approach to writing tasks if boys are to be encouraged to see their work more positively.

Creating an Appropriate Culture for Writing

It is a truism that in order to get better at writing, developing writers need to be given adequate space and time to write, for as Frank Smith asserts, we learn to write by writing, flexing our composition muscles and solving language problems as they arise (Smith 1982). There needs then to be some provision for all pupils to spend stretches of time working on compositions that absorb their interest and for which they receive adequate support and praise. These need not necessarily be narratives. Boys in the Nottingham school, who reported working on a news site for their school web page, were motivated by a tangible outcome for their work, as well as by access to both laptops and school networked computers.

In the first stages of schooling, teachers can encourage children to write by devising writing areas embedded within creative play around a particular theme matching the children's current interests—a fire station or hospital emergency department, for example (see Bearne 1998, pp. 96–7). Jackie Marsh has described the motivating power for young writers of a writing area connected to some aspect of popular culture (Marsh 1999; Thompson and Marsh 2000, p. 17), and other teachers have described how creative play areas designated as fire stations, Chinese restaurants, garden centers, and news agents may stimulate writing activities (Bearne 1998, p. 96).

Not every written piece needs to extend to reams of writing, but opportunities need to be provided for pupils to become engaged in more extended writing from time to time. It is my preliminary finding that in the wake of the National Literacy Strategy there has been greater emphasis on short, underdeveloped gobbets of writing, often selected to demonstrate a particular aspect of language study, e.g. the use of commas, or of reported speech than opportunities to write at length.

There is also a positive side to the Literacy Strategy. Teachers are generally now far more aware of the importance of providing explicit knowledge of genre and convention, as one path to success and all pupils, boys and girls alike, are being supported in a broader range of written forms. This means that adequate attention has to be given to planning different aspects of textual composition, ensuring that writing is seen as an essential part of learning activity and not confined to story production, or handwriting practice. The production of nonfiction genres, however, needs not to remain unrelentingly serious. Boys in particular, but not exclusively, enjoy writing which parodies and mocks the serious intent of others. Here is a ten-year-old boy's work on instructions which avoids the repetition of bland instructions for making tea or boiling an egg, which I have encountered most frequently as examples of this particular genre.

How to Make a Zog

Ingredients		*Utensils*
Shredded snake skin	300g	Mixing bowl
Oodles of ooze	150g	Whisk
Blood agar	1tsp.	Oven 350° Fahrenheit
Green dye	50g	
Red marbles	2	
Rotten algae	5tsp.	
Flick-knife blades	12	
Peanut	1	

Method
1. Pour shredded snake skin, oodles of ooze and blood agar into a mixing bowl
2. Whisk briskly
3. When the mixture froths add green dye and red marbles
4. Whisk rotten algae with flick-knife blades in a separate bowl

5. Combine the two mixtures
6. Now add a peanut for the brain and place in loaf tin
7. Preheat oven to 350° (Gas mark 9)
8. Put on middle shelf
9. Leave to cook for 22 hrs.
10. Remove from tin

You now have a Zog!!!

Recipe by David
Age 10

In setting out to support writing in school, it is also essential to give it status within the community, by creating appropriate rewards and establishing areas where work is both displayed and acknowledged. I found high levels of motivation for writing among both boys and girls in the Nottinghamshire school. They frequently enter work for a wide range of writing competitions, both locally and nationally, including the composition of media texts, and have received many commendations for their work. The school also prominently displays a wide range of all the children's work and presents awards in assembly for achievements in writing.

A Final Note on Gender

I began this chapter by suggesting that the differences in writing, which I was about to discuss, were not generalizable uncritically to the work of all boys and all girls. Neither will the key issues be identical for all school communities. Social class and race are significant factors in orienting pupils towards certain kinds of school activities and achievements, and these factors also need to be taken into account when assessing how well the writing tasks devised for a particular class of children match their need for support and development. Gender, then, is always only a part of the story, but as I have shown above, a careful analysis of differences in both pupils' choice of subject and their preferred genre style can assist teachers in understanding the range of support that their pupils will need to improve performance in the writing curriculum.

Notes

1. In reproducing the pieces, I have regularized most of the pupils' spelling and punctuation, as my argument rests on the selection of subject and style for writing, rather than the technical aspects of their work.
2. This is a practice I have found very useful both as researcher and practitioner. The pupils' own selections can be used as the start of a writing conference in which a full picture of the individual's abilities can emerge.
3. In the secondary phase it is particularly useful to draw on a range of work from across the curriculum so that the full picture of a pupil's achievement or difficulties is formed.

4. See, for example, the Writing Continuum produced as part of The First Steps program researched and developed by the Education Department of Western Australia. These course materials which have also informed the National Literacy Strategy in the United Kingdom show clearly how children's writing develops from personal to more formal report and discursive writing.

References

Bearne, E. (1998) *Making Progress in English*. London: Routledge.

Education Department of Western Australia (1994) *First Steps: Writing continuum*. Melbourne: Longman.

Fisk, N. (1973) *Grinny*. Harmondsworth, England: Puffin.

Hughes, T. (1963) *How the Whale Began*. London: Faber.

Jordan, E. (1995) "Fighting boys and fantasy play: The construction of masculinity in the early years of school," in *Gender and Education* 7(1), 68–95.

Marsh, J. (1999) "Batman and Batwoman go to school: Popular culture in the literacy curriculum," *International Journal of Early Years Education* 7(2), 1999.

Millard, E. (1994) *Developing Readers in the Middle Years*. Buckingham: Open University Press.

Millard, E. (1997) *Differently Literate: Boys, girls and the schooling of literacy*. London: The Falmer Press.

Millard, E. (1999) "Mad about the boys," *The English and Media Magazine* **38**, Summer, pp. 13–15.

National Curriculum Council: National Writing Project. (1990) *Responding to Writing*. Walton-on-Thames: NFER/Nelson.

Paley, V. G. (1984) *Boys and Girls: Superheroes in the doll corner*. Chicago: The University of Chicago Press.

Pidgeon, S. (1993) "Learning reading and learning gender," in Barrs, M. and Pidgeon, S. (eds.), *Reading the Difference*. London: Centre for Language in Primary Education.

Plath, S. (1981) *Collected Poems* (edited T. Hughes). London: Faber and Faber.

Sadler, M. (1986) *Alistair's Time Machine*. London: MacMillan, Papermac.

Sendak, M. (1963) *Where the Wild Things Are*. New York: HarperCollins.

Sheeran, Y. and Barnes, D. (1991) *School Writing, Discovering the Ground Rules*. Milton Keynes: Open University Press.

Smith, F. (1982) *Writing and the Writer*. Oxford: Heinemann Educational.

Steedman, C. (1982) *The Tidy House, Little Girls Writing*. London: Virago.

Thompson, P. and Marsh, J. (2000) "Literacy, TV and video: Thoroughly modern media," *The Primary English Magazine* **5**(3).

Weinberger, J. (1996) *Literacy Goes to School: The parents' role in young children's literacy learning*. London: Paul Chapman.

Wells, G. (1987) *The Meaning Makers: Children learning language and using language to learn*. London: Hodder & Stoughton.

Wray, D. and Lewis, M. (1997) *Extending Literacy: Children reading and writing nonfiction*. London: Routledge.

Part III

Nonfiction Issues

Chapter 10

Developing Nonfiction Writing: Beyond Writing Frames
David Wray and Maureen Lewis

Nonfiction Writing: Some Classroom Examples

Nonfiction writing causes problems for young writers, more so than fiction writing. To pick out some of these problems, we begin by looking at some examples.

The first piece was written by Joe, a seven-year-old student, who was asked, in a science lesson, to explain how the rain cycle works. Here is his explanation:[1]

How does rain fall?

The rain comes from the sky. Miss Jones put some water in a kettle and it boiled up. The steam came out of the spout, and she put a piece of glass in the steam. The glass went all misty and then it made drops of rain. When the rain fell off the glass, it was wet and it looked slippy. Miss Jones said that was how rain fell.

The second piece is an extract from the writing of ten-year-old Lee, who was asked to write to explain why the Battle of Hastings was fought. Here is the first half page (of three pages altogether) of his explanation:

The Battle of Hastings

Duke William of Normandy left Normandy with about 600 ships and 12,000 men on September 27th in 1066. William and his barons had been preparing the invasion of England since early spring of that year. He had fought many notable battles. His ship, the Mora, arrived ahead of the fleet. William waited and ate a hearty breakfast. As his fleet straggled into place behind him, they moved eastward to the first sheltered bay to provide protection for his armada.

William fell on the beach, grasped the sand, and declared , "This is my country." Next, the ships were disembarked. A fort was built inside Pevensey Roman Fort as an H.Q., while the army camped behind it. William scouted the land. Taking his army around Pevensey Bay, he camped 8 miles to the east, north of what is now known as Hastings, and waited.

Finally, ten-year-old Kerry has written a discussion paper about boxing.

Boxing

There is a lot of discussion about whether boxing should be banned. The people who agree with this idea, such as Sarah, claim that if they do carry on boxing they should wear something to protect their heads. They also argue that people who do boxing could have brain damage and get seriously hurt. A further point they make is that most of the people that have died did have families.

However, there are also strong arguments against this point of view. Another group of people believe that boxing should not be banned. They say that why did they invent it if it is a dangerous sport. They say that boxing is a good sport; people enjoy it. A furthermore reason is if they ban boxing it will ruin people's careers.

After looking at the different points of view and the evidence for them, I think boxing should be banned, because five hundred people have died in boxing since 1884.

Most teachers would agree that, while each of these three pieces of writing may be interesting and "creative," the first two are inadequate responses to the task the students were given. They are both written in ways which owe more to imaginative stories than the structures expected of writing in Science and History respectively (there is a strong suspicion that parts of the second piece may have been copied directly from reference material). A large number of students appear to have similar problems in writing, and their difficulty is one of matching the way they write, the style they choose, and the structure they use, to the particular purposes for writing that you encounter in various curriculum subjects.

Yet in the third piece of writing, the student has apparently solved this problem. Her writing is structured to fit the demands of a discussion paper; it shows evidence of appropriate choice of vocabulary and sentence structure. Because of these features, it gives the appearance of a much more mature piece of writing. How has Kerry been enabled to do this? It is central to the argument of this chapter that the answer lies in the nature of the teaching she has received, which has ensured that she is aware of the structural and language demands of particular writing tasks and she does not approach them with misguided assumptions about how writing works in this context.

What are the essential characteristics of this teaching? They are twofold. Firstly, it rests upon an analysis of the problems students face in producing effective nonfiction writing and attempts to help them overcome these problems. Secondly, it is guided by a model of effective teaching. We will explore both these aspects further.

The Problems of Nonfiction Writing

Writing causes several problems for those not skilled at doing it (and even for those who are!). We have identified four major problem areas.

1. The Blank Page Problem

Most writers will agree that the most difficult part of writing anything is the first line or two. Getting started can be so difficult, even for experienced writers, that they invent a number of "delaying tactics" (sharpening pencils, making coffee, walking around the room) to put off the awful moment. A blank page can be very daunting, and for many less experienced writers it can result in the abandonment of the writing task. "Please, Miss, I can't think what to write" will be recognizable to many teachers as a familiar response of some students to writing tasks. The blank page has overwhelmed them.

2. Writing Is Different from Talking

When talking to another person, the language user receives constant support for his/her language. Talking usually takes the form of a dialogue; that is, one person says something, this prompts the other person to say something, which in turn prompts the first person to reply, and so on. Talkers thus receive continual prompts for their language production. These prompts also help the language user to join in the ongoing dialogue. We naturally adapt the way we speak depending upon our relationship with the listener, and clues as to an appropriate way to join in a conversation come from the way the other person speaks.

Writers, on the other hand, do not receive such prompts. They are by themselves, forced to produce language without support from anyone and to work out for themselves an appropriate register for that language.

Of course, in a classroom, there is potential support available from a teacher who may be at a student's shoulder prompting with such suggestions as:

"That's an interesting idea. Tell us more about that."
"You've described that well. Can you give some more information about why it was there?"
"How exciting! And what will happen next?"

It is difficult, however, in a classroom that may contain thirty or more student writers, for a teacher to be able to provide enough of this support to meet the needs of the whole class.

3. The "And Then" Syndrome

Inexperienced writers tend to have a limited range of ways of joining together ideas in writing. Most teachers will recognize this by the prevalence of "and then" in their students' writing, as if this were the only way of linking ideas in writing. Mature writing, of course, is characterized by more elaborate ways of joining together ideas, using such connectives (connecting words) as *furthermore, moreover, nevertheless, on the other hand,* and so on. Teachers need to find ways of deliberately introducing these alternative connectives to students and helping them use them effectively in their writing.

4. *The Structure of Texts*

It does seem to be the case that students often lack experience of different types of texts, especially nonfiction texts, and their organizational structures. They need some support in distinguishing between these types in terms of linguistic features such as vocabulary, connectives, and structure. A concept which can help explain and categorize these linguistic differences is that of text genre.

According to genre theory, pieces of writing which share a common purpose will tend to share a common structure. One language purpose might be to provide instructions for someone else to carry out a task, as, for instance, in a recipe. Such instructions, spoken or written, will tend to follow the following pattern:

- a statement of the goal (e.g. This is how to make a chocolate cake)
- a list of materials necessary to achieve this (e.g. You will need . . .)
- a series of steps to carry out (e.g. First you . . . , Then . . .)

Language patterns such as this tend to become so routine that we are barely aware of them, yet clearly they have to be learned. Many students will find such structures difficult because they do not have the right expectations about texts. It is quite common, for example, for students to write instructions in the form of a narrative: "I got some sugar and put it in a mixing bowl. Then I . . ." This suggests that teachers need to teach students to use a range of appropriate language structures for appropriate purposes.

In order to do this, teachers themselves need to be aware of various text structures. As we have outlined elsewhere (Lewis and Wray 1995), there appear to be six basic factual genres: Recount, Report, Discussion, Persuasion, Explanation, and Instructions. Research suggests that primary students get a great deal of experience of writing recounts but rarely experience the other genres. This imbalance is important because in later school life and in adulthood these other genres are very heavily used and are crucial to success. Secondary school examinations, for example, demand the ability to write cogent arguments and discussions, and if students have not been taught how to structure these forms of writing, they will be disadvantaged.

A Model for Teaching Writing

The model of teaching on which we have based our work is summarized in the following diagram (the thinking underpinning this model is fully outlined in Wray and Lewis 1997).

demonstration
↓
collaborative activity
↓
scaffolded activity
↓
independent activity

The model stems from the ideas of Vygotsky (1978), who put forward the notion that learners first experience a particular cognitive activity in collaboration with expert practitioners. The learner is firstly a spectator, as the majority of the cognitive work is done by the expert (parent or teacher), then a novice as he/she starts to take over some of the work under the close supervision of the expert. As the learner grows in experience and ability, the expert passes over greater and greater responsibility but still acts as a guide, assisting as necessary. Eventually, the learner assumes full responsibility for the task, with the expert still present in the role of a supportive audience. The model seems to make good theoretical sense, yet it can be a little difficult to apply it fully to teaching in a busy, overpopulated classroom. In particular, it seems that students are too often expected to move into the independent writing phase before they are really ready, and often the pressure to do so is based on the practical problem of teachers being unable to find the time to spend with them in individual support. What is needed is something to span the collaborative and independent activity phases.

We have called this the scaffolded phase—a phase where we offer our students strategies to aid writing, but strategies that they can use without an adult necessarily being alongside them. One such strategy we have developed which has become popular is the use of writing frames. These can act both as a way of increasing a student's experience of a particular type of nonfiction writing and as a substitute for the teacher's direct interventions which encourage students to extend their writing.

What Are Writing Frames?

A writing frame consists of a skeleton outline to scaffold students' nonfiction writing. The skeleton framework consists of different key words or phrases, according to the particular generic form. The template of starters, connectives, and sentence modifiers which constitute a writing frame gives students a structure within which they can concentrate on communicating what they want to say, rather than getting lost in the form. However, by using the form, students become increasingly familiar with it.

We have space here for only a few examples of the writing frames we have developed. Figures 10.1 and 10.2 give examples of frames for two of the six factual genres we described earlier. Further, photocopiable examples can be found in Lewis and Wray (1997 and 1998) and a more extensive account of the thinking behind writing frames in Lewis and Wray (1995).

Although I already knew that _____

I have learned some new facts. I learned that _____

I also learned that _____

Another fact I learned was _____

However, the most interesting thing I learned was _____

Figure 10.1 A "Recount" Writing Frame

There is a lot of discussion about whether _____

The people who agree with this idea, such as _____, claim that _____

They also argue that _____

However, there are also strong arguments against this point of view _____ believe that _____

Furthermore _____

After looking at the different points of view and the evidence for them I think _____ because _____

Figure 10.2 A "Discussion" Writing Frame

Writing with a frame overcomes the four writing problems highlighted earlier.

1. It no longer presents writers with a blank page. There is comfort in the fact that there is already some writing on this page. We have found that this alone can be enough to encourage weaker writers to write at greater length.
2. The frame provides a series of prompts to students' writing. Using the frame is rather like having a dialogue with the page, and the prompts serve to model the register of that particular piece of writing.
3. The frame deliberately includes connectives beyond the simple "and then." We have found that extended use of frames like this can result in students spontaneously using these more elaborate connectives in other writing.
4. The frame is designed around the typical structure of a particular genre. It thus gives students access to this structure and implicitly teaches them a way of writing nonfiction.

How Writing Frames Can Be Used

The use of a writing frame should always begin with discussion and teacher modeling before moving on to joint construction (teacher and student[s] together) and then to the student undertaking writing, supported by the frame. This oral, teacher modeling, joint construction pattern of teaching is vital, for it not only models the generic form and teaches the words that signal connections and transitions, but also provides opportunities for developing students' oral language and their thinking. Some students, especially those with learning difficulties, may need many oral sessions and sessions in which their teacher acts as a scribe before they are ready to attempt their own writing.

It is useful for teachers to make "big" versions of the frames for use in the teacher-modeling and joint construction phases. These large frames can be used for shared writing. It is important that the student and the teacher understand that the frame is a supportive draft and words may be crossed out or substituted. Extra sentences may be added or surplus starters crossed out. The frame should be treated as a flexible aid not a rigid form.

We are convinced that writing in a range of genres is most effective if it is located in meaningful experiences. The concept of "situated learning" (Lave and Wenger 1991) suggests that learning is always context-dependent. For this reason, we have tended to use the frames within class subject work rather than in isolated study skills lessons.

When the students have a purpose for writing they can be offered a frame when:

- they first attempt independent writing in an unfamiliar genre and a scaffold might be helpful to them;
- a student/group of students appear, stuck in a particular mode of writing, e.g. constantly using "and then . . . and then" when writing an account;
- they "wander" between genres in a way that demonstrates a lack of understanding of a particular genre usage, e.g. while writing an instructional text such as a recipe they start in the second person (*first you beat the egg*) but then shift into a recount (*next I stirred in the flour*);
- they have written something in one genre (often a personal recount) which would be more appropriate in a different genre, e.g. writing up a science experiment as a personal recount.

In all of these situations, we would stress that writing frames are just one of a range of strategies and writing experiences a teacher would offer to assist learners.

Moving Beyond Writing Frames

Writing frames have a clear appeal to teachers in that they can quickly transform students' nonfiction writing from the pseudo-narratives we showed earlier to more appropriately structured and worded pieces. There is, however, a danger, if they are not used circumspectly, that formulaic writing can result. We are concerned that frames can in fact be overused and offer the following comments to avoid this.

It should be obvious that students should use the frames less and less as their knowledge of a particular form increases. At this later stage, when students begin to show evidence of independent usage, the teacher may need only to have a master copy of the frames available as help cards for those occasions when students need a prompt. A box of such help cards could be a part of the writing area to which students are encouraged to refer for help with their writing. Such support fits with the general "procedural facilitation" strategy for students' writing suggested by Bereiter and Scardamalia (1987). It also seems to be a way into encouraging students to begin to make independent decisions about their own learning.

Also, as students become familiar with the frame structures, there are a number of alternative support structures which can be used, such as prompt sheets containing lists of possible ways of connecting ideas together. A number of these are found in Lewis and Wray (1998), and an example of such a prompt sheet is given in Figure 10.3.

Opening paragraph What is your main argument?	
Arguments What is the most important point you want to make?	
What supporting evidence can you add?	
What is your next point?	
Supporting evidence? Details?	
Continue in this way with any other points you want to make.	
Conclusion Remind the reader what your main point is and ask them to support you.	

Figure 10.3 A "Persuasive" Writing Prompt Sheet

Final points

The following points seem to us to be crucial to the success of writing frames as a teaching strategy.

- Use of a frame should always begin with discussion and teacher modeling before moving on to joint construction and then to the student undertaking writing supported by the frame.
- Not all the students in a class will need to use a writing frame.
- Writing frames should be used when a student has a reason for doing some writing, and the appropriate frame can be introduced if the student needs extra support. The frame in itself is never a purpose for writing.
- It should be made clear to the students that the frame is just a draft, and they should be encouraged to cross out, amend, and add to the frame as suits them.
- Frames are only a small part of the varied and rich writing experiences we offer students. They will need wide experience of text written in a range of genres as well as opportunities to write in a variety of contexts.
- Generic structures are not rigid, unchangeable forms. It is not appropriate to teach them in this way.

Note

1. The pieces of student writing included in this chapter are used to illustrate particular points about writing structure and language use. Since transcription skills are not the issue here, the pieces have been typed and edited to include correct spelling, punctuation, etc.

References

Bereiter, C. and Scardamalia, M. (1987) *The Psychology of Written Composition.* Hillsdale, NJ: Lawrence Erlbaum.

Lave, J. and Wenger, E. (1991) *Situated Learning.* Cambridge: Cambridge University Press.

Lewis, M. and Wray, D. (1995) *Developing children's non-fiction writing.* Leamington Spa: Scholastic.

Lewis, M. and Wray, D. (1997) *Writing Frames.* Reading: University of Reading, Reading and Language Information Centre.

Lewis, M. and Wray, D. (1998) *Writing Across the Curriculum.* Reading: University of Reading, Reading and Language Information Centre.

Vygotsky, L. (1978) *Mind in Society: The development of higher psychological processes.* Cambridge, MA: Harvard University Press.

Wray, D. and Lewis, M. (1997) *Extending Literacy.* London: Routledge.

Chapter 11

Notemaking Techniques for Young Children
Bobbie Neate

Notemaking—The Black Hole of Teaching

Notemaking is probably the most important tool for academic learning that any student will acquire. However, few have ever been taught these vital life skills (Neate 1992). Every good teacher tells children to make notes, but there appears to be a general lack of knowledge about how to teach them (OFSTED 1998, 1999). Most adults were never taught how to make notes from different types of texts. Even fewer of those were taught notemaking skills in their formative years.

First let me define *notemaking* (in relation to notetaking)—a term which I have now used, for a number of years, to help educationalists clarify the difference between two different activities which, on the surface, appear quite similar.

Notetaking is when a learner responds to a speaker or a TV program by taking down relevant words to help them remember salient features, facts, numbers, etc., of the talk or lecture. These notes may be used to write up the learner's new knowledge. (Notes can also be lists of words, or words sketches, which are used for planning an essay/assignment/meeting).

Notemaking, however, is more specialized; it is reserved for notes made when reading a written text. It is a term that applies to the retrieval of information from written texts either on screen or on paper. Notemaking demonstrates a reader's ability to select (and reject) pertinent sections of the text relevant to the needs or purpose of that reader. These notes often form the basis of a "write-up in one's own words" (a learning process on which the academic system is based). Notemaking, therefore, is something we do when we read (not when we listen) to help us focus on the meaning of the text(s) in hand. The notes may also be used as a memory jogger, but without meaningful retrieval they are useless.

There is no doubt that notemaking is a crucial skill. The very process is vital to our learning—it is a skill we exercise all the way up the educational ladder. In order to make effective notes (ones that actually help our understanding), we have to read and understand and "interrogate"

154

texts. We also have to reorganize them in our minds. But most important of all, we have to make the very ideas/concepts/strategies put forward by a writer "our own." We make the notions "our own" by being able to write about new learning as if it belongs to us. Hence, we have to select and reject the salient features of the text(s) we are reading.

Students of all ages read academic works (including "project" books, textbooks, academic journals, and articles on screen); in an educational setting, they are expected to regurgitate their "readings" in the shape of a basic project, essay, or thesis. Historically, teachers have helped their students with the selection of work to be read (basic instruction) and with the writing styles of their work. Teachers also look and comment on their students' writing attempts. However, at the *real* point of learning—i.e. understanding the text, selecting the relevant words or sections of text and recording them—teachers often fail to intervene. They tend not to look and comment on their children's notes. Nor do they know enough about notemaking to be able to teach a notemaking strategy that will actually help the child on a particular text. The real learning factor has been left out of the teaching equation when children are asked to "write up" what they have read and learned.

The evidence in the UK is that very few adults were ever taught how to make notes from written texts when they were young (DfEE 1998). There is also evidence that, unless students are taught flexible notemaking strategies at a young age, they are unlikely to be able change their reading and notemaking habits when they are older (Pugh 1978; Nisbet and Shucksmith 1986; Bulman 1985).

In the past, primary schools overemphasized work on narrative texts almost to the exclusion of work on informative texts (now all this has changed with the National Literacy Strategy); however, nowadays we should be asking ourselves, "How many children in a class are going to *need* informative reading when they leave school?" as opposed to "How many children in a class are going to *need* narrative reading when they leave school?" And "How many in a class are going to have to write *informative* texts when they leave school?" as opposed to "How many in a class are going to have to write *narrative* texts when they leave school?" The answers can be persuasive in influencing teachers who overvalue the tradition of story reading and writing (Neate 1996, 1999a, 1999b).

There is no one method of teaching notemaking that will work on all text types. There is no one magic answer (a fact that is often not fully appreciated). Therefore, children need to be explicitly taught how to make notes on different text types. The notes children make need to be analyzed, checked, and discussed with each pupil. If they do not become a shared and valued part of learning, children will fail to become efficient and effective learners. Too many of our adult students fall into this category.

An effective/efficient performer is comparable to an express train—they gather up their passengers and get to their destination in the quickest most direct way.

Untrained notemakers lack purpose—why do children often copy great swathes of text from a project book? Usually because they lack a specific purpose—if they only have a vague question such as, "I want to find out about dinosaurs" then everything and anything in a book called *Dinosaurs* is relevant to that child's needs. The child has failed to read with a purpose suitable to their needs.

Too many British students find themselves in a similar scenario when they do their assignments or essays. They take copious notes from their textbooks and then find that the notes are useless because they did not read the texts with a tight, specific purpose (i.e. to write the specific information needed in their essay).

I carried out research on students and teachers who were undertaking a course on the teaching of notemaking, and below are examples of the most commonly quoted responses to a variety of questions.

1. *What notes did you make as a child?*

"No notes in primary school 5–11."

"From biology textbooks and magazines at University but not at primary school at all."

"Some in years when I was 11–14. It was mostly copying word for word."

"Read books—wrote down salient points which I then found to be useless."

"Primary school—weekly task of taking notes from reference books when looking up answers to general knowledge—nobody looked at them."

"Secondary—notes from teachers' talks."

"Didn't do any."

"Copious notes at college."

"Listened to information as it was read out—closed book and rewrote."

"Primary—don't remember making notes. Secondary—involved copying from books—just tried to take as much information down as possible—didn't really organise anything."

2. *How did you make your notes?*

"Copied off board."

"Tried to find key words—but failed."

"Left out words—still wrote in sentences."

"Underlining."

"Bullet points."

"Started copying verbatim."

"I was limited. I wrote what I thought was important, wrote down points or phrases in linear form—from book or memory."

"Linear notes using a type of shorthand, used a highlighter pen."

3. *Who taught you?*

"I was self-taught."

"Never taught."

"A bit at secondary."

"I have never been taught and I don't know if I have improved."

"Was taught but no one checked or supervised notes."

"Taught to 'speed read' but not make notes."

4. How successful were you?

"Unsuccessful for essay writing."

"Used keywords, sometimes forgot what the point of the text was."

"I remembered the topic but not what to say about it."

"Notes—very poor—content wrong."

"My quality of writing was always dependent on my notes—if I understood and made 'good' notes I got higher marks."

"Made notes but could not understand them."

"Often had too much irrelevant stuff in my notes."

"I wrote 'mega notes.' I changed them, added to them, subtracted from them but they were useless. I never used them and always found myself re-reading the original book."

"Highlighter useful when I used colour codes."

5. Do you change your strategies according to what you are reading?

"No."

"I only have one strategy."

"No, I still pick up keywords as reminders of what to memorise but sometimes I forget what the original point was, so I took the wrong keywords."

"I try to be more concise now but otherwise same strategy."

"No, strategies firmly entrenched. I can't change."

These responses are not unusual in Britain, but they are worrying because they demonstrate that too many adults are untrained and self-taught notemakers. Hence, they lack precision in their notes.

I include here some sample comments from children about notemaking.

"I have only done one (notemaking activity) before. That was last year" (age 9).

"We have to leave out the 'and's' and 'a's.' We are not supposed to include them" (age 10).

"We are just not to put in the little words" (age 10).

"I can't put it in my own words—it just does not work" (age 9).

These comments reinforce that teachers are still equating abbreviating with the skill of notemaking.

In summary, higher education students and children have told me that the following problems crop up too frequently in their attempts to write up their new-found knowledge (gleaned from texts).

• Getting started—they do not know how or where to start (usually because their notes have not been specific enough).

• They do not know how to reorganize the text(s) read.

• They cannot make sense of their own notes.

• They do not limit the amount of words in their notes.

• They cannot get rid of the original structure.

• They cannot change the author's original words.

• They realize that they do not understand the text—but only when they have finished reading the text (they do not admit this to themselves at the point of reading and making notes).

If children were given clear guidance in their early years in school, most of these problems would be solved. Children are more adaptable and learn to adapt their reading habits much more successfully than adults (Neate 1999a). In other words, adults know they need help but often find it almost impossible to change bad habits.

However, knowing about good notemaking strategies is not the only solution; often children hold authors in too much awe and fail to appreciate that a book is not suitable to their needs. It is an interesting but relevant thought that teachers fail to teach children to become critical readers of informative texts. They allow children to struggle with very difficult or with inappropriate genres and expect them to cope. Teachers intuitively know when one text is better written than another one, but they often fail to alert the novice reader to this fact. Some teachers even worry that if children are allowed to criticize texts, they will become overcritical and never read another information book—this is far from the case in practice. My cause for concern is the amount of poor models of informative writing in existence. Some texts have poor organizational features, lack a logical organization, are sometimes written in an inappropriate register, and often lack the very features of the particular genre that they are meant to represent. These books may be "fun," but they do not promote a particular nonfiction reading or writing strategy, nor are they written in the correct genre. They promote reading a text from beginning to end and may be more appropriate for fiction list.

Finding a suitable text in order to make notes is clearly a prerequisite to good notemaking skills. There are three further points that I would like to make before I discuss individual strategies that are significant for good notemaking.

1. Purposeful Reading

With all notemaking strategies, readers must have a specific purpose when dealing with a text. If the reader reads with a purpose (or purposes), they are:

- much more likely to make effective notes;
- much less likely to deviate;
- much more likely to increase their understanding.

2. Delay Write-up

Children (and adults) should not make notes and write up on the same day. If they do this, all that will happen is that the child will remember the original text and not absorb the meaning behind the words. Notemaking is all about making somebody else's text "your own." Changing the original text in some way is vital. When the children are learning, make them store their notes for three to seven days before asking them to write up the notes.

3. Cooperative Learning

Children learn best when they are carrying out the notemaking activities with a partner. If the notemaking activity encourages talk, discussion, and agreement, the readers are more likely to take the task seriously.

I demonstrate this to groups of teachers by giving them a fairly simple fungi text and asking them to make notes. I do not give them a purpose; I just ask them to make notes. Even though I have been talking about the importance of making notes with a purpose, often ninety-five percent of the teachers will forget about the importance of reading with a purpose and just launch into their old habits. I then stop the teachers and ask them about their notemaking attempts. I then ask them to make notes on the same text but this time with a partner. They also have to fill in a chart. In the chart (Figure 11.1), they are not allowed to put more than three words in any box. They also have to agree on the three selected words. Teachers are always very surprised to find how much more purposeful and effective their notemaking is when they are suddenly pushed into a position where they have to work with a partner. They also frequently mention how much fun the chart is and how motivated they are to complete the task.

Name	Place found	Color of cap	Height grows to	What is strange	Poisonous/ taste	Latin name

Figure 11.1 Chart for Notemaking on Fungi

Individual Notemaking Strategies

No one method is the answer on all texts, because different text types demand different notemaking strategies. Children achieve more if they learn one strategy at a time (adults can learn to mix and match).

Basically, I advise children to use charts when the texts have comparisons in them. If they need to write in the report genre, charts provide an excellent basis. If they need to write an explanation, making notes with pictures helps. Also, if the text they are making notes from is an explanation or a procedural text, then I advise them to make notes using this strategy. Patterning is the strategy to use if the children are using more than one text, especially those that offer different opinions. Underlining or marking of texts should be used on difficult texts that need a thorough perusal.

1. Underlining

How to do it:
- Decide on what you want to find out.
- Find a suitable text that might answer your question.
- Work with a partner.
- Place an acetate sheet over the selected text.
- Write your question at the top of each page.
- Read all the way through the text.
- Underline a few words with a water-based colored pen.
- Carefully choose your words—be selective.
- Write your question and underlined words on a piece of paper—write them as a list.

Further extensions
- Read for another purpose or question—use a different colored pen.
- Write these underlined words as another list.
- When you have answered all your questions, put the original text away. Store your notes carefully.
- After a few days, get out your list of words (your notes).
- Maybe reorganize them.
- Either tell somebody what you have found out (orally), or
- Write down your research using the notes.

Advantages
- Underlining works on any text type.
- You highlight the important points in the text.
- It helps you read with a purpose.
- It helps you answer your own questions.
- It helps you to be selective and reject unnecessary words.
- It aids understanding.
- It helps you become more focused.

When to use this kind of notemaking
- When you are reading for a particular purpose
- When you want to be selective
- When the text is not well laid out
- When the text is not a procedural genre; when the text does not have specific comparisons in it
- When you are new to notemaking
- When you have good questions

Comment from child after doing underlining
"I am not sure this notemaking is easier, and not sure about the writing up of it either." (After writing)—"Oh I see now—you are meant to change it around . . . I think this writing is easier but the notemaking needs more thinking" (age 9).

2. Notes with Pictures

How to do it:
- Choose a suitable text.
- Decide what you want to find out.
- Cover any pictures on the page (if there are pictures already there, they will influence the reader).
- Read the text all the way through.
- Start your picture.
- Remember, only you need to understand your drawings, so don't worry about getting them to "look right."
- Keep re-reading the text.
- Check that you have all the details you need. (You might want to add a few words to the drawings when you are experienced.)
- Put your drawing and text away.
- After a few days, bring out your picture notes.
- Use your notes to tell somebody what you have learned.
- Write up about your research pictures.

Advantages
- The notes are personal.
- Each picture is different, so they are easy to remember.
- It helps you to read with understanding.
- It helps you be selective and decide what is important.
- The pictures are easy to remember.
- It helps you read the text very carefully.

When to use this kind of notemaking
- When the text is about how something works, how something is made, how something changes
- When there is a sequence or an order in the text (Figures 11.2, 11.3, and 11.4).

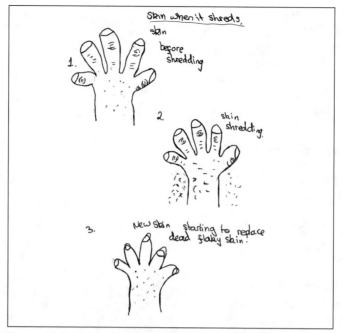

Figure 11.2 Notemaking on the Process of Skin Replacement

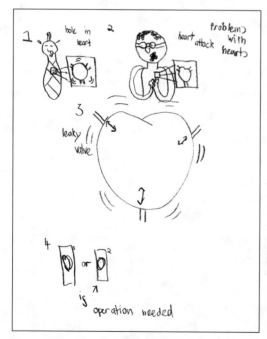

Figure 11.3 Example of a Child's Notemaking Using Pictures

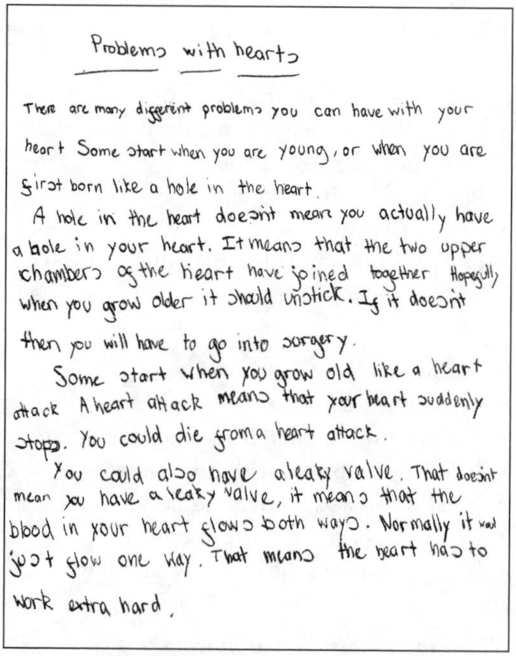

Problems with hearts

There are many different problems you can have with your heart. Some start when you are young, or when you are first born like a hole in the heart.

A hole in the heart doesn't mean you actually have a hole in your heart. It means that the two upper chambers of the heart have joined together. Hopefully, when you grow older it should unstick. If it doesn't then you will have to go into surgery.

Some start when you grow old like a heart attack. A heart attack means that your heart suddenly stops. You could die from a heart attack.

You could also have a leaky valve. That doesn't mean you have a leaky valve, it means that the blood in your heart flows both ways. Normally it would just flow one way. That means the heart has to work extra hard.

Figure 11.4 Write-up After Leaving Notes for Four Days (age 8)

Comment from child after making notes with pictures
"It is easier because before, I didn't know what to do. Before I found a page that looked interesting and then just wrote it all down" (age 8).

3. Notemaking Using Charts

How to do it:
- Work with a partner.
- Find a suitable piece of text.
- Decide what you want to find out.
- Decide what to compare.
- Draw a rough chart.
- Judge how the information fits into your chart.
- Draw another chart, leaving space for further information.
- Read the text all the way through. Put in as few words as possible per box.
- Check that you have all the information you need.
- Put the chart and original text away.
- After a few days, bring out the chart. Tell somebody what you have learned, using the chart as a reminder.
- Use the chart to organize your writing.

Advantages
- It helps you notice similarities and differences.
- It helps you to be selective.
- It helps you to decide on the most important words.
- The chart can show that some information may not be in the text.
- It helps you to read with a purpose.
- Writing up from a chart is easy, and it has a natural order.

When to use this kind of notemaking
- When there is something to compare
- With texts such as those on trees, plants, animals, people, types of houses, or countries
- When there is similar information about two or more things (Figures 11.5 and 11.6)

Comments from children
"Charts make it easier—you know what you are looking for" (age 8).
"You have two brains if you work together" (age 8).
"You can have a talk and if we don't agree, look again" (age 7).

4. Patterns

How to do it:
- Select a suitable text.
- Use underlining method (on acetate) to write all your questions.

Name of animal	grass Snake	Sticklebacks	Toads	Rabbit
Eggs or babies	eggs	eggs	eggs	babies
Home of young	Compost heap	nest	ponds	burrow
Care of young	itself	male	its Self	female
Development 1. 2. 3. 4.				
Time before reaching adult	after 3 years	½ and years	3 or four years	four months
How long they live	X	X	40 years	X

Figure 11.5 Chart Comparing Four Animals

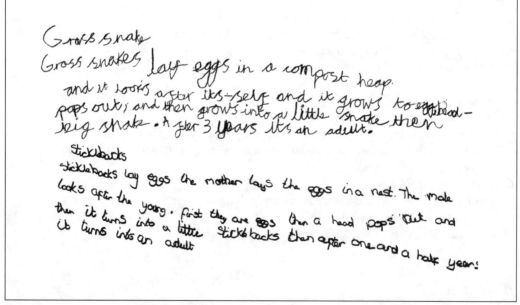

Figure 11.6 Write-up from Chart (Figure 11.5)

- Write down the selected words as a list.
- Look at your lists—collect the words that go together and put them into groups.

Further extensions
- Use another piece of paper and draw a central picture.
- Write one spoke of words.
- Write the most important words next to the center.
- Out of this, draw another line or lines.
- Write another spoke as you need.
- Put the pattern and original copy away (Figure 11.7).
- After a few days, get out your pattern (your notes).
- Tell somebody what you have learned—one spoke at a time—or write up what you have learned for somebody else to read.

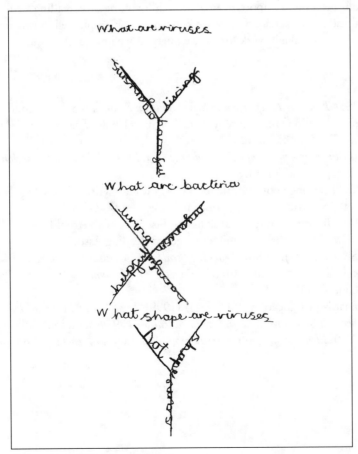

Figure 11.7 What Are Viruses?

Advantages
- Patterns are easy to remember.
- They are very colorful.
- They can be used on all texts.
- You can be creative.
- Writing is made easy and is well organized.

Conclusion

If only governments and schools would give notemaking the prominence it deserves, our children would be better equipped and less likely to make "mega" notes, which, in the words of one student, were "a complete waste of good time—why did I do it? And I never learned, I kept doing it."

Research on the Internet is becoming more and more important. Weaker students find a suitable site, press the print button, and think they have done the research. Never have real notemaking skills been more important to all our children, because reading with only basic skills is an ineffectual and futile exercise. Unless we know how to manipulate information, how to make sense of it, and how to make it work for us, we might as well not bother.

References

Bulman, L. (1985) *Teaching Language and Study Skills in Secondary Schools.* London: Heinemann.

Department for Education and Employment (DfEE) (1998) *The National Literacy Strategy: Framework for Teaching.* London: DfEE.

Neate, B. (1992) *Finding Out About Finding Out: A guide to children information books.* Hodder & Stoughton (reprint Infopress).

Neate, B. (1996) "Learning about nonfiction books through writing," *Reading,* July 1996 **30**(2).

Neate, B. (1999a) "A curriculum based on genre," *Primary English* **5**(1).

Neate, B. (1999b) "Information retrieval skills," in Fisher, R. with Arnold, H. (ed.) *Understanding the Literacy Hour.* Hertfordshire: United Kingdom Reading Association.

Nisbet, J. and Shucksmith, J. (1986) *Learning Strategies.* London: Routledge.

Office For Standards in Education (OFSTED) (1998) *The National Literacy Project: An HMI evaluation.* London: OFSTED.

Office For Standards in Education (OFSTED) (1999) *The Annual Report of Her Majesty's Chief Inspector of Schools: Standards and quality in education 1997/8.* London: OFSTED.

Pugh, A. K. (1978) *Silent Reading: An introduction to its study and teaching.* London: Heinemann.

Chapter 12

Using Graphic Organizers to Write Information Texts
Steve Moline

We often ask children to research a topic (by "making notes") without giving them enough explicit guidance in how to plan their writing. This results in a number of structural problems in the children's texts, such as incomplete information, gaps in logic and a lack of direction. The main reason for this appears to be that while notes can provide plenty of detailed "points," they do not help with planning the structure of a text. Children complain that they don't know where to start or how to organize the details in the notes they have made, while teachers comment that the children often miss the guiding concept of the texts that they attempt.

This chapter offers some solutions to these problems by focusing the children on the design of their texts. Graphic organizers such as flow diagrams, tables, webs, and storyboards can be used to summarize the source material and to plan the final draft of their writing.

What Are Graphic Organizers?

A graphic organizer is a text that provides a visual structure for the information it holds. Its structure organizes the details to capture the text's guiding concept, and to provide a framework for writing a final draft.

Examples of graphic organizers discussed here are listed in Figure 12.1. They have been selected for their usefulness when writing such information genres as a report, an explanation, or a procedure.

Why Use Graphic Organizers?

The traditional way to write information texts in classrooms has been to make brief notes while reading the source material, then to attempt a final draft based on these notes. Some problems with this method are:

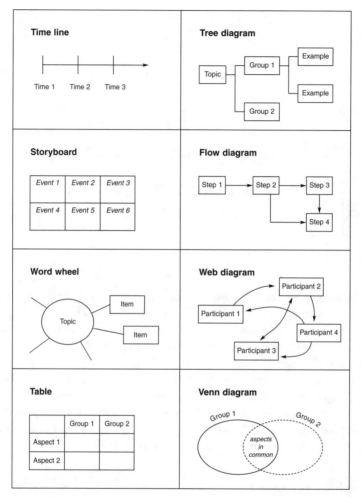

Figure 12.1 Some Graphic Organizers Suitable for Planning Information Texts

- Children get lost in the detail. They may wander off-task, leave out key information, repeat some of the information, fail to link some events or reasons, or come to inconsequent conclusions.
- Children complain that they "don't know where to start." Their notes do not offer a guide to what comes first or last, or how the details are related to each other, or how they could best be sequenced.
- Children have difficulty picturing the shape or direction of their text while they are writing it, and lose a clear idea of its purpose; the task seems meaningless and the writer becomes discouraged. The forest of detailed notes seems overwhelming without a map.
- Teachers comment that the children's work seems aimless: While plenty of information (little bits of data) has been provided, the guiding concept of the text often becomes lost.

All of these problems are caused by the same weakness: Our usual practice of "making notes" tends to focus on details at the risk of overlooking the text's structure and function. Making notes is an excellent way of recording precise and nuanced details, but the notes by themselves lack a "map" of the text's organizing principle, for example, the recursive "shape" of the water cycle or the classifying principle at work in a report about mammals. It is a waste of time collecting miscellaneous facts about stages in the water cycle if children miss the point that there is an underlying structure that connects each step in the process. No amount of additional facts about clouds or lakes can provide this.

Graphic organizers can act as frameworking tools to overcome these problems. For example, when planning an explanation of the water cycle, children may choose to use a flow diagram which sequences the steps of the process; or when writing a report about mammals, a tree diagram can be used to classify the topic into groups and sub-groups and to fit the examples to these groups. In both cases, the diagram offers both a sequence to follow when writing the final draft, and a grasp of what the text is essentially about. Organizers are not intended here to replace the practice of making detailed notes; rather, the two activities are best viewed as having complementary advantages. These are summarized in Table 12.1.

Matching Genres and Graphic Organizers

Each information genre has a different purpose and therefore a different structure. In most cases, a genre can be matched to a visual text that performs some or all of its organizing functions. In the following pages, we look at the functions of each genre, matching it with graphic organizers that help children with planning their final draft. A summary of how graphic organizers can be matched to genres is provided in Table 12.2.

Table 12.1 Notemaking and Graphic Organizers Compared

	Advantages	*Disadvantages*
Notes	• are ideal for recording details and examples • capture nuances, subtleties, and ambiguities	• lack organization (such as the sequence of cause and effect in an explanation, or logic links in an argument) • do not identify missing data, gaps in logic, irrelevant details, inconsistencies, misplaced examples • lack a framework for the writing task (leading to omission of details, wandering off task, lack of closure)
Graphic organizers	• can capture the guiding concept or organizing principle of a text • provide a framework for organizing the final draft • suggest headings for paragraphs and topics for sentences • highlight missing data or weak links in reasoning • visualize the information in a form that more memorable for some children	• tend to simplify and generalize the topic • may omit details in order to focus on the guiding concept of the text • tend to overlook subtleties, nuances, or ambiguities that are better captured in carefully phrased notes

Table 12.2 Matching Information Genres and Graphic Organizers

Genre	Graphic organizer
Recount	• time line • storyboard
Procedure (Instructions)	• storyboard • flow diagram
Information report	• word wheel • table • tree diagram
Explanation	• storyboard • flow diagram • web diagram
Persuasion (Argument)	• word wheel • flow diagram
Discussion	• table • Venn diagram • web diagram

Recount

Recounts retell events in the order in which they occurred (Table 12.3). Personal recounts include the writer's responses and sometimes end with a comment, whereas factual recounts adopt a neutral tone to the subject and end by summarizing outcomes.

When writing a recount, children need to sequence the events chronologically. However, they commonly miss out some events, or place them out of order. The reason for this seems to be that when we record our past experiences, we tend to recall the events that impressed us first, and add the others later. A time line or storyboard helps children to sequence the events, but in different ways.

Table 12.3 Planning a Recount

Structure of a recount	Graphic organizers for planning a recount	Possible topics
1 Orientation 2 Sequence of events in time order 3 Outcomes or comments	• **time line** to arrange events in time sequence • **storyboard** to show how the subject changes over time	**Age 6** My life so far **Age 8** Our day at the museum **Age 10** How telephones have changed **Age 12** Effect of sunlight on plants (science experiment)

A time line focuses the writer on the exact times when the events occurred as well as the order in which they happened. The writer's notes can be used to provide the details, but the time line offers a structure that can be followed when preparing the final draft. A storyboard is more useful when describing how a subject has changed over time, such as the development of the motor car or the telephone. Storyboards consist of a series of diagrams, each with a caption: The diagrams highlight key changes (such as to the design of the telephone), while the captions support each diagram with additional information (such as the date of each new development).

Figure 12.2 shows how notes and a time line have been combined to write a recount of a visit to a local zoo. Notes provide the details, remembered in no particular order, while the time line provides a structural overview without the details, and the two have been combined in the final draft.

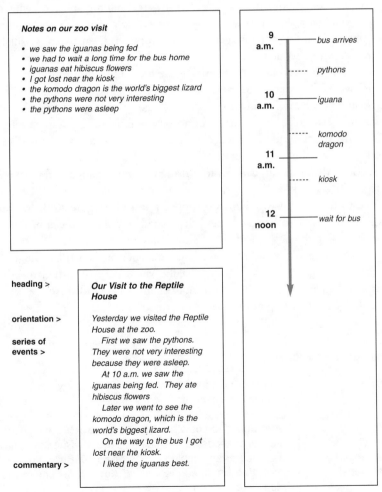

Figure 12.2 A personal recount of a zoo visit is first recollected as a series of notes, then planned as a time line and the two combined in a final draft.

Procedure (Instructions)

Procedural texts list materials and provide a method (a series of instructions) to enable the reader to carry out a task (Table 12.4).

Children need to be aware of the reader's needs when writing a procedure. The list of materials should be complete and exact (sometimes giving quantities, as in a recipe), and the method requires careful organization, so that the task can be carried out successfully. Sequencing is critical to the success of a procedural text. Children often need to revise their method section, checking for missing steps and for steps placed out of order (asking, does the reader need to do *this* before doing *that?*). Children sometimes find it difficult to imagine the needs of a reader who is less familiar with a task than they are.

Procedures often involve noting changes to the subject as it is being prepared or assembled. This is why recipe books frequently include step-by-step photographs, or why the assembly instructions that come with your new sound system provide a sequence of diagrams. These are both examples of storyboarding the instructions. In a storyboard, each step is usually numbered, providing the reader with a sequence to follow.

Frequently, children need help in organizing the method section of the text, to ensure that the instructions "work" in practice. Storyboarding can help children to clarify the order of the steps and to visualize how an item will appear at each stage. If children draw each stage on a small square of paper, they can move the squares around on the table or the floor to establish the best sequence. When this is done, the squares are numbered and put into a pile; children then work through the pile as they write the final draft.

More experienced writers can benefit from using a flow diagram as a frameworking tool for sequencing steps, since this kind of diagram is especially helpful where two or more strings of instructions need to be brought together to complete a task. In Figure 12.3 the three parts of a hamburger need to be prepared separately, and this added complication can be understood more clearly by first visualizing the task as a "forked" flow diagram.

Children may also need to consider whether the reader of their final text would benefit if each step is illustrated, storyboard-fashion, especially where parts are fitted together in precise ways. Sometimes a diagram of the subject is a more economical (and therefore practical) way of instructing the reader than writing out the same information in sentences.

Table 12.4 Planning a Procedure

Structure of a procedure	Graphic organizers for planning a procedure	Possible topics How to...
1 Goal 2 Materials (list) 3 Method (arranged as a series of steps)	• **storyboard** to show how the subject changes as it is being prepared or assembled • **flow diagram** to sequence steps in a method	**Age 6** Make a salad sandwich **Age 8** Send an email message **Age 10** Build a model boat **Age 12** Assemble your tent

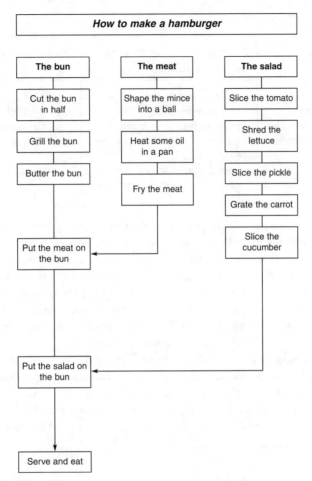

Figure 12.3 A "forked" flow diagram helps to sequence the steps and to organize parallel strings of steps.

Information Report

A report opens with a definition of the topic and usually classifies the topic into groups, or lists its components. In the remainder of the text, these groups or components are described in detail (Table 12.5).

When preparing notes for a report, children usually have no trouble assembling "bundles of facts" or providing examples; they have more difficulty showing how the facts are related within groups, particularly when smaller groups belong within larger ones, rather like Chinese boxes. For example, in a report about mammals, divided first into carnivores and herbivores and then into the cat family and others, listing some of the big cats as examples, it is not surprising that children lose their way, giving undue emphasis to some groups or details while forgetting to include others.

Table 12.5 Planning a Report

Structure of a report	Graphic organizers for planning a report	Possible topics
1 Definition 2 Classification into groups or components 3 Description of examples	• **word wheel** to list groups and/or examples • **table** to sort a topic into groups and list examples for each group • **tree diagram** to sort a topic into groups and sub-groups	**Age 6** Pets **Age 8** Dinosaurs **Age 10** Habitats **Age 12** Telecommunications

The outcome can be to lose the original purpose of the text, which is, first of all, to show the organization of mammals and only secondly to describe some typical examples.

Graphic organizers that offer a suitable structure for planning a report include word wheels, tables, and tree diagrams. Word wheels can be used for simpler reports which do little more than describe examples, as shown in Figure 12.4A. Different topics (Mars, Venus) can be broken down into their attributes (dust storms, clouds) by extending the diagram outwards. Numbering the topics provides the writer with a sequence to follow when writing the final draft. However, a word wheel makes it difficult to draw comparisons between attributes.

Tables, on the other hand, divide a subject into its components (shown in the column headings across the top of the table) and aspects to be considered or compared (shown in the row headings down the side of the table). When planning a report on the nearest planets, the writer might start by listing the planets at the top of the table, and identifying some aspects of each planet down the side, as in Figure 12.4B. This enables the writer to check whether there

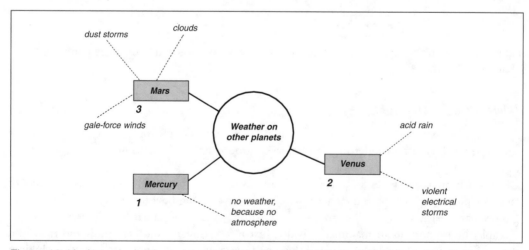

Figure 12.4A A word wheel can be extended to include attributes (dust storms) as well as topics (Mars, Venus).

Our nearest planets			
	Mercury	**Venus**	**Mars**
land forms	• craters • mountains • high cliffs • plains	• volcanoes • high plateaux • glowing rocks	• craters • volcanoes • canyons • sand dunes • ice caps
atmosphere and sky	• constant "night sky" even when sun is shining	• completely covered with dense clouds • always dark	• pink sky • thin clouds • two moons • sun looks much smaller
weather	• no weather because no atmosphere	• acid rain and violent electrical storms	• gale-force winds and dust storms • some clouds but no rain

Figure 12.4B A table can be used to organize notes into both components (Mars, Venus), and aspects (land forms, weather). The structure of a table allows us to compare aspects by reading across the rows from left to right.

are any gaps in the information that has been collected (the table would show an empty box), and to make comparisons by reading across the table. In these ways, a table is a better analytical tool than a word wheel for preparing a report.

The table also provides a sequence for working through the notes when writing the final draft. If the writer chooses to arrange the report as a series of descriptions of each planet, then the headings of the table would form the headings (and paragraph topics) of the report, the writer working down through the information in each column. Alternatively, if the intention is to compare the planets, then the aspect headings (land forms, etc.) would work as paragraph topics and the writer would find similarities and differences by moving across the table from left to right.

A tree diagram also classifies a topic (represented as its "trunk") into groups (its "branches"), but, unlike tables, tree diagrams can be extended into ever smaller sub-groups if this is needed. Even quite simple reports can require this breaking down of the subject into its smaller groupings, especially when examples are added and described (as in Figure 12.5), whereas tables are not generally used to do this.

Figure 12.5 shows how a tree diagram can be used both to summarize a report and to plan one. If children are encouraged to construct a tree while reading this kind of text, they will have a stronger understanding of how reports systematically follow a classifying structure. If they use a tree when planning their reports, they can also use it as a "map'"when working through the details of their final draft. They can use the first-level groups (house/tent/caravan [trailer]) as paragraph topics, and the second-level groups (such as brick/timber) as sentence topics.

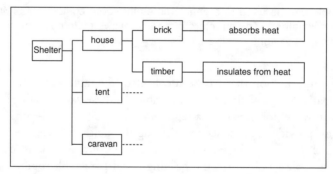

Figure 12.5 The classifying structure of a report can be understood more clearly if it is visualized first as a tree diagram.

Explanation

Like recounts and procedures, explanations often require the writer to think sequentially (Table 12.6). Explaining *how* is to connect causes to effects; explaining *why* is to relate reasons to consequences.

In an explanation, all the steps in the process need to be included for the explanation to "work." Children often produce explanations that omit a critical step, repeat steps, or place them in a sequence that does not make sense as an explanation. Attempting an explanation based only on notes of isolated details, without a "map" to follow, is the most likely cause of these problems.

Where a simple linear process is being explained (such as how bread is made), a storyboard can help children with planning their explanations. The numbering of the boxes in the storyboard helps the writer to focus on the correct sequence, while the graphics can summarize the significant ways in which the subject changes. Where a cyclical process is explained (such as an

Table 12.6 Planning an Explanation

Structure of an explanation	Graphic organizers for planning an explanation	Possible topics
1 Statement or question to be explained 2 Explanation arranged as a series of steps	• **storyboard** to show how something is made or changes over time • **flow diagram** to sequence steps in a process • **web diagram** to relate participants in a network or system	**Age 6** How bread is made **Age 8** A forest food web **Age 10** The water cycle **Age 12** How we are governed

insect's life cycle), the storyboard can be organized like a clock face (as in Figure 12.6), providing clockwise directionality to the text. The arrows dispense with the need for numbering, and the writer could start the explanation with either the egg or the adult.

If a process has several preconditions or more than one outcome, a flow diagram is more useful than a storyboard, since it allows the writer to track parallel strings of events. In Figure 12.7, the process of respiration has been visualized as a flow diagram which identifies multiple causes and effects. This clarifies the guiding concept of respiration for the writer and provides a clear sequence to follow when writing out the explanation.

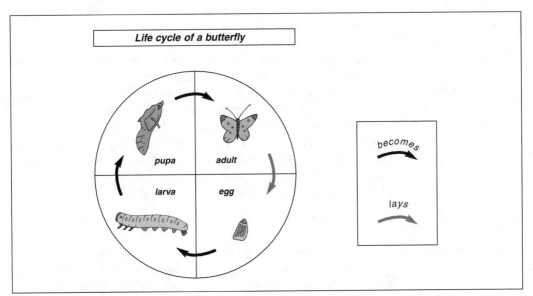

Figure 12.6 A "clock-face" storyboard can be used to explain cyclical processes. Arrows are assigned meanings and show the direction of the text.

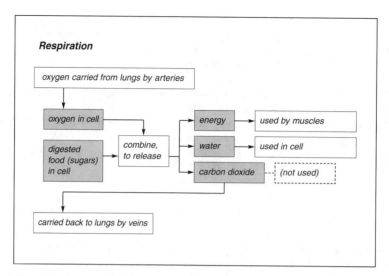

Figure 12.7 A flow diagram can be used to connect multiple preconditions or outcomes. Here the preconditions are oxygen and sugars, and the outcomes are energy and water.

Some explanations involve a number of participants that interact within a system or a network of relationships. The participants may be animals in a food web, characters in a novel, or providers of goods and services in a community. In a habitat such as the seashore, the participants may even include inanimate rocks, water, and sunlight. A web diagram can be used to identify the participants and the relationships they have with one another. Participants may be represented as boxes, while relationships are shown as labeled arrows. The diagram can be used as a checklist, although it does not always provide a sequence in which to write out the explanation, since the details in web diagrams, like those in maps, can be read in almost any order and still make sense. Children can, however, make sequencing decisions after completing the diagram by numbering the participants (or the relationships) in the order in which they intend to explain them.

In Figure 12.8 the different parts of a seashore habitat have been identified in boxes, and the interactions between them have been recorded as labeled arrows. Having decided to discuss the living and nonliving factors separately, the writer has highlighted the nonliving participants to distinguish them from the animals and plants, and then numbered all the participants in the order in which they would be addressed in the final draft.

Persuasion (Argument)

Persuasive texts seek to encourage the reader to adopt the writer's point of view. Although these texts include advertising and political speeches which appeal to emotions, the kinds of persuasive texts discussed here are limited to rational arguments in which a case is presented logically.

Children often enjoy writing these kinds of texts, which allow them to express their preferences forcefully. Arguments nevertheless require detachment when analyzing the strengths and weaknesses of the reasons offered and the links between them. Making a list of reasons for a point

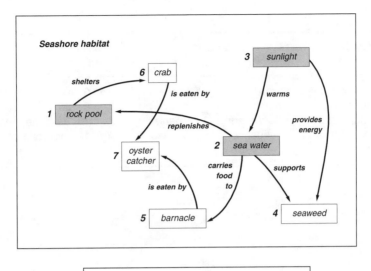

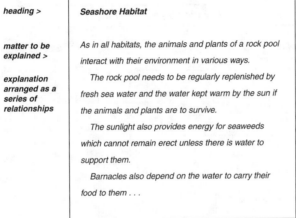

Figure 12.8 In this web of relationships in a seashore habitat, the writer has used shading to distinguish the participants as living or nonliving, and numbered them in the order in which they are to be explained in the final draft.

of view comes easily; however, children usually need extra support when developing the analytical skills that logical thinking demands of them (Table 12.7).

The simplest framework for planning an argument is a word wheel. Young children can use this kind of diagram to list a number of equally ranked "one-step" reasons for an opinion. Children can number the "spokes" when deciding the order in which to present their reasons.

When planning a more sophisticated argument which has several strings of reasons, a flow diagram helps the writer to "think through" all the steps, identifying gaps and inconsistencies. In Figure 12.9 the writer has chosen to argue for electric cars in preference to petrol cars. The diagram helps the writer to arrange complementary strings of reasons for and against, which lead to a conclusion

Table 12.7 Planning an Argument

Structure of an argument	Graphic organizers for planning an argument	Possible topics
1 Statement of opinion 2 Series of reasons arranged logically 3 Restatement of position 4 Call for action	• **word wheel** to list "one-step" reasons • **flow diagram** to organize a sequence of linked reasons	**Age 6** Dogs are the best pets **Age 8** Join our club **Age 10** Save the great white shark **Age 12** Everyone should vote

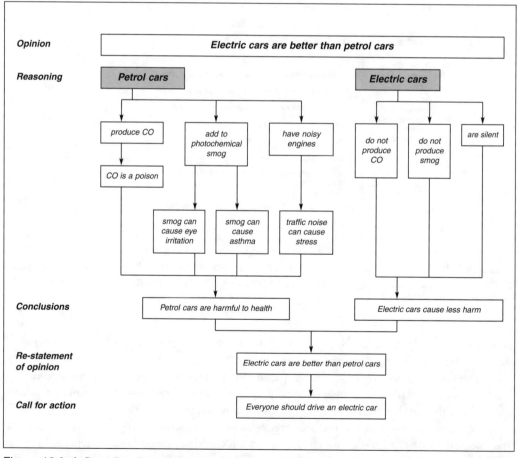

Figure 12.9 A flow diagram systematically draws out strings of reasons when making a more complex argument.

that one kind of car is more harmful than the other. This in turn supports the writer's preference for electric cars, leading to a "call for action" that everyone should drive an electric car. The diagram helps the writer to see how each reason or conclusion follows from what has gone before, and to match up the three strands of the argument for electric cars to be sure that all three "answer" the objections to petrol cars.

Where gaps or inconsistencies reveal themselves in the diagram, the writer can add or modify reasons before attempting the final draft. When writing out their arguments, children can also use the diagram as a guide to sequencing the argument:

> *First I will discuss three problems with petrol cars, then I will show how electric cars avoid these problems.*
> *Petrol cars can cause three health risks...*
> *Electric cars, on the other hand...*
> *It follows that petrol cars are more harmful...*
> *Therefore, electric cars are better than petrol cars.*
> *For these reasons, everyone should drive an electric car.*

Discussion

In a discussion the writer considers two or more sides of a topic where opinions differ. The writer adopts a neutral tone and avoids taking sides, summarizing conflicting views and sometimes noting where opinions may overlap (agree). The text concludes either by recommending one side's point of view or by offering a new combination of views that may resolve the conflict (Table 12.8).

Discussions often require more detachment than persuasive texts. More than one argument needs to be analyzed, and the writer's task at the end may involve selecting the stronger reasons from both sides, synthesizing them in a new argument. Understanding the needs of conflicting stakeholders in a dispute requires an objectivity that does not always come easily to younger writers. For these reasons, it could be said that this is a more sophisticated genre than the others discussed here.

Table 12.8 Planning a Discussion

Structure of a discussion	*Graphic organizers for planning a discussion*	*Possible topics*
1 Statement of two or more conflicting views 2 Background information 3 Arguments for and against 4 Conclusion that *either* recommends one side over the others, *or* proposes a way to resolve the conflict	• **table** to list and compare opposing attitudes or arguments • **Venn diagram** to highlight where conflicting views may overlap (agree) • **web diagram** to show relationships between stakeholders in a debate or controversy	**Age 6** Favorite animals **Age 8** Is homework always necessary? **Age 10** For and against video games **Age 12** Should we log some rainforests?

Simple discussions are nevertheless manageable by young children, who can plan their text using a table that lists different points of view, with their reasons, side by side for comparison. For example, they can use a table to survey their friends in order to find favorite animals or foods and the reasons for their choices.

More experienced writers can use a table to arrive at a decision by examining alternatives. In Figure 12.10 the writer has been set the task of choosing the most suitable materials for an energy-efficient house. Different materials are listed across the top of the table, and aspects to be compared down the side, enabling the writer to compare alternatives systematically and to make a choice in favor of one material, or to choose a combination of materials. Each material can be "scored" by reading down the columns, or compared on the basis of different criteria by reading across the rows. In this way, a table can assist children to make considered decisions when preparing a formal discussion of the issues.

A Venn diagram can locate agreement where two apparently opposed points of view overlap, and can be used to find common ground in a dispute, leading to a resolution of the conflict. In Figure 12.11 the arguments for and against bringing pets to school have been arranged in two loops. Points of agreement have been placed where the loops overlap, allowing the writer to offer two possible compromises: All pets could be brought to the school once a year for a pet show, or some (specified) animals could be brought into the classroom for study over longer periods.

In preparing a discussion that involves more than two points of view, it sometimes helps to identify the relationships between the stakeholders. We can "map" these relationships in a web

Materials for energy-efficient housing			
	timber	**mud brick**	**aluminum**
cost to buy	less expensive than steel	nil cost if we make them	most expensive
insulation properties	insulates well in hot climate	retains heat in cold climate	poor insulation
effects on environment	depletes forests	materials taken from site only	high energy use in manufacture
maintenance	re-paint/repair every 10 years	no painting; some repairs	very low maintenance
safety risks	fire risk; resists earthquakes	earthquake risk; resists fire	resists fire and earthquake

Figure 12.10 Children can "score" the alternatives (by reading down the columns of the table), or compare them on the basis of the aspects shown on the left (by reading across the rows of the table).

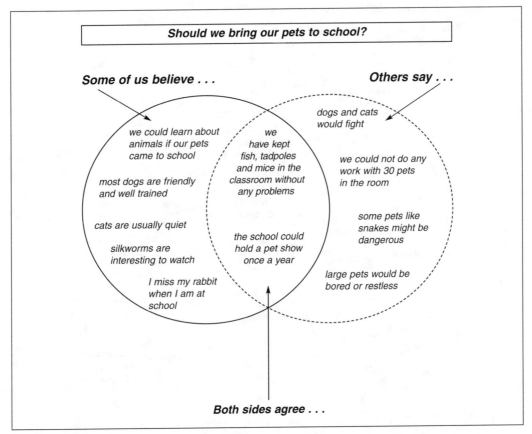

Figure 12.11 A Venn diagram can be used to identify points of agreement between opposing sides of a discussion.

diagram in which the roles of each participant are defined by labeled arrows, as in Figure 12.12. While this diagram does not summarize the arguments themselves, it does help the writer to identify the motivations for those arguments, explaining why the stakeholders disagree. This in turn can help the writer to formulate suggestions for resolving the conflict by discovering which parties are potentially in agreement or have hidden motives that are not expressed in their arguments, and which parties need to be brought together if the conflict is to be resolved.

Designing a Research Task

So-called genre writing should not be seen as an isolated "writing" activity. Information writing is best done as part of a research task, which involves reading the source material, recording details in note form, planning the written text using a graphic organizer, and completing the final draft. The structure of such a research task is shown in Figure 12.13.

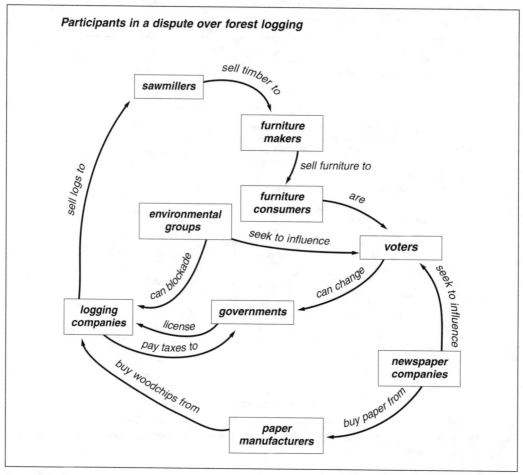

Participants in a dispute over forest logging

Figure 12.12 A web diagram helps the writer to identify the relationships between the participants in a dispute.

The key to the success of this structured activity is the task sheet, which should be designed to support the writer at each stage of the procedure.

A task sheet, therefore, should:

- have clear goals
- offer a procedure to follow, such as is shown in Figure 12.13
- include examples of completed texts in the same genre (but on a different topic)
- provide examples of graphic organizers and notes (but on a different topic)
- list the key features of both the structure and the language of the genre
- provide for opportunities to review work in progress

At each step, the teacher should be available to the children as they work in their groups, as they will need guidance and support. It is not enough simply to hand out the task sheet.

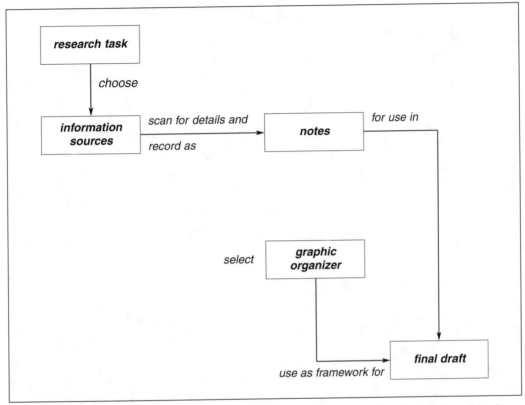

Figure 12.13 Provide the children with a "map" of the research task before they start work on it.

Further Reading and Viewing

The ideas in this chapter have their origins in the following:

Moline, S. *I See What You Mean: Children at work with visual information.* Longman/Pearson (Australia), Stenhouse (USA), Pembroke (Canada), 1995.

Moline, S. *The Information Toolkit* (Books 1–3). Oxford University Press (in press).

Moline, S. *What Is Visual Literacy?* (video). Longman/Pearson (Australia), Stenhouse (USA), Pembroke (Canada), 1997.

Part IV
Getting Ready for Publication

Chapter 13

Developing Understanding of Punctuation with Young Writers and Readers

Nigel Hall

Punctuation is a very strange object for beginning writers and readers. It consists of a variety of often very tiny, almost invisible marks that do not seem to make any difference to their reading and writing. As most teachers will recognize, young children have a wonderful capacity to write without using punctuation and then read aloud their writing perfectly. However, along come teachers and tell them that they have to use these minute marks, and teachers do so with copious reminders and much red ink. But, as so many teachers will testify, children often manage to continue ignoring punctuation, leaving teachers tearing their hair in exasperation. In this chapter I want to explore why punctuation often makes no sense to beginning writers and readers and examine some strategies that might help children develop an understanding of punctuation that is more meaningful and useful to them.

Children usually arrive in school as fairly fluent users of oral language. Their abilities and experience will vary, but, inevitably, teachers spend more time trying to keep children quiet than they do persuading them to talk. Most children feel comfortable with oral language and use it without having to think about how they do it. Punctuation, of course, is not a feature of oral language. Although many children will have begun an acquaintance with written language before arriving in schools, it is in schools that the emphasis changes from simply using oral and written language to do things in the world to focusing on how written language works. The experience of literacy in schooling is dominated by the requirements to analyze language (whether it be sounds, letters, grammar or textual features) rather than to use it meaningfully. For children familiar with using language solely to make meanings, this imposition has the effect of making all this new knowledge seem like something "out there" which is being imposed upon them for little reason. Some of this "out there" knowledge comes to make sense fairly easily; other parts of it retain a mystifying status and instead of being incorporated meaningfully into a child's world, remain for a long time as things which are important only because teachers say they are. Punctuation is a classic example of an aspect of literacy experience which for a long time (and for some, a very long time) appears to be externally imposed by teachers as if it were a kind of punishment for writers. The consequence is that many adults tend not to look back kindly on their own experiences of learning to punctuate, and many people never feel comfortable using punctuation.

Why Punctuation Can Appear Meaningless to Young Writers and Readers

I have now spent many years researching how young children come to learn about punctuation, and in this section I want to share some of the typical punctuation practices I have seen in classrooms. Of course, not all teachers, children, and classrooms are the same, but the many conversations about punctuation I have had with practicing teachers in several countries have convinced me that what I will describe is fairly typical in many classrooms.

Beginning to read and write is hard. It demands the orchestration of a range of complex activities. For a writer, the burden is even greater; they have to control the creation of the meaning, the grammatical representation of this meaning, its conversion into a set of phoneme/grapheme relationships, and represent all this neatly on a piece of paper, using an awkward instrument. No wonder children make choices about what they should concentrate on when writing, just as a learner of any age makes decisions when learning a complex activity. Try and remember learning to drive. At first it is impossible to do everything at once; coordinating it all successfully comes along later. Punctuation is often a last choice of young writers, but I would want to claim that, to a large extent, the way we as teachers approach punctuation and resource its learning plays a large role in encouraging children to see it as meaningless.

1. Most beginning readers and writers have their priorities straight; they have read their teacher's (and schooling's) real agendas and are spending their reading lives concentrating on decoding words, and their writing lives making sure the handwriting is neat and the spellings are correct. At no time in my research studies did I ever hear a child come up and ask a teacher if their punctuation was correct. All day, everyday, children sought reassurance that their spellings were correct. The consequence here is that although teachers might tell children that punctuation is important and necessary, teachers themselves are dominated, understandably, by phonics, handwriting, and spelling; children are not stupid—they get the message. Thus, effort is directed toward those things believed to be really important and away from things perceived as less significant.

2. Most punctuation marks are small, and probably the most important, the period, is the smallest of them all. It should be no surprise that children find the exclamation mark and the question mark the easiest to remember; they do, after all, look a bit like letters. I gave several groups of young children a brief copying exercise. All they had to do was to copy a few sentences which contained a wide range of punctuation marks. Many did not copy the punctuation marks at all. Even some of the more able children, who were already exploring punctuation marks, copied the visually salient marks but left out the periods (see Figure 13.1). It is very hard for a learner to focus on the least visually salient aspect of writing when so many other things command attention.

"Hello!" said the old man. "Where
are you going?" The boy just
looked at him. "I don't know!" The
boy was lost. He didn't know
where to go.

Figure 13.1

3. Although teachers do talk about punctuation, quite a lot of the talk I have observed and recorded tends to emphasize naming and labeling the marks. Typically, this kind of work consists of identifying the punctuation marks in a text and reciting/learning the name of the mark. This is obviously an important thing to do; having a language of punctuation will help in many situations. But, labeling and naming, while useful, do not help children understand why these marks are important, or what they do. For this, explanation is required. Without it, children can be very interested, even enthusiastic, as the children I observed were, but it leaves them treating the punctuation as marks which have names rather than as marks which have uses. An extra problem is that, as teachers, we seem to have a mania for teaching children the "rules," and they often get much better at reciting a rule than using it. Arthur (1996) reported on a lesson in a British classroom during which the children, when asked what goes at the beginning, could all shout, "A capital letter," but when doing the following piece of writing, most of them omitted it.

4. The tendency to focus on naming and labeling probably occurs because of the mess that often results when explanation is explored. Without going into a long historical lesson, punctuation is, and always has been, a complex object. Across historical time it has changed quite dramatically. In the West, the early use of punctuation was almost totally elocutionary; indeed, the origin of Western punctuation lies not in what writers did but in what readers did (Parkes 1992). At a time when oral reading predominated over silent reading, readers put in their own punctuation so that they could declaim the text orally. It was not until many centuries later that a shift began to take place which moved away from punctuation as an elocutionary marker towards punctuation as a grammatical marker. We have suffered ever since, as the two often sit very uncomfortably beside each other (see Hall 1996). Should teachers stress elocutionary marking—as they often do? Whenever teachers say, "Take a breath" or "Read it aloud to see what it sounds like" or "You need to make a longer pause when you see a period," they are using rather doubtful elocutionary marking, something which can also be seen clearly in the first-ever book about punctuation for children, *Punctuation Personified*, anonymously published in 1824 (see Figure 13.2).

ENSIGN SEMICOLON, marked thus;

See, how Semicolon is strutting with pride!
Into two or more parts he'll a sentence divide.
As 'John's a good scholar; but George is a better;
'One wrote a fair copy; the other a letter!'
Without this gay ensign we little could do;
And when he appears we must pause & count TWO.

A COLON, marked thus :

The colon consists of two dots, as you see;
And remains within sight whilst you count one, two, three;
'Tis us'd where the sense is complete, tho but part
Of the sentence you're reading, or learning by heart.
As 'Gold is deceitful: it bribes to destroy.
'Young James is admired: he's a very good boy!'

Figure 13.2

Such explanations can cause children perpetual confusion, and they try to listen for spaces that are simply not there in silent reading. On the other hand, starting with grammatical explanations is going to be rather tough for young writers and readers, despite the efforts of Carey (1958, p. 23) to convince us it is easy:

> Every school boy knows that full-stops come at the end of sentences; and seeing that a sentence has got to contain at least one main clause, with its own finite verb, quite apart from any subordinate clause that may be added, one would have thought that this was about all that need be said on the subject.

The answer might be to take a leaf out of the book of those children who have shown us how they finally made sense of punctuation, and I will come to that later. But, of course, when teachers are confused (and sometimes wrong), children get confused, and once they are confused, they tend to adhere to their beliefs that punctuation is not something useful to them.

A second problem with the move to explanation is that, unfortunately, many teachers are themselves unsure about, or inconsistent in their use of, punctuation. Only recently I observed a lesson in which part of it was devoted to the apostrophe. On the board was a teacher-written sentence about something else the children had to do later; it had three errors in it, two of which were the omission of apostrophes signifying possession.

5. It is an unfortunate fact of classroom life that the general reading experience of children tends to confirm any beliefs that punctuation does not have any function. This is caused by the design and layout of the books the children read. It is not intentional, as book designers and authors have, quite reasonably, been making access to the texts as easy as possible. But making something easier often means taking something away, and when that happens, important clues can disappear. A very large number of young children's books, whether trade books or basal readers, have only one sentence per page (and sometimes only one sentence in a whole book—for instance, *Rosie's Walk* by Pat Hutchins). If there is one sentence on a page, then capital letters and full stops are redundant. The child starts where the words begin and stops when there are no more words. The child does not have to pay any attention whatsoever to the punctuation. Even when books have two sentences on a page, nearly all of them will start each sentence on a new line despite where the previous sentence ended, for instance:

> *John came into the room.*
> *He walked past the cupboard towards the window.*
> *It was locked.*

Thus, once again, the child does not need to pay attention to the punctuation, as space does the work of conveying information about the units of written language. Equally, when beginning writing, there is often an emphasis on writing one line. The teacher writes a line and the child copies underneath; the child writes a line and draws a picture or vice versa. Often, when a child writes two sentences, the new sentence begins on a new line. There are even materials (such as Breakthrough to Literacy) which seem to build this in, as it has individual sentence markers.

Capital letters and periods have no function when only one sentence exists. Such punctuation only becomes both useful and necessary once two sentences are written. Punctuation does not really serve to indicate when a sentence begins and ends, as many teachers are inclined to suggest, but to demarcate and indicate the relationship between two units of meaning. The marks used to demarcate the units convey important messages to the reader about the relationship between the two units. A comma between two units conveys a different relationship from when there is a period. One-sentence pages or books, however helpful they may be in other respects, do not help to develop children's understanding of how punctuation works.

The above five factors tend to cohere, almost conspire, to act against young readers and writers perceiving punctuation as meaningful (Hall 1998). Punctuation is easy to overlook, is often confusing when one does look, does not seem needed to read books or to write, and, anyway, has to take second place to more important things. It should be no surprise that teachers can struggle to persuade children that punctuation does have a use. Of course, children's general competence in some other areas of literacy does improve as their experience grows and they can begin to focus on other things, teachers consistently remind children not to forget to put capital letters and periods, and children begin to read books which have more complex text structures. But, as so many teachers will testify and as the research evidence confirms, the move to incorporating punctuation into written texts takes some strange paths. Children's early use of punctuation is often based on graphic principles (Hall 1999; Ferriero and Pontecorvo 1999). Who hasn't seen rows of periods placed down the edge of lines of writing, who hasn't seen children put a period between every word, who hasn't seen experienced child writers putting a capital letter at the start of story and a period right at the end, and that's it. Some may even have seen children assigning the "dots" randomly through a piece of writing. The move to graphic principles occurs because to children they seem to offer a more plausible theory of use than the overcomplicated explanations offered by teachers. Placement of punctuation by graphic principles is easy to learn and sometimes even produces a correct response. However, they clearly are more likely to be wrong than right, and being stuck in the use of graphic principles will seriously hold back a child's development as a writer. Children need to move from graphic principles, which are a dead end, to the use of linguistic principles, which open up the world of punctuation.

Facilitating Young Readers' and Writers' Understanding of Punctuation

The factors which will help young writers and readers develop a sense of punctuation as something meaningful are both general and specific. Some derive from a consideration of the above factors and some derive from other perspectives. What does seems clear is that endless exercises, learning of rules, reminders, and punishments for getting it wrong are not conducive to developing an understanding of punctuation. That is exactly how so many people who have problems with punctuation when writing began their writing careers. I offer the following ten general suggestions. These derive from my own research and that of the few other people who have investigated the topic.

1. Meaningful understanding of punctuation happens when the experience of learning to write and read is itself meaningful. Quite some time ago, Calkins compared two third-grade (eight- to nine-year-olds) classrooms (Calkins 1980). In one, writing was an experience in which children wrote for a purpose, reflected on their writing, and explored its effect upon readers. They were experiencing writing as real authors who had the power to shape and modify their texts to influence readers. In the other classroom, writing was more regulated, had to be right the first time, involved more standardized text forms, and was not reflective, and punctuation was learned by rules and definition. In the first class, the children used many more types of punctuation, more often and more appropriately, than did the children in the other class. The way the children in the first class talked about punctuation was about how it made a dif- ference to the text. The children in the second class talked about punctuation by reciting for- mal definitions. The children in the first class had incorporated punctuation into their repertoire of writing skills and were becoming effective and natural users of it, whereas for the other children, punctuation was a more distant, formal concept.

2. Within a classroom, even when writing is taught meaningfully, punctuation needs to be talked about in a different way. We need to make it clear through the language we use that punctua- tion is a tool that an author can use in making decisions. It is part of the way authors create an impact upon a reader. Thus, when discussing punctuation in someone's text (both adult and child authors), the discussion should be focused upon why the author chose to use that bit of punctuation in that place. So rather than say, "Where does the text show us" or "Who can find the bit where . . ." use phrasing which emphasizes the author's role: "How did the author make us frightened?" "How did the author let us know it was really exciting?" "Why did the author do this rather than that?" Punctuation fits so easily into this style of analysis and reinforces the notion that punctuation is a decision-making process and that authors, even young authors, have choices. Children who see punctuation as a tool that is available to them can be excited about its possibilities. In such circumstances, children will actively experiment with punctuation as they make their authorial decisions. Alongside this has to run the experience of hearing what readers have to say about their texts and discovering whether these effects work. Authors' cir- cles can provide just such feedback. It should also go without saying that children need to be writing a lot of continuous text in order to meet authorial challenges frequently.

3. I said above, given the opportunity, children will experiment with punctuation. This must be encouraged even though, inevitably, experiments will not always work. Anyway, what counts as punctuation is not always easy to decide. The relatively small number of marks that have conventionally been taught as punctuation are, in these days of typographical freedom, no longer sufficient. Apart from the introduction of new formal marks, such as the interrobang (and even children can invent new formal marks, see Martens and Goodman 1996), and less formal marks such as emotions—once very popular on bulletin boards—space, typography, color, etc., can all be used to demarcate units of language. A more contemporary definition of punctuation is offered by McDermott (1990). He suggests that punctuation "is the use of spacing, conventional signs and certain typographical devices to promote understanding and to guide correct reading, whether silent or aloud."

Should we be acknowledging that children are growing up in an increasingly creative typographical world and might be quite sensitive to how one can use typography as punctuation? The child in Figure 13.3 was responding to a teacher comment in his dialogue journal book.

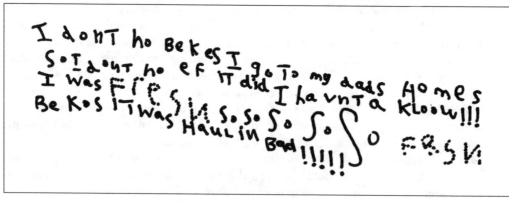

Figure 13.3 *Translation* I don't know because I go to my dad's home so I don't know if it did. I haven't a clue! I was freezing, so, so, so, so, so freezing because it was hailing bad!

4. The classroom environment must support thinking about and noticing punctuation. All texts on display that need punctuation should have it. Any notices, signs, etc., should be punctuated when it is appropriate. Children's work, with their own varieties of punctuation, should be well displayed to give credence to your support for their experimentation. Equally, the use of punctuation must be made public by having the teacher and other adults using it in front of the children. The use of talk books, daily message sheets, and dialogue journals offers teachers the chance to be creative with punctuation that will be seen by children. On the first page of the dialogue journal entry, the teacher uses some question marks (see Figure 13.4). The five-year-old respondent noticed this and was attracted by the possibilities. She did not get it all right, but use of question marks offered the opportunity to discuss the correct usage.

5. It is difficult for teachers to radically change the texts children read. However, if sentences are largely demarcated by space and punctuation is redundant, then teachers need to find ways to stress the continuity of the text and signal the real function of punctuation. Teachers must seek examples of texts which do contain sentences which run on continuously. Every time a sentence butts up against another one, there is an opportunity to examine why the period and capital letter are there. Even more importantly, all children must be encouraged to always write the equivalent of two sentences or more; drop all one-sentence writing, even with total beginners. Teachers should also be modeling the writing of multisentence texts which run continuously, and be thinking aloud as they do so. If children are using two-sentence continuous texts, both as readers and writers, then they cannot rely on space to tell them how the text is demarcated; they need to pay attention to the punctuation.

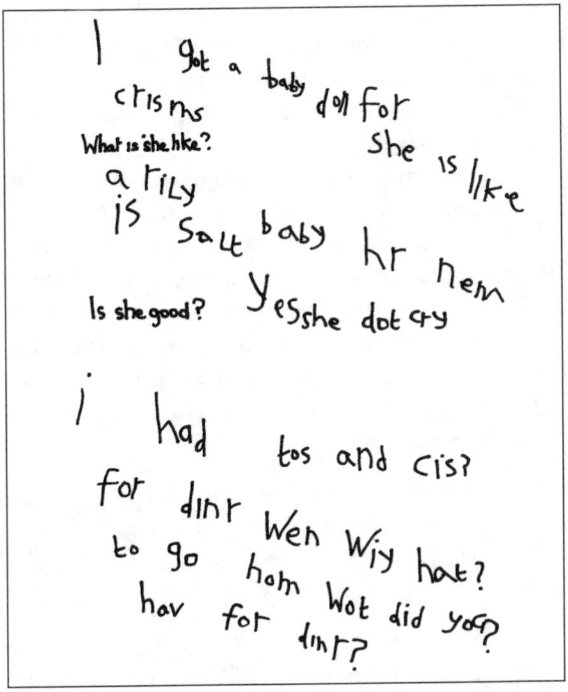

Figure 13.4

Translation

Child: I got a baby doll for Christmas.
Teacher: What it is she like?
Child: She is like a real baby. Her name
          is Charlotte.
Teacher: Is she good?
Child: Yes, she doesn't cry.
          I had toast and cheese for dinner
          when we had to go home. What
          did you have for dinner?

6. When children are beginning to become writers and readers, then whatever your preferred explanation about punctuation, use it and only it. Do not try to use elocutionary explanations alongside grammatical explanation or explanations relating to meaning. Pick one and stick with it! If you don't, you simply increase the possibilities of confusions. This does not mean you should restrict children's own attempts to find explanations; simply limit your own to one type. The children I have studied were not really offered much in the way of explanation at all. So how did they move on? The children who moved most swiftly to using a linguistic base for their punctuation adopted meaning as their principal criterion. By this I mean that they seemed to identify units which made some kind of complete sense. Indeed, some authors of textbooks have used this as a definition of a sentence. However, for these children it was not the conventional sentence boundary that was adopted at first, but a boundary between units which made sense to them.

Last night I went to the park I played soccer and scored three goals. after that I went to my auntys house I had lemonade and cakes when I was there.

For this child, the meaningful units could be characterized as "going to the park" and "going to his aunty's"; they are demarcated by a period and, if lucky, a capital letter. Such a move is a critical one. It reveals that the child has a linguistic strategy rather than a graphic strategy, and, in my experience, once children have made this conceptual leap, they move on fairly quickly. Of course, sometimes this will mean that phrases rather than sentences are demarcated (as in some of the children studied by Cazden, Cordiero, and Giacobbe 1985). The above child, a few months later, was demarcating sentences relatively conventionally and accurately. It is, of course, at such a point that children are more likely to begin to understand formal grammatical explanations for punctuation usage.

7. Do read, and ask children to write, a range of text forms. Different types of text makes use of different types of structures, and some punctuation marks may be easier in one text form than in another. For instance, punctuating stories is often problematic for young writers because, for them, the text can appear seamless; the story just runs on, so how does one demarcate it? But in information writing or descriptions, the text is often a set of attributes, and it can be easier to see demarcation points when collections of facts or attributes are involved. For instance, the child in the example below, who was struggling to demarcate her stories fully conventionally, was able to make a much better job of a set of memories (and the piece is punctuated as written, although spelling has been corrected):

I like you very, very much! You are kind. You hardly shout. Do you remember the party and we played and ate lots of food and remember the Christmas party and I got a pencil case. Remember when we first came in Year 2. I was scared and when you read a story I wasn't scared then. You shouted because some of use didn't colour neatly. You shouted at some of us because we didn't write neatly.

8. If there is an ethos in a classroom in which talk about learning is a real presence, and if children are curious about punctuation, then talk about punctuation will become part of the writing process. Children share knowledge and can be better at explaining things to each other than we are to them. They do not always get it right, but let's face it, neither do we! One five-year-old developed his own explanation for his use of speech marks. He argued that his plentiful distribution of quotation marks (see Figure 13.5) told people that it was him doing the talking; in other words, it was his authorial voice and the ownership this implied that was being marked. While he was confusing authorial voice with character voice, his explanation was at once so comprehensible to the other children that within a couple of days they were

Figure 13.5

Translation
The car was in the garden.

all doing it. While this is an incorrect decision about quotation marks, it nevertheless reveals a child who was reflecting deeply on what they meant, and such reflection is always to be encouraged rather than eliminated.

9. Do encourage children's interest in all punctuation marks. Some books and some programs will give you the impression that there is a particular order in which punctuation marks need to be learned and, therefore, taught. Some will even counsel not introducing certain marks. This chapter has focused more on sentence demarcation than on other uses of punctuation because that is often what most bothers teachers, but there is no reason why children cannot get interested in any of the punctuation marks. Indeed, it is absolutely critical that a broad interest is encouraged. Noticing one punctuation mark and thinking about its use is the key to noticing another and comparing it. Children who are interested in punctuation and are experimenting with it in their writing will want to try out any mark they see.

In one class I studied, the five- and six-year-old children had been reading a traditional rhyme, which was laid out on the page as follows:

>   *Miss   Mary   Mack*
> *Mack*
> *Mack*
> *Was dressed in black*
> *black*
> *black*

Another teacher, noticing what they were reading, gave them a book in which the text was arranged differently:

> *Miss Mary Mack, Mack, Mack,*
> *Was dressed in black, black, black.*

The children were fascinated by the commas, which they had not seen before. A few days later, I visited the classroom. Some of the children had been writing their own rhymes (see Figure 13.6).

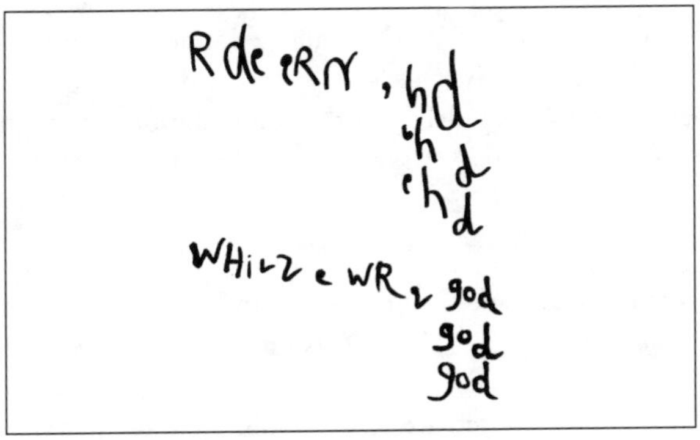

Translation
Red Riding Hood, Hood, Hood,
Was very good, good, good.

Figure 13.6

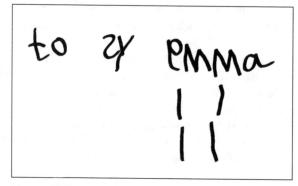

Translation
To see grandma, grandma, grandma.

Figure 13.7

This poem ran for about seven pages, and this child's hand had clearly gotten tired. So, towards the end, she adopted a new device—ditto marks (see Figure 13.7).

No one in the class, not the teacher and not the children, had ever mentioned ditto marks, but here she was using them quite appropriately. How did she know these marks? She had seen her elder sister using them! So please do not underestimate even very young children's capacity to note and use more unusual punctuation marks.

10. Many of the situations I discuss above are about creating a climate in which children develop an active interest in punctuation. There are, however, many times when a teachable moment arrives and some straightforward, direct teaching can suddenly make sense to a child. A teacher can often be guided by the child. I watched a six-year-old girl who had, on her own, started to put quotation marks into her writing and was not getting them quite right. It was easy to take a few minutes and talk with the child, showing her how it had been done in a book and explaining the principle which was operating. She immediately went back to her writing and corrected what she had done with no additional explanation or help from me. The moment was appropriate and so was the direct teaching.

Conclusion

There are no foolproof methods in teaching, and the suggestions above cannot guarantee that every single child will become a proficient and enthusiastic user of punctuation. However, I do believe they significantly increase the chances of children deciding that punctuation can be interesting, fun, and highly functional for them in their own lives as writers and readers.

References

Arthur, C. (1996) "Learning about punctuation: A look at one lesson," in Hall, N. and Robinson, A. (eds.) *Learning About Punctuation*, pp. 92–127. Portsmouth, NH: Heinemann Educational Books.

Calkins, L. M. (1980) "When children want to punctuate: Basic skills belong in context," *Language Arts* **57**, 567–73.

Carey, G. V. (1958) *Mind That Stop*. Harmondsworth: Penguin Books.

Cazden, C., Cordiero, P., and Giacobbe, M. (1985) "Spontaneous and scientific concepts: Young children's learning of punctuation," in Wells, G. and Nichols, J. (eds.) *Language and Learning: An interactional perspective,* pp. 107–23. Brighton: Falmer Books.

Ferriero, E. and Pontecorvo, C. (1999) "Managing the written text: The beginning of punctuation in children's writing," *Learning and Instruction* **9**, 543–64.

Hall, N. (1996) "Learning about punctuation: An introduction and overview," in Hall, N. and Robinson, A. (eds.) *Learning About Punctuation*, pp. 5–37. Portsmouth, NH: Heinemann Educational Books.

Hall, N. (1998) "Young children and resistance to punctuation," *Research in Education* **60** (November), 29–40.

Hall, N. (1999) "Young children's use of graphic punctuation." *Language and Education* **13** (3), 178–93.

McDermott, J. (1990) *Punctuation For Now*. London: MacMillan.

Martens, P. and Goodman, Y. (1996) "Invented punctuation." in Hall, N. and Robinson, A. (eds.) *Learning about punctuation*, pp. 37–54. Portsmouth, NH: Heinemann Educational Books.

Parkes, M. B. (1992) *Pause and Effect: An introduction to the history of punctuation in the West.* London: Scolar Press.

The experience on which much of this chapter is based derives from two ESRC-funded research projects: "Learning to punctuate: A conceptual and ecological investigation" R000221380, and "Learning to punctuate between the ages of six and seven: A conceptual and ecological investigation" R000221796.

Chapter 14

Teaching Spelling Through Writing: Five Avenues
Sandra Wilde

Helping children learn to spell doesn't need to be difficult or time consuming when it's integrated into the writing process. Both students and teachers can be helped to think about the spelling that goes on during writing, making it fun and meaningful rather than a complicated, tedious, separate subject.

Young Alex was writing about what he liked to do on the mountain (Figure 14.1). He used his knowledge of letters and sounds, as well as the word *mountain* written where he could see it in his classroom, to write, "I like to hike up the mountain" (even though he was still a little unsure about which way the letter *p* faces). As he went to write, "I like to ski down the mountain," can't you just imagine him saying to himself "ssskkkiii," and then thinking about the letter *x* and how similar it sounds to the *sk* in *ski*? (After all, ski contains the sounds /s/ and /k/, while *x* contains the sounds /k/ and /s/.) So Alex spelled *ski* as XE.

Although news articles about spelling bees (the national one in the United States is now telecast on the cable sports network ESPN) and memories of spelling lists and tests may predispose us to think of learning to spell as being about words, it's really about writing. Every time we write, we have to either know or think about the spellings of the words we're using. How better to learn about spelling, then, than through writing? As I've learned over the last twenty years or so about how children learn to spell, and thought about how teachers can support that process (Wilde 1992), I've come up with ideas about what I believe are important aspects of learning how to spell. I'll describe here five avenues for helping spelling develop that are connected to the process of learning to write. Three of them involve encouraging children to think about aspects of spelling, while the other two focus on what the teacher can think about and do.

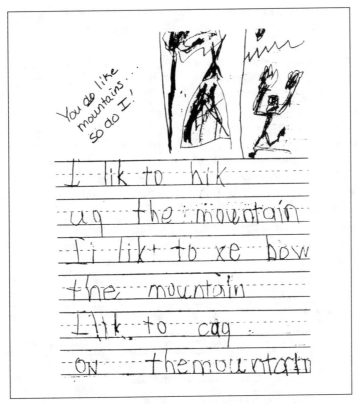

Figure 14.1 You do like mountains...so do I!

1. When You Write, Think About How Words Might Be Spelled

When adults write, we don't particularly need to think about spelling since we know how to spell almost every word we want to use. For children, though, particularly young ones, writing is an active process of constructing spellings based on their developing knowledge of how sounds and letters go together, what words look like, and so on.

We see this in Alex's writing. An invented spelling (used here as a rough synonym for "misspelling") is always a sign of thinking; the writer has literally, in the absence of knowing a word, invented his best approximation. Alex's spelling of *ski,* as we've seen, is most likely a representation of the right sounds in the wrong order; HIK and LIK are obviously logical, since each sound is represented by a letter. Even CAP for *camp* has a logic to it; when *m* and *n* appear before other consonants, they're likely to be omitted by young writers, not because children don't hear them but because they aren't pronounced as strongly as they are on their own. (Try saying *cam* and *camp* to see if you can feel how the *p* affects the *m*.)

The teacher's role in this? Primarily just to provide the opportunities to write, and encourage the thinking to take place. There's a mistaken belief that letting young writers spell words wrong will let them develop bad habits, but this just isn't true. Research in Henderson and Beers (1980) shows that children's spelling grows and develops over time, not only becoming more correct, but also becoming more sophisticated on the way to correctness. A piece of writing by six-year-old Kim about her favorite book shows what this looks like (Figure 14.2). It reads: "Charlotte's Web. I like the part when Wilbur gets his medal, but another pig wins too." Some of the spellings are obvious phonetic ones, but why the extra *e* on five words (almost a third of the total words)? Why a *t* instead of a *d* in *medal*, when it clearly sounds like a *d*?

The first is pretty easy to answer. A lot of words in English end in silent *e*. Mature writers know that these are usually (although not always) words with long vowels, but young children know only that there are a lot of them! They thus tend to overgeneralize silent final *e*'s, adding them in a seemingly random way since they don't yet have any good theory in their heads of when to use them. With more experience, both with individual words and with the spelling patterns they represent, children's use of the silent *e* becomes more conventional. But just the presence of the silent final *e* shows that the child has moved beyond merely phonetic spelling.

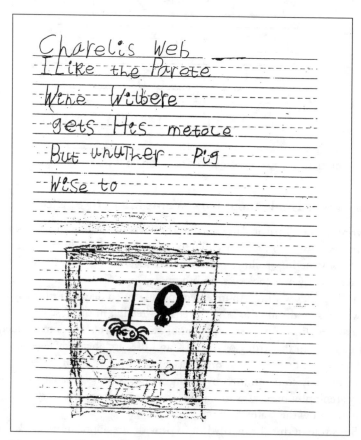

Figure 14.2 Charlotte's Web

The reason for Kim's use of *t* in *medal* is less obvious but just as logical. When a *t* sound occurs between vowels in English, it frequently ends up being pronounced like a *d*. For this reason, *medal* and *metal* are pretty much homophones. And indeed, we wouldn't be at all surprised if Kim had been writing about metal and spelled it with a *d*, since that's what you hear. Why the reverse, though, when in this case the phonetic spelling of the consonant would have been the correct one? It's over-generalization again. When a child starts seeing words like *metal*, *water*, and *atom* in print, and realizing that what she hears as *d* is spelled with a *t*, she may well start assuming that the same holds true for words like *medal* and *soda*. Thus, she may go from spelling both groups of words with a *d* to spelling both groups with a *t*, and will eventually figure out which spelling goes with which words.

If a teacher were to assume that Kim can't hear that *medal* has a *d* in it and planned remedial instruction, it would just confuse the issue. But if the teacher realizes the logic behind children's spelling, he or she will know what aspects of it reflect normal development as well as the idiosyncrasies of our spelling system. But with young children, when in doubt don't try to teach too much, since most early learning about spelling (once children know the alphabet and can write with invented spelling) comes from seeing words in print and trying them out in their writing.

2. When You Write and Especially When You Edit, Have a Variety of Strategies for Coming Up with the Right Spelling

Take a look at seven-year-old Bert's story about a big dinosaur fight (Figure 14.3). It reads:

One day tyrannosaurus challenged triceratops and his friends in a hockey game. It would be tyrannosaurus and diplodocus against triceratops and allosaurus. So! Anyway, tyrannosaurus was winning. Somebody cheated on triceratops's teams and got put in jail. But the pteranodon came to the rescue and they won! And they went home happy.

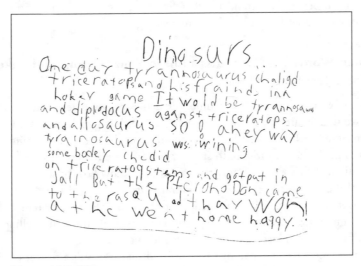

Figure 14.3 Dinosaurs

Isn't it interesting that, in the midst of a number of relatively unsophisticated spellings, he managed to spell five different dinosaurs' names almost perfectly (only one vowel was wrong)? Bert's teacher had immersed her class of seven-year-olds in a unit on dinosaurs. She encouraged them to write about dinosaurs every day, and one of the resources available to them was a lengthy list of dinosaur names that they had compiled together and continued to add to. Most of the children referred to this large-print chart as they wrote.

When children are writing, they'll often invent spellings for words they don't know, and this is indeed the most efficient strategy most of the time, but it need not be their only one. Teachers can fill the classroom with sources of words: charts like the dinosaur one that relate to what children are writing about; dictionaries and word books; atlases and other reference books; word walls with commonly used words; small laminated cards or Post-Its with words you know your children have trouble spelling. You can also teach children how to use these resources and others. What are some good strategies for finding a word in the dictionary? What do you do if you can't find the word? When and how can you use a spellchecker successfully?

As children get older, it becomes more and more important for them to learn how to proofread their own writing. After all, the ultimate goal of spelling instruction is to develop writers who can produce a final draft where the words are spelled right. They aren't helped to do this if the teacher merely circles misspellings for them, or lowers their grade because of them. It also isn't particularly relevant to do proofreading exercises in a spelling book or to edit each other's writing. No, if you want to learn to correct your own spelling, you need to be taught how, and then do so, ideally with writing that you're editing because it'll be seen by a wider audience.

The teacher's role here is threefold. First, to help children realize the importance of spelling for final drafts (not so much because the writing can't be read otherwise as because it's part of what writers do as they practice their craft). Second, to help them learn how to find words that might be misspelled in their writing. Ironically, this gets harder as you get better, since your invented spellings are closer to being correct and it's therefore easier to miss them. Third, to develop the strategies I mentioned earlier for getting the right spelling.

3. Think About Words That You Miss a Lot in Your Writing, and Take a Little Extra Time to Just Learn Them

When children are writing big words like dinosaur names or countries of the world, particularly in first drafts, we usually aren't that fussy about whether they get them right. One of the great advantages of invented spelling is that it enables them to use any words they want in their writing, no matter how difficult those words are to spell. If children are required to spell everything right, they're likely to limit their writing to only the words they know how to spell.

However, I did start getting concerned several years ago when I heard the same comments and questions over and over again from teachers of children aged nine or ten: "Their spelling is terrible. I don't mind if they invent on the big words, but why are they still spelling so many common words wrong? They don't seem to care about spelling at all."

As I listened closely to these comments, I realized that it wasn't a matter of children having trouble with *most* common words; rather, the same ones came up over and over again. They were spelling *they* THAY. *Girl* and *first* were GRIL and FRIST. They couldn't remember which words started with *wh*. Sometimes *with* came out as WHITH or some other variation that showed that the *h* was confusing them. I think you probably know the words I'm talking about.

Of the most common words in English, a relatively small number of them continue to give writers problems even after they've picked up the spellings of most of the others. Since *they* rhymes with *hay*, it's logical to think there's an *a* in it. In *girl*, you do hear an *r* right after the *g*, but hey, there's an *i* in there somewhere, isn't there? And so on. What makes it so hard is, as Frank Smith (1994) has pointed out, it's not that you can't remember the right spelling, but that you can't forget the wrong one. Do you find yourself that this is the case with words that you have trouble with? For instance, for *they*, a young writer might be thinking, "Is it *a* and I think it's *e?* Or is it *e* and I think it's *a?*" Clearly, he needs a way to pin it down and remember it.

I've started doing a mini-lesson with children that's tremendously effective in dealing with this issue. First, we talk about words that they always get right every time they write them. I ask them, for instance, if they always spell *the* correctly. What about their own names? If you're doing this lesson at the appropriate developmental level (i.e., they spell most very common words correctly), not only will they say yes, they may even laugh at you. "Of course I spell *the* right!" We agree that, although the words they always get right vary a little from one person to another, there are a lot of them, and that it would be silly to spell these "easy words" wrong, because you don't even have to think about them; you just know them.

Next we talk about the words that you'd probably have to invent if you were going to write them: the big words, the dinosaurs, the science and geography words, perhaps the names of authors like Jon Scieska. As far as strategy goes, we agree here too: It makes more sense to just make your best attempt at these "hard words," knowing that you can always correct them but not wanting to slow down your thought process to look them up during the first draft.

Then we move on to the real focus of the lesson: the words that you feel that you should know but you're always getting wrong, that you have to correct a lot when you proofread, that you always try to remember but can't keep straight. The words like *they* and *with* and *girl* and *because*. Then my suggestion is: Would it be worth it if you could spend just one extra second and get these words right every time? Obviously, yes. I pick a word, then—let's say *they*—and talk about how you could take that one extra second to make sure you're spelling it right. How about just thinking that it's *the* plus a *y?* Or that just as "he" is part of "they," the word *they* contains the word *he?* With a simple mnemonic device like this, you have a way to pin down the spelling.

For a word like *because,* where the hard part is remembering where all those vowels go, you might want to write the word on the outside of your writing folder where you could take your one extra second to take a quick look before you write it. If you use the word enough in your writing, you'll probably find that, after a while, you've internalized the spelling and don't need to look any more.

This is a powerful tool—try asking children to pick one "one-second word" a week to work on—that's closely tied to writing, since it's about gaining more control over the words that appear over and over again in everyone's writing. The idea also is to go from taking the extra second to then learning that one word so well that you'll never have to think about its spelling again.

4. Teachers: Think About the Spelling Patterns You See in Your Children's Writing

Teachers can draw on children's writing to create instruction about spelling patterns that is meaningful and developmentally appropriate. First, let's look at a few sentences from a condolence letter written by an eight-year-old around the Thanksgiving holiday. (It's an unfortunate example of an inauthentic assignment!)

> Dear Mr. and Mrs. Turkey,
> I am sories [sorry] that your son did [died] in a dinner. I feill [feel] sad for you.

When you look at the three invented spellings in this excerpt, you'll notice that in all three, Anna had the wrong spelling of the word's long vowel. These vowels are easy for children to represent in invented spellings, even at an early stage of development, since they sound the same as the names of the vowel letters, but they're relatively hard to spell correctly because there are so many different ways to spell them, many of them requiring more than a single letter.

When children start to spell these sounds in their writing in a variety of ways, such as two vowels together or by using a silent final *e,* it's a sign that they've moved beyond phonetic spelling to a more complex understanding of vowel patterns, even though they often don't know which pattern applies to which word. When you see this pattern emerging in the writing of a number of your children, it's a sign that this is a good time for some targeted instruction. I'd focus primarily on the idea that there are a variety of ways to spell these sounds, but that some of them are more common than others. (For more details, see Wilde 1992).

Similarly, a piece by nine-year-old Gordon included the spellings COMEING and STOPED. He was consistent, as reflected not only in these spellings, but also throughout his writing, in knowing the spellings of the two suffixes involved, whereas younger children may well spell them phonetically (e.g. *stopped* would be spelled STOPT). Yet he didn't yet know the rules for necessary changes in the root words when these suffixes are added to some words; he, and classmates at a similar developmental level, would clearly be ready for instruction that helped them discover these principles. For instance, I might provide a list of words like come/coming, bite/biting, take/taking, and ask them to figure out what the rule is.

5. Teachers: Think About What's Happening with Children Whose Writing Shows They Have Trouble with Spelling

This is a complex subject since there are so many possible answers to why children may be struggling with spelling. But the major point I'd like to make here is the value of the teacher's *thinking* about what's going on with the child rather than looking for a way to define or label it. I find, in talking with teachers about children like these, they sometimes tend to think diagnostically in the sense of suggesting that the child has some particular kind of deficit, but I think that common sense is usually the best place to start.

Let's look at a few sentences from a piece of writing by Deirdre, a mathematically talented eleven-year-old:

The proble [problem] ask how meny miles dos light go in one year. Whe I stard [started] I now I was going t have to do the problem in stepes. Frist I had to know how fast light travels in one scent [second] so I asked my dad and he said 300,000 km.

Out of fifty words, eleven (22 percent) are misspelled, which is certainly higher than it should be at this age. But when you take a close look at the spellings themselves, they aren't really too far off. Six of them (PROBLE, MENY, DOS, WHE, T, STEPES) are off by only one letter (missing, added, or changed). FRIST has all the right letters but in the wrong order. Some of the words she got wrong here were spelled correctly elsewhere in the piece.

Thinking about Deirdre's spelling in common-sense terms, I'd ask two questions. First, does she read very much? At this age, it's uncommon to miss so many relatively common words and to not spell the *-ed* suffix consistently unless you're not much of a reader. Second, if she read back over her piece, would she be able to spot the invented spellings and then correct them? Since many of her inventions were spelled correctly elsewhere and since she sometimes left off the final letter of words, my hunch was that she wrote quickly to get her ideas down but could probably do a reasonable job of editing.

In Deirdre's case, she was indeed not much of a reader. Fortunately, she shortly afterwards discovered Judy Blume's novels and began to read them voraciously, and her spelling improved quite a bit. Now, several years later, she still has to work at spelling and makes good use of a spell-checker, but is achieving top grades in the sciences at college.

When the full version of Deidre's sample was shared with a group of teachers, their initial responses, while acknowledging the quality of her mathematical thinking, posited a variety of possible explanations for her spelling problem, most of them deficit-based. They also wondered about emotional causes. Astonishingly, one of them referred to a mention of her dad's roommate to wonder, apologetically, if perhaps her dad was gay and the shock of discovering it was affecting her spelling!

The reality, if we use common sense and just look at the children's writing, is typically much simpler and less convoluted. Here are some clues to how to interpret what we see in the writing of weaker spellers:

- If she's a strong reader and there are appreciably more words misspelled than is typical for her age, there's a good chance she doesn't have a lot of natural spelling ability and will always have to work harder at it than other students.
- If the same word is sometimes spelled correctly and sometimes not, she may be writing quickly without necessarily attending much to spelling.
- If her final drafts have almost as many invented spellings as the first drafts, she may not have learned, or learned enough about, how to proofread.

Conclusion

More and more I've come to believe that the only kind of spelling curriculum that makes sense is one that's grounded in children's writing. The only real reason for caring about spelling is because it makes your life easier as a writer. As adults we know that if we can't produce a piece of writing where the spelling is close to perfect, we'll be criticized about it, possibly lose out on job opportunities, and so on. Some adults have even limited their lives—in terms of career choices, or continuing their education—because they feel insecure about their spelling. We can talk to children all they want about passing spelling tests in order to get good grades, or because it's good for them, but personally I'd sooner see children try to get better at spelling for the same reason I do: because it's part of being a writer.

References

Henderson, E. H. and Beers, J. W. (1980) *Developmental and Cognitive Aspects of Learning to Spell.* Newark, DE: International Reading Association.

Smith, F. (1994) *Writing and the Writer* (2nd ed.) Hillsdale, NJ: Lawrence Erlbaum.

Wilde, S. (1992) *You Kan Red This? Spelling and Punctuation for Whole Language Classrooms K–6.* Portsmouth, NH: Heinemann.

Chapter 15

Raising Awareness of Grammar Through Shared Writing

George Hunt

Shared writing is a practice that forms the central source of creative literary activity in many primary classrooms. By "shared writing," I am referring to any situation in which an oral composition by a child or, more frequently, a group of children is written down by a teacher or other person more competent in transcriptional skills. The scribe usually uses a flip-chart or other large writing surface in order to emphasize the collaborative nature of the writing process, to provide opportunities for the clear demonstration of aspects of this process, and to facilitate a shared reading of the emerging text. These texts can subsequently be edited, redrafted, and published, eventually becoming a valued part of the reading resources of the class or the school. Shared writing is a long-established practice, and its value has been recognized by advocates of both holistic and skills-based approaches to literacy (CLPE 1990; DfEE 1998). Its efficacy in helping learners of all ages and abilities to become readers and writers is also well attested (Smith 1994). In this chapter I would like to explore the potential of this approach for raising children's awareness of grammar. Before doing this, however, it would be apt to point out the benefits of the approach, and to set it within its pedagogical framework.

Strengths of Shared Writing

1. Children who are inhibited by their limited knowledge of writing conventions are enabled to build up a body of personally meaningful texts rapidly, as the scribe takes over the physical task of writing while helping the learners to "orchestrate the constraints" imposed by these conventions (Harste *et al*. 1984). The high visibility of the emergent text provides a vivid demonstration of how spelling, punctuation, and layout operate, while also providing a creative and personally satisfying stimulus for attending to these conventions (Tuxford and Washell, in CLPE 1990).

2. Because these texts are created from the children's own imaginations, they express the authorial "voice" of the group, which can therefore claim authentic ownership of them (Graves 1983).

3. Because they are written down from the children's dictation, their syntactic patterns mirror those of the children's speech, thus rendering the text more readable (Perera 1984). At the same time, because these speech patterns are captured on the page, they become available for modification and development. With due respect to the authors' voices and stages of readiness, the teacher can show how dictated speech can be reshaped into structures more typical of the sentence and discourse organization of written language. Regular experience of such reshaping in the course of shared writing can help to develop learners' speech and hence their independent writing (Perera 1990).

4. Collaborative effort alleviates the solitude of the author's task and centralizes writing as a social event in which children share a variety of perspectives on the problem-solving nature of the process. Negotiations regarding content, vocabulary, sentence structure, and discourse can create a sense of mutuality, contributing to what Bruner (1986, p. 127) has referred to as "joint culture creating as an object of schooling and as an appropriate step en route to becoming a member of the adult society in which one lives out one's life." Oral language is of course central to this process, and the role of a mutually stimulating joint focus of attention in eliciting rich conversation is well attested (Wells 1987). The creation of the text provides the teacher with opportunities to "think publicly" alongside the learners, modeling both specific language structures and general compositional strategies such as frequent re-readings of the text-so-far and the speaking aloud of possibilities for the next chunk in order to weigh choices about vocabulary and syntax. It provides the learners with opportunities to converse with the teacher and with each other amidst these processes, and thus to make them their own.

Grammar

Explicit teaching about grammar fell into disfavor during the 1960s because of a belief that it was failing to improve pupils' language and was instead causing disaffection from language study (HMSO 1964). Although some of the research reports which confirmed this have been challenged (Tomlinson 1994), the point is that this research merely reiterated what teachers, and pupils, knew already. There was a perception that activities such as the identifying and labeling of grammatical forms without a context to demonstrate the relevance of these activities was drudgework; that the drilling of rules and definitions based on misconceived applications of Latinate grammar to English trivialized language study; that an emphasis on error detection and the superiority of standard English pathologized everyday language and alienated pupils who spoke nonstandard varieties (Carter 1990).

After a period in which the subject virtually disappeared from the curriculum, a new style of grammar teaching emerged in the UK during the 1980s, setting grammar within the wider field of "knowledge about language." This approach is functionally orientated, and its theoretical paradigm is systemic grammar (Halliday 1985). Classroom activity is based on the critical exploration of a variety of written forms and speech events, and is firmly grounded in the social contexts in which language is used and abused (Carter 1990).

More recently this approach has been preempted by a resurgence of prescriptivism which has brought back many of the practices that fell into disfavor after the publication of the Lockwood Report in 1964 (HMSO 1964). Primary-aged pupils are again, as part of the National Literacy Strategy, being required to learn dubious definitions of parts of speech (a verb is a doing word; an adverb tells us more about a verb) and to underline grammatical features in decontextualized passages. In some cases these practices are being presented to pupils with no attention being paid to their needs and interests. A group of ten- and eleven-year-old readers was recently seen trying to complete a photocopiable worksheet which required them to underline conditional clauses in a passage about bicycle maintenance. The text was not a genuine cycle manual and appeared to have been sown with conditional clauses in order for the pupils to have something to underline. The children were all underachieving readers and were having difficulty understanding the text. When asked why they were doing work which seemed ill suited to their needs, the teacher acknowledged that the work was inappropriate, but was being conducted because knowledge of conditional clauses was part of the nationally prescribed schedule of objectives for Year 6, and that all pupils in that year therefore had to "cover" them, using photocopiable worksheets from a published package in which the school had invested in order to ensure that this coverage was comprehensive.

These two potentially antagonistic movements to reintroduce grammar reflect the controversial nature of the subject and the fact that there are contending notions of the purpose of the study of grammar. The "critical awareness" element, articulated largely by teacher–educators and educational linguists, argues that the study of oral and written texts in their social contexts can raise the learners' awareness of how language is used to consolidate or shift power relations, and is therefore potentially empowering. The "back-to-basics" element, articulated largely by politicians and journalists, argues that grammar is a discipline associated with conformity to rules of good linguistic and social behavior. Neither of these views has a great deal of evidence to support it. One of the reasons why traditional grammar was abandoned was because it was failing to raise standards (HMSO 1964), while more recent approaches, such as those advocated by the Language in the National Curriculum project (LINC), have not been given sufficient opportunity to prove themselves. However, case study materials in such sources as Bain *et al.* (1992) and Collerson (1997) suggest that exploratory approaches to grammar can inspire learners' curiosity about language while providing them with a useful metalanguage, with which to talk about the subject.

What both of these approaches have in common is a belief that grammar study should be justified in instrumental terms. An alternative view (Crystal 1988) is that we should study it for the same reasons we study basic anatomy or geography: Language is a fundamental aspect of human experience and therefore deserves study in its own right. A related view (Cameron 1997) is that grammar is not a set of goal-driven activities, either for learner empowerment or for the improvement of speech and writing: It is a way of reflecting on the formal and functional aspects of language. "The skills it develops are not specifically language skills (though they do have a verbal component); they are reasoning, argument, problem solving and critical reflection" (p. 232).

These two notions—language as an object of interest in its own right, and grammar as critical reflection—return us to the link between grammar and shared writing. Grammar can be regarded as a set of choices for expressing meaning involving the appropriate organization of form and structure. In normal speech, we do this unconsciously, and it is in this sense that linguists maintain that everybody knows grammar, because everybody can organize structures into patterns that make sense to other members of their speech community. In the case of writing, however, we have time to reflect consciously and critically on these choices. By participating in the conversations that surround the joint creation of a text, children begin to articulate these choices, thus developing the metalinguistic awareness that Donaldson (1978) describes as the first step in mastering the manipulation of symbols. In Bruner's words, they are persuaded to "view expressions as if they were, so to speak, opaque objects to be examined in their own right, rather than transparent windows through which we look out upon the world" (Bruner 1986, p. 125). The physicality of the shared writing experience—the objectifying of thought and speech into publicly visible, manipulable shapes—enables learners to focus on the purely *formal* aspects of language, while the creative endeavor provides a purpose for the introduction of technical vocabulary to facilitate talk about these aspects. If the endeavor takes place in an environment in which learners are accustomed to seeing themselves as writers, the abstract demands of grammar education might be realized in the course of a communicative activity which produces a tangible product. The following examples are intended to illustrate these points.

Example 1

A group of six- and seven-year-old children had been brought to school through streets scattered with the debris from a storm that had swept through the country the night before, causing severe damage and some deaths. The event had been so dramatic that only a handful of children arrived in class that day, and their talk was all about the terror and excitement of the storm. The teacher decided to engage them in the shared composition of a recount of what had happened the previous night, suggesting that this was a very special event that they would probably want to talk about in years to come. Because the children had been in bed when the storm occurred, their memories were mainly of the sounds that had woken them up. The teacher started to jot these down on the chalkboard as the children recalled them. The initial list read:

> *trees going crash*
> *my bedroom door going bang bang bang*
> *bins rattling*
> *dogs howling*
> *windows smashing*

Up until this point, the purpose had been to brainstorm main points for a conventional recount, but then the following exchange occurred:

Child 1:   Those last three, they've all got "ing" on the end.
Teacher: I suppose it's because we're talking about what things were do -ing.
Child 2:   And what we were hear -ing.

The teacher asked if the first two contributions could be made to fit the pattern, and the children readily produced:

trees crashing
doors banging
bins rattling
dogs howling
windows smashing

Then a child noticed that the first and last items rhymed, so the teacher rewrote the list with the rhyming items as a couplet, and invited the children to come up with more rhyming ideas, reminding them of Robert Southey's poem *The Cataract of Lodore*[1] (Philip 1990), which they had recited and enjoyed earlier in the term. The challenge of finding rhyming pairs which would change the recount into a poem fascinated the children, and after fifteen to twenty minutes, a long list of couplets had been written down by the teacher and was ready to be reshaped by the children into the final version of the text, which is given below:

wind howling
dogs growling
doors banging
cans clanging
branches slashing
trees crashing
rain teeming
babies screaming
buildings shaking
windows breaking
glass shattering
storm battering
bins rumbling
tiles tumbling
everybody crying
people dying

The children were pleased at having produced both an accurate, if somewhat dramatized, set of impressions of the storm, and an artefact with an interesting formal pattern. Discussion of this pattern created the context for consolidating use of the terms *verb* and *noun*. It would not have added anything to the experience of the authors to point out that their text consisted of a set of noun phrases, detached from an "understood" common subject–verb stem (*we heard* or *there were*), with each consisting of a noun and an "-ing" participle, though a teacher presenting the text to an older group might use such vocabulary.

It might be informative to compare this episode with that of the ten- to eleven-year-old children struggling to identify conditional clauses in the bicycle maintenance text. In the latter example, the content of the lesson was dictated by a prescribed objective and by a contrived text whose structure was unnaturally tailored to the demands of this objective. The abstract notion of a conditional clause was presented without any kind of experience which might have demonstrated the usefulness of the term.

In writing the storm couplets, the children were working from vivid experience to the creation of their own text. Their "poetic" writing was loosely related to a model that they had recently encountered and enjoyed. The use of grammatical terminology arose naturally from their own observations of patterned, communicative writing. Significantly, it was one of the children who pointed out the formal similarity of the repeated participles, shifting the direction of the writing event towards a playful manipulation of formal, functional, and phonological features.

However, there are powerful objections to the idea that a focus on grammar should always be embedded in "authentic" writing and, even more troublingly, depending on children's own discoveries about formal aspects of language. What if there had been no storm and therefore no inventory of nouns and participles to draw the children's attention towards regularities? Should teachers rely entirely on such episodes of serendipity? These questions are particularly pressing for teachers working under command curricula specifying which aspects of grammar and language forms should be studied and at what age they should be taught. Under less constrained systems, frequent shared writing of a variety of texts will almost inevitably generate repeated attention to a wide range of grammatical features: All texts are *ipso facto* permutations of items from word classes; specific genres require specific features, such as the use of the passive voice in reports or of imperative sentences in instructional texts; the transition from speech to writing enables the teacher to point out features (such as extended subject noun phrases) more typical of the latter than the former. But when the curriculum demands, for example, "coverage" of adverbs in Year 4 term 1, as in the National Literacy Strategy, the teacher is forced into more focused intervention than was the case in the first episode. The next two examples show how the teacher can focus on particular aspects of grammar in the course of cross-curricular writing.

Example 2

A class of nine-year-olds had been studying the myths of Greece and Rome, and had particularly enjoyed an oral rendition of the story of "Philemon and Baucis" by a visiting storyteller. This story describes how Zeus and Hermes sought hospitality from mankind after a long journey, and were denied it by all but an elderly priest and his wife, whom they rewarded with eternal life. There was a group of underachieving writers in the class with whom the teacher was conducting a program of shared writing, so he chose this story as the basis for a simple, collaborative retelling. The children took it in turns to do this orally before beginning to dictate to the teacher how the story should be written. The teacher wrote the children's retelling out on a flip-chart, but at various points stopped the flow of the discourse in order to prompt reflection on alternative possibilities for vocabulary and syntax. Describing the mood of the two disguised Olympians by the end of the day, the children dictated:

> *They were cold and tired. They felt hungry.*

The teacher underlined the word *hungry* and flipped to a clean page in order to create a word web of alternatives for the adjective. The first prompt was "Can you suggest any other words we could use for this adjective?" The children responded with the synonyms *starving, famished,* and *peckish*. (Almost immediately, one child remarked that the last suggestion did not sound right for a god.) The teacher then asked if it was possible to replace the word with more than one word. Suggestions included *really starving, very hungry indeed,* and *like having a good feed*. In choosing which one of these might be an appropriate substitution, the word *phrase* was used to summarize these expressions. (The opportunity was there to distinguish between the two adjective phrases and the subordinate nonfinite clause, but this would not, of course, have been developmentally appropriate; however, the distinction is a potentially useful one for the teacher to know about in assessing the range of structures that children can use.) Next, the teacher wrote in the prompt *as hungry as,* and the children generated the similes *a wolf, a toothless wolf, a pack of toothless wolves,* and *a penniless beggar outside a chippy* (a fish and chip shop). When the objection was raised that "chippies didn't exist in those days" an alternative "*a starving beggar outside a feast*" was added to the web.

The teacher then prompted the group to think about recasting the original sentences. Three possibilities were written up on a fresh sheet:

> *They were cold and tired and hungry.*
> *They were cold, tired, and hungry.*
> *They were cold. They were tired. They were hungry.*

After reading the alternatives aloud in various ways, they decided that the third sounded "the plod-diest," and hence the most appropriate. Furthermore, they also decided to forgo the more flamboyant alternatives they had produced for the word *hungry,* settling on the three short, simple, staccato sentences as the final version. So, a tour around a brief extract had enabled the group to consider concepts such as synonymy, phrase expansion, and sentence restructuring. The terms *phrase, synonym,* and *simile* were used in the actual session, and when the class as a whole looked at the word web later, the term *noun phrase* was used to summarize the set of structures which had been produced to complete the simile stem. It is interesting to note that although all of this was done in order to convey meaning more effectively, from a purely grammatical point of view the most important lesson was a purely structural one: that a functional component (in this case a subject complement) can be realized by a variety of different forms. In this case, the lesson was of course, implicit, reinforced through the year by many similar sessions. The abiding questions concern when and to what extent such formal considerations should be made explicit.

Example 3

A group of nine- and ten-year-olds had been surveying local wildlife during a science project. They had made observational drawings of wildflowers, and had used guidebooks to identify them, labeling the drawings with common and scientific names. The teacher pointed out that many of the common names (foxglove, buttercup, harebell) were compound words based on the plants' appearance, incorporating picturesque metaphors, somewhat akin to the compound expressions of Anglo-Saxon poetry. Sometimes, because of language change, the process was less obvious (daisy, dandelion). The children were set the challenge of examining the plants afresh, and renaming them by creating new compounds. Ideas were pooled and the most popular were used to label a display of the drawings. Thus, daisy became sunsplash; foxglove, beesax; and bluebell, banana-bell (when looked at through a hand-lens, the individual florets of this plant resemble slightly unfurled bananas).

This was a brief, cross-curricular project in which reflection on word form was used to make links between morphology, etymology, and literature. It does, however, invite the comment that approaching these concepts via botany is going a long way around. The final example will show how shared writing can be used in investigations in which language itself is the direct object of study.

Example 4

A group of ten-year-old children had been collecting nonwords by playing "antiScrabble" (a game following the same rules as Scrabble but disallowing any words that are already in the dictionary; see Hunt 1994) and by making onset and rime nonsense generators (see Figure 15.1).

	at	ell	ing	oom	ush
b	*	*	bing	*	*
cl	clat	clell	*	cloom	clush
fr	frat	frell	fring	froom	frush
shr	shrat	shrell	shring	shroom	shrush
spl	*	splell	spling	sploom	splush

Figure 15.1

A selection of words was written out on a chart and the teacher's first prompt was, "What kind of words might we have here?" As well as obvious responses such as "stupid ones" and "weird ones," suggestions included "names of funny noises," "nicknames for people" (perhaps based on Bing), and "the names of rivers." It was interesting that the nominal function and onomatopoeia were the first dimensions of language that suggested themselves to the children. Nobody volunteered the names of any conventional word classes until the teacher invited the children to use a selection of words to complete the frame below:

Stephen _____ed his new _____s on Saturday.
He walked _____ly home. His dad was _____ious when he heard about it,
but Stephen felt un_____.

Discussion of the completed frames elicited the realization that the prefixes and suffixes made you think about "what the words were doing" in the sentences, as did the kinds of words that the nonsense items preceded and followed. The procedure was repeated, this time using the popular strategy of substituting the nonsense words in *Jabberwocky* (Carroll 1855). A group effort yielded the stanza:

And as in splellish thought he stood
The Fratfrellfring with eyes of flame
Came shrooming through the clushy wood
And clatsplushed as it came!

As well as demonstrating the role of affixes and word order, the need to fill di- and trisyllabic spaces entailed a discussion of compounding and of whether or not the longer words had to be compounds. It was decided that Fratfrellfring, as the name of the creature, was not a compound, whereas clatsplush, equivalent in structure and meaning to handclap, was.

The final step of the activity was to select some of the words and to write formal dictionary definitions of them, using both a school dictionary and Lewis Carroll's own definitions of the terms from *Jabberwocky* as models. This involved identifying the word class of the new word and embedding it into a sentence in order to demonstrate its usage.

This activity was a direct investigation of language structure, but it was firmly grounded in play, providing a reminder that productive grammatical activity can have a lot in common with the kind of exploratory meddling that children indulge in with construction kits. Although the investigation started with phonological play and culminated in the invention of meanings for words, its main objective was to play about inside the grammatical hemispheres of morphology and syntax. Permutating nonsensical stems with detached affixes compels the children to focus on form and function; meaning is subsequently brought to the words in an act of creative imagination. Thus, the activity integrates grammar with both phonology and semantics.

The above examples are meant to illustrate that grammar can be explored within, and can be used to inform, creative activity. They are also intended to suggest open-ended ways of playing with and talking about language that might be applied to activities other than shared writing; some of these activities were subsequently used during independent writing, for example, and the last activity led to some of the children making their own word games. All of the activities require some knowledge of grammar on the part of the teacher, and none of them is likely to lead to lasting learning unless topics are revisited in different ways, so that "children meet the same notions many times over but always in a memorable way" (Tuxford and Washell 1990). The forum of shared writing provides a sociable and productive way of providing guided discovery learning of a topic that all too often is taught through arid and ineffective transmission.

Note

1. Robert Southey's evocation of the Lodore waterfall in the Lake District consists largely of an inventory of "onomatopoeic verbs of sound and movement."

References

Bain, R., Fitzgerald, B. and Taylor, M. (eds.) (1992) *Looking into Language*. London: Hodder & Stoughton.

Bruner, J. (1986) *Actual Minds, Possible Worlds*. Cambridge, MA: Harvard University Press.

Cameron, D. (1997) "Sparing the Rod: What teachers need to know about grammar," *Changing English* 4(2), pp. 229–39.

Carroll, L. (1855) "Jabberwocky," in Green, R. L. (1956) *The Book of Nonsense*. London: Dent.

Carter, R. (ed.) (1990) *Knowledge About Language and the Curriculum: The LINC Reader*. London: Hodder & Stoughton.

CLPE (1990) *Shared Reading, Shared Writing*. London: CLPE.

Collerson, J. (1997) *Grammar in Teaching*. Newtown, NSW: Primary English Teaching Association.

Crystal, D. (1988) *Rediscover Grammar*. Harlow: Longman.

DfEE (1998) *The National Literacy Strategy Framework*. London: DfEE.

Donaldson, M. (1978) *Children's Minds*. London: Fontana.

Graves, D. (1983) *Writing: Teachers and children at work*. Portsmouth, NH: Heinemann.

Halliday, M. (1985) *Introduction to Functional Grammar*. London: Edward Arnold.

Harste, J., Woodward, V. and Burke, C. (1984) *Language Stories and Literacy Lessons*. Portsmouth, NH: Heinemann.

HMSO (1964) *The Examining of English Language (The Lockwood Report)*. London: HMSO.

Hunt, G. (1994) *Inspirations for Grammar*. Leamington Spa: Scholastic.

Perera, K. (1984) *Children's Writing and Reading*. Oxford: Blackwell.

Perera, K. (1990) "Grammatical differentiation between speech and writing in children aged 8 to 12," in Carter, R. (1990) *Knowledge about Language*. London: Hodder & Stoughton.

Philip, N. (1990) *A New Treasury of Poetry*. London: Blackie.

Smith, B. (1994) *Through Writing to Reading*. London: Routledge.

Tomlinson, D. (1994) "Errors in the research into the effectiveness of grammar teaching," *English in Education* **28**(1), pp. 20–26.

Tuxford, P. and Washell, A. (1990) "'There's them things again:' Shared writing and the exploration of linguistic awareness," in CLPE (1990) *Shared Reading, Shared Writing*.

Wells, G. (1987) *The Meaning Makers*. London: Hodder & Stoughton.

Notes on Contributors

Robin Campbell is Emeritus Professor of Primary Education at the University of Hertfordshire. Before working at the university, he was a teacher and head teacher of primary schools in the UK; subsequently he has worked on literacy projects in South Africa and taught graduate school in the United States. He has had ten books published. Most recently that has included *Literacy from Home to School: Reading with Alice* (Trentham Books) and the edited book *Facilitating Preschool Literacy* for the International Reading Association.

Janet Evans is Senior Lecturer in Education at Liverpool Hope University College. Formerly an Early Years and primary school teacher, she has recently finished two years as Literacy Consultant with the National Literacy Strategy. She has written seven books on language, literacy, and mathematics education for Early Years and primary educators, along with articles and chapters in edited books. Janet has taught in India, Nigeria, Australia, America, and Canada and was awarded two scholarships which enabled her to work and study in the United States. She has presented papers at many international conferences along with organizing and teaching on numerous in-service conferences. Janet still manages to find time to work in schools, doing action-based research with young children and their educators. Her last book, *What's in the Picture: Responding to Illustrations in Picture Books* (Paul Chapman), reflects her ongoing research interest in children's literature, reader response, and literature circles focusing on the picture story book genre.

Rosalie Franzese has an MA in Reading. She is an outstanding, experienced demonstration teacher, a professional developer, and an adjunct professor at New York University. Using the work of Moustafa and of Dorn, French, and Jones (*Apprenticeship in Literacy: Transitions across Reading and Writing*, Stenhouse 1998) in classrooms with economically disadvantaged children, she has developed successful instructional strategies to help children spell by analogy.

Nigel Hall teaches at Manchester Metropolitan University where he is Professor of Literacy Education. He is the author, co-author, or editor of a large number of books about young children's play, language, and literacy and early writing. He has also written over fifty articles and over thirty chapters about literacy in other people's books. He co-directs "The Punctuation Project" and has just been awarded a third Economic and Social Research Council (ESRC) funded project to research punctuation in relation to primary school children.

David Hornsby was with the Ministry of Education (Victoria, Australia) for many years and taught at every year level. He lectured in education at the Royal Melbourne Institute of Technology and La Trobe University. For four years he was a curriculum consultant in primary and secondary schools and then returned to the primary classroom. He is now working in teacher education, in educational publishing, and as a curriculum consultant in schools. David is invited to present at conferences worldwide. He has completed ten lecture tours of the United States, and has also worked with teachers in England, Ireland, Indonesia, and Singapore. His latest book, *A Closer Look at Guided Reading* (Eleanor Curtain), has just won the award for being the best book in the Primary Teacher Reference category of the "Australia Awards for Excellence in Educational Publishing."

George Hunt is lecturer in language and education at the University of Reading. Previously a classroom teacher, he has worked in several London primary schools, teaching across the entire age range. He has also worked as a teacher trainer in The Commonwealth of Dominica and in Mongolia, where he is currently involved in the International Reading Association's Reading and Writing for Critical Thinking Project.

Charmian Kenner received her PhD from Southampton University for research on children's writing in a multilingual nursery and now works as a consultant and lecturer on bilingualism and family literacy. She is currently based at the Institute of Education in London where she is working on a two-year research grant awarded by the Economic and Social Research Council (ESRC), conducting case studies of five-year-olds learning to write in more than one script system. Charmian has written several articles and contributed chapters to books on bilingualism. Her latest book, *Home Pages: Literacy Links for Bilingual Children,* has just been published by Trentham Books.

Maureen Lewis, currently a Regional Director for Initial Teacher Training for the National Literacy Strategy, is a Senior Lecturer in Language and Literacy at the University of Plymouth and is well known for her work as co-director of the influential Nuffield, Exeter Extending Literacy (EXEL) Project. She was a teacher for many years before beginning her research career, and in her position at the University of Plymouth she spent as much time as possible working in classrooms with teachers and children. She has written many books, chapters, and articles about literacy, including books on writing frames and the award-winning book, *Extending Literacy: Children Reading and Writing Non-Fiction*, co-authored with David Wray. She has recently been involved in research, looking at the impact of the literacy hour in England, at the challenges of supporting literacy across the curriculum in secondary schools, at ways of engaging the interest of boy readers, and at the use of Information, Communication, and Technology (ICT) in literacy teaching.

Elaine Millard is a Senior Lecturer in Education at the University of Sheffield and the Director of its Literacy Research Centre. Prior to this, from 1968 to 1988 she worked as an English teacher in a wide variety of 11–18 comprehensive schools in Sheffield and Nottinghamshire. From 1989–1990 she was employed as an Advisory Teacher by Nottingham Local Education Authority, and she has recently evaluated Key Stage 3 (11–14 years) Pilot Literacy Projects for Derbyshire, Durham, and Sheffield. Her research interests span issues in the development of literacy at all levels, from early reading to critical theory. Her current research is focused on gender, race, and class differences in the development of home and school literacies, including computer literacies. Her recent publications include *Differently Literate: Boys, Girls and the Schooling of Literacy* (Open University Press), *Gender in the Secondary School Curriculum* (Falmer Press), and her forthcoming book with Jackie Marsh, *Popular Cultures, Popular Literacies: Using Popular Culture in the Primary School* (Paul Chapman Publishers).

Steve Moline is a consultant, writer, illustrator, and graphic designer who writes for children under the name of David Drew. He has produced more than one hundred information books for children, including the series *Informazing, Realization and InfoActive*. He has also written, for teachers, *I See What You Mean: Children at Work with Visual Information*. This book was the first on that subject for school teachers; he has also co-produced a training video for teachers, *What is Visual Literacy?* Steve pioneered nonfiction "big books" in the 1980s. Since 1990 he has conducted workshops for teachers on information literacy and visual literacy in the UK, the United States, Canada, Australia, New Zealand, and India. He is currently preparing *The Information Toolkit*, a teacher reference series on using graphic organizers to help children plan and write information, to be published in 2000–2001 by Oxford University Press.

Margaret Moustafa is a Professor of Education at California State University at Los Angeles. She is an experienced elementary school teacher and author of *Beyond Traditional Phonics: Research Discoveries and Reading Instruction* (Heinemann 1997), "Children's productive phonological recoding" (*Reading Research Quarterly*, 1995), and co-author of "Whole-to-parts phonics instruction: Building on what children know to help them know more" (*Reading Teacher*, 1999). Using the research findings of other scholars as well as her own research findings on how children learn a phonic system, she developed whole-to-parts phonics instruction as a powerful, systematic, explicit way of teaching children a phonic system which is compatible with their natural cognitive processes.

Bobbie Neate has written extensively on reading for information and she has always stressed the value of teaching children to read nonfiction at a very early age. Her first publication, *Finding Out About Finding Out*, won a book award for the teaching of literacy and was one of the first texts which helped teachers promote nonfiction reading in primary schools. Bobbie has been a primary school teacher, a lecturer in higher education, a special needs teacher, a literacy adviser, and a consultant in reading research skills. She was nonfiction editor of the Longman Book Project. She has now set up her own publishing business, which aims to teach children how to read for information. Many of the published texts teach young children how to make effective notes.

Dawn Nulty is deputy head teacher at Our Lady's Catholic Primary School, Warrington, England. Previously she worked as Information, Communication and Technology (ICT) coordinator and class teacher at St Columba's Catholic Primary School, Knowsley. She has been involved in staff development from both a school and authority perspective and is an active promoter of the benefits and use of Information Technology (IT) in literacy. Dawn has written several articles on literacy and IT and has conducted presentations at Higher Education conferences in both Liverpool and Manchester. She is currently working to obtain a masters degree in Education at Liverpool Hope University College, Liverpool.

Gervase Phinn is a freelance consultant, author, and speaker. He taught for over fourteen years in a range of schools before becoming General Adviser for Language Development in Rotherham and later Principal Education Officer with North Yorkshire County Council. He is a Fellow of the Royal Society of Arts and Visiting Professor in Education at the University of Teeside. Gervase has lectured widely and has published many articles on the use of English in Education along with collections of his own plays, stories, and poetry. He has made numerous appearances on television chat shows, and his latest novel, *Over Hill and Dale* (Michael Joseph), the sequel to *The Other Side of the Dale*, has been serialized on BBC radio. Some of his other recent publications include *Lizard Over Ice* (Nelson) and *Classroom Creatures* (Roselea Publication), both poetry anthologies, and *Young Readers and Their Books* (David Fulton Publishers).

Sandra Wilde is Professor of Curriculum and Instruction at Portland State University (Oregon) where she works with both prospective teachers and those interested in becoming literacy specialists. She is the author of numerous books, including, most recently, *Miscue Analysis Made Easy*. She is best known for her work on invented spelling, particularly her 1992 book, *You Kan Red This*. She is currently working on a brief critical dictionary of testing and standards.

Lesley Wing Jan taught in both the Australian State and Independent systems before her current position as Co-ordinator of Learning and Teaching at a large Melbourne school. She conducts professional development programs for teachers throughout Victoria and across Australia and has appeared in several teaching videos. She has taught about literacy teaching and learning at the tertiary level and has a particular interest in literacy teaching across the curriculum, monitoring children's progress and student self-assessment. She is a member of the Review Board for *The Australian Journal of Language and Literacy* (Australian Literacy Educators' Association) and was a member of the English CSF 2000 Review Committee. Lesley has written many books, including *Write Ways: Modelling Writing Forms* (Oxford University Press); *Spelling and Grammar* (Ashton); *Modelling Writing in the Early Years of Schooling* (Catholic Education Commission), and has co-authored three with Jeni Wilson: *Thinking for Themselves* (Eleanor Curtain); *Student Self Assessment* (Eleanor Curtain) and *Integrated Assessment* (Oxford University Press).

David Wray taught in primary schools and is currently Professor of Literacy Education at the University of Warwick. He has published over twenty-five books on aspects of literacy teaching and is best known for his work, with Maureen Lewis, on the Nuffield Extending Literacy (EXEL)

Project, which has been concerned with helping learners of all ages access the curriculum more effectively through literacy. The work of this project was made an integral part of the National Literacy Strategy in England, and David was a founding member of the Advisory Group to the original National Literacy Project. His major recent publications include *Extending Literacy* (Routledge); *English 7–11* (Routledge); *Developing Children's Non-Fiction Writing* (Scholastic), and *Writing Frames* (Reading and Information Centre, University of Reading).